Book Yourself Solid

for COACHES *and* CONSULTANTS

Book Yourself Solid

for *COACHES* and *CONSULTANTS*

The Fastest, Easiest, Most Reliable System *for*
Getting More Clients Than You Can Handle,
Even if You Hate Marketing *and* Selling

Michael Port
New York Times Bestselling Author

with **Matthew Kimberley**

WILEY

Published by John Wiley & Sons, Inc., Hoboken, New Jersey.
Published simultaneously in Canada.

For general information on our other products and services or for technical support, please contact our Customer Care Department within the United States at (800) 762-2974, outside the United States at (317) 572-3993 or fax (317) 572-4002.

Wiley also publishes its books in a variety of electronic formats. Some content that appears in print may not be available in electronic formats. For more information about Wiley products, visit our web site at www.wiley.com.

Library of Congress Cataloging-in-Publication Data:

Names: Port, Michael, 1970- author. | Kimberley, Matthew, author. | John Wiley & Sons, publisher.
Title: Book yourself solid for coaches and consultants : the fastest, easiest, and most reliable system for getting more clients than you can handle / Michael Port with Matthew Kimberley.
Description: Hoboken, New Jersey : Wiley, [2025] | Includes bibliographical references and index.
Identifiers: LCCN 2024020706 (print) | LCCN 2024020707 (ebook) | ISBN 9781394225682 (hardback) | ISBN 9781394225705 (adobe pdf) | ISBN 9781394225699 (epub)
Subjects: LCSH: Marketing. | Strategic planning. | Consultants.
Classification: LCC HF5415 .P6368 2025 (print) | LCC HF5415 (ebook) | DDC 658.8—dc23/eng/20240601
LC record available at https://lccn.loc.gov/2024020706
LC ebook record available at https://lccn.loc.gov/2024020707

Cover Design: Paul McCarthy

SKY10081019_080124

This book is a love story disguised as a business book.
It's a love story between you and all the inspiring clients you will serve.

Contents

Contents

Michael's Note

In early 2000 I was utterly dissatisfied and completely disillusioned with my work as the vice president of programming at an entertainment company. The environment felt like a prison—long hours, unresponsive colleagues, and no personal engagement. Sound familiar? I decided to embark on a new career path as a professional business consultant: a marketing and business coach. I secretly passed the time reading, researching, studying, and honing my skills. After much planning, my freedom date was marked on every calendar in my apartment with a huge victorious smiley face. My resignation letter was signed, sealed, and ready for delivery. I could hardly keep my legs from sprinting out the door to follow my heart and head (both of which had checked out long ago).

On that auspicious day, I received the envelope with my bonus inside, ran to the bank, cleared the check, and proudly delivered my letter of resignation. The joy, pride, and satisfaction that I felt at that moment were incredible. I floated home and woke up the next day to plunge into my career as a coach serving others.

I didn't bask for long in the glory, however, before I realized I was in for trouble.

Call me crazy, but I really thought clients were just going to fall into my lap. I expected them to meet me, fall in love with me, and trade their money for my services. Instead, I moped about my very costly New York City apartment, panicking, feeling sorry for myself, and doing trivial busy work that wasn't going to generate a dime of income.

Within six months I was desperate, which heralded a new phase of my life. I was fed up. I'd reached my limit. I was not going to throw in the towel and give up on my career. My innate need to support and provide, to serve the people I was meant to serve, kicked into high gear one chilly New York morning. Plus, what choice did I have? I didn't think homelessness would look good on me. Rather than dwelling on the cold reality of my financial struggle and the bitter temperature outside, I worked every single day for no fewer than 16 hours just to pay the bills (I don't recommend this as a strategy, by the way). I poured myself into more resources and studied everything I could get my hands on about how to attract clients, communicate effectively, sell, market, and promote my services. First and foremost, I wanted to learn how to love marketing and selling by turning it into a meaningful pursuit.

Obviously, it worked, or I wouldn't be writing this and you certainly wouldn't be reading it. Within 10 months, I was booked solid with more clients than I could handle. But the personal checks I cashed were not the most valuable part of my business. The real heart of what I was creating was the marketing system that propelled my business and income every month. I started sharing my marketing process with a small group of trusted clients, and I watched their success unfold before my eyes. I could hear confidence, pride, and accomplishment in their voices. Their businesses took off.

My clients, who were service professionals of all kinds, started to get booked solid: massage therapists, mortgage brokers, accountants, therapists, acupuncturists, dentists, hair salon and spa owners, bookkeepers, web and graphic designers, business consultants, chiropractors, professional organizers, financial planners, virtual assistants, health care providers, insurance brokers, attorneys, personal trainers, travel agents, photographers, physiotherapists, Pilates and yoga instructors, coaches, Realtors, reflexologists, sales professionals, naturopaths, and others were getting more clients than they could handle. Well, not all of them. But most of them did—the ones who did the work.

I immediately began to engineer a completely replicable system that I could pass on to you. That system is the Book Yourself Solid system, and you're holding it in your hands, the same system that more than a million people have used since 2003.

When the book was released in April of 2006, *Book Yourself Solid* was the number-two best-selling book on Amazon.com. Not in a category but number two in *all* books. No one was more surprised by that than me. It has since become an evergreen resource for professional service providers all over the United States, the United Kingdom, and Canada. It's been translated into Spanish, Vietnamese, Bulgarian, Polish, Bahasa Indonesian, Orthodox Chinese, Korean, and others. It's included in curriculums at graduate-level business schools and is touted as recommended reading by professional associations like the National Association of Realtors, which called *Book Yourself Solid* a "must-read."

The thing about a published book is that once it's printed, it's done. Yet, over the years, I've found ways of improving it. As a result, I've changed important parts of the system, fine-tuned others, and added new, up-to-date material. This edition of the book keeps the best of the Book Yourself Solid system, clarifies essential parts, and trims the fat, doing away with anything that you don't absolutely need to know, and critically, has been completely rewritten, with the help of my friend and colleague, Matthew Kimberley, to be for you: the coach.

If I've learned anything over the past 20 years, it's that you don't need more information; you need better-organized information that is easier to consume and make use of. I believe this new edition of the book should make for even easier reading, faster and more effective consumption, and bigger, more impressive, and more profitable results.

It is realistic for you to become a successful coach or consultant. But you need to learn the skills necessary to promote your work and become the go-to person in your field before it's too late. There is no question that the Book Yourself Solid system can change your business and your life.

You love what you do. You're great at what you do. You stand in the service of others, and you are a remarkable human being for doing so—now it's time to get booked solid.

This book offers a way toward a profitable, meaningful, and absolutely booked-solid business, overflowing with as many clients as your heart desires, clients who energize and inspire you, clients with whom you do your best work, clients who will pay you handsomely.

I hope you feel the same exhilaration in building your coaching business as I do every day. I expect that the Book Yourself Solid system will not only inspire you but will keep you keenly focused on learning and relearning, experimenting and honing all that is within you. I am certain the secret to your success isn't just in the work that we do together. It lies within you. *Book Yourself Solid* will simply help facilitate your greatness.

We are all on this path together, learning from one another. We are all seeking joy, love, success, and happiness. Continue to trust that you are making a huge difference in the lives of your clients, yourself, and society as a whole.

Here's to you—to focusing on getting as many clients as your heart desires. Please come to the Book Yourself Solid system with an open heart and mind. Completely remove, or at least set aside, any preconceived ideas fluttering in your head. Let the process be revealed to you step-by-step.

The Book Yourself Solid way is one of abundance, joy, and meaning. It's my deep honor to serve you. Now, let's get to booking you solid.

Warmly,
Michael Port

Note on the Text

You might call yourself a coach, or a consultant, or a trainer, or an advisor, or indeed none of these.

What's important is that you have chosen to be in the business of change.

You help good people, companies, organizations, and communities become better than they are today, with your unique set of skills, expertise, and wisdom.

Throughout the book I have used the term *coach* and *coaching* as a useful shorthand and to save you the time from reading *coaching or consulting or training or advisory business* whenever I allude to the work that you do.

Whatever you call yourself, you're doing important work. I'm here to help you do more of it with the people who matter most to you.

Preface

The Book Yourself Solid system is supported by both practical and philosophical principles.

From a practical perspective, there may be two simple reasons why you don't serve as many coaching clients as you'd like to today. Either you don't know what to do to attract and secure more clients or you know what to do but you're not actually doing it. The Book Yourself Solid system is designed to help you solve both of these problems, including the information you need to book more clients for your coaching business. If you already know what to do but aren't doing it, I hope to inspire you into action and help you stay accountable so you build the business of your dreams. Moreover, you'd be surprised to learn that marketing isn't really what gets you clients. It's what you do once someone becomes aware of you that books you the business. The Book Yourself Solid system is designed to show you how to create the awareness you need for the products and services you offer and then exactly what to do to book the business once someone becomes aware of you.

From a philosophical perspective, I believe that if you have something to say, if you have a message to deliver, and if there are people you want to serve, then there are people in this world whom you are *meant* to serve. Not kinda, sorta, because they're in your target market . . . but *meant* to. If this doesn't resonate for you now, I believe it will when you have read this book and begun to follow the Book Yourself Solid way.

The system is organized into four modules:

1. Your Foundation
2. Building Trust and Credibility
3. Simple Selling and Perfect Pricing
4. The Book Yourself Solid Six Core Self-Promotion Strategies

We will begin by building a foundation for your business that is unshakable. If you are truly serious about becoming a successful coach, you must have a steadfast foundation on which to stand. You will then be ready to create and implement a strategy for building trust and credibility. You'll be considered a credible expert in your field, and you'll start to earn the trust of the people you'd like to serve. You'll price your offerings in the sweet spot of the client's desires, and you'll know how to have sales conversations of the highest integrity that work. Then, and only then, will you execute the six core self-promotion strategies, thereby creating awareness for the valuable services you offer by using promotional strategies that are based on your talents—strategies that feel authentic and honest.

To help you design a coaching business overflowing with clients who inspire and energize you, this book includes written exercises and Booked Solid Action Steps that will support you in thinking bigger about your business. I walk you through the actions you need to complete on the path to serving as many clients as your heart desires.

You will want to retain your responses to the written exercises for regular review. I have prepared a complimentary downloadable workbook that includes all of the written exercises and Booked Solid Action Steps contained in this book. Simply visit our website and download the workbook so that you may begin today to take the necessary steps to get more clients than you can handle.

Go to www.bookyourselfsolid.com/coaches and download your free copy of the workbook so you have it in your hands before you turn another page. So, your first action step is to get your workbook. Although you'll no doubt get great value just from reading this book, the true value—and your success—lies in your decision to take an active role and to participate fully by doing the exercises and taking the Booked Solid Action Steps I've outlined.

Please work through *Book Yourself Solid for Coaches and Consultants* in sequential order. No skipping, jumping, or moving ahead – the Book Yourself Solid Six Core Self-Promotion Strategies are effectively implemented only after your foundation, credibility-building, pricing, and sales strategies are in place. One of the main reasons that coaches say they hate marketing and selling is that they're trying to market without these essential elements, which is like eating an egg before it's cooked—of course, you'll hate it. So no matter how compelled you are to skip ahead, I urge you to *please* follow the system and watch the process unfold. Remember, self-promotion just creates awareness for the products and services you sell. It's what you do once someone becomes aware of you that earns you the business. All the marketing in the world won't do you much good if you have a weak foundation (or none at all), can't demonstrate credibility, don't know how to earn trust, price your offers, or have an effective sales conversation.

So many talented and inspired coaches like you run from marketing and sales because they have come to believe that the marketing and selling process is pushy and self-centered and borders on sleazy. This old-school paradigm is not the Book Yourself Solid way. It is the typical client-snagging mentality. And you must *never* fall into this way of thinking and being. If you do, you'll operate in a mentality of scarcity and shame as opposed to one of abundance and integrity.

Ask yourself these questions:

- How can I be fully self-expressed in my work to create meaning for me and those whom I serve?
- How can I work only in the areas of my greatest strengths and talents so that I can shine?
- How many relationships with people of purpose did I make and deepen?
- How can I better listen to and serve my ideal clients?
- How can I wow people with substance?
- How can I over-deliver on my promises to my clients?
- How can I cooperate with other professionals to create more abundance?

If you keep asking yourself these questions, set a solid foundation for your business, build trust and credibility within your marketplace, learn how to price and sell your offerings, and use the six core self-promotion strategies, you'll have a booked solid coaching business in no time.

Acknowledgments

The first line of the acknowledgments section in virtually every book goes something like this: to list everyone I want to thank for their contributions to this book would be a book in itself. You really don't know how true that is until you write your own book.

I've written six books and each time I finish one, I make the people around me promise that they'll punch me in the eye if I say I'm going to write another one. Needless to say, I make sure to have ice packs at the ready. It seems like books are written by one person in solitary confinement in a cabin in the Berkshires or the French Alps. But rarely is that the case. This book and all my books are better because of the people around me. This book in particular is better because of the diligent work of my friend and coauthor, Matthew Kimberley. Matthew, my family, friends, colleagues, and clients offer their ideas, relentlessly, at times. You and I are the better for it. So, if you determine that what I've put on paper has merit, you can thank the people around me. They're the ones who deserve the credit. I just form the sentences while holding an icepack on my eye.

Module ONE

Your Foundation

To be booked solid requires that you have a solid foundation. That foundation begins like this:

- Choose your ideal clients so you work only with people who inspire and energize you.
- Understand why people buy what you are selling.
- Develop a personal brand to make you memorable and unique.
- Talk about what you do without sounding confusing or bland.

Over the course of Module One, I'll step you through the process of building your foundation so that you have a platform on which to stand, a perfectly engineered structure that will support all of your business development and marketing, and—dare I add—personal growth. That's because being in business for yourself, especially as someone who stands in the service of others, requires constant personal reflection and growth.

1

Over the years, I've found that many people want to hurry through the foundation and just get to the marketing. Please resist this temptation. Remember: marketing rarely gets you clients. What you do once someone becomes aware of you is what actually books you the business. I'm aware that I've said this three times now. I'll say it again later. It bears repeating. You need a solid foundation on which to stand first.

Building your foundation may seem like a lot of work. Maybe it is. That all depends on your definition of work, I suppose. But having a solid foundation that feels secure to your potential clients is the first key to business success.

Building your foundation is a bit like putting a puzzle together. We're going to take it one piece at a time, and when we're done you'll have laid the foundation for booking yourself solid.

1

The Red Velvet Rope Policy

He who trims himself to suit everyone will soon whittle himself away.
—Raymond Hull

Imagine that a friend has invited you to accompany her to an invitation-only special event. You arrive and approach the door, surprised to find a red velvet rope stretched between two shiny brass poles. A nicely dressed man asks your name, checking his invitation list. Finding your name there, he flashes a wide grin and drops one end of the rope, allowing you to pass through and enter the party. You feel like a star.

Do you have your own red velvet rope policy that allows in only the most ideal clients, the ones who energize and inspire you? If you don't, you will shortly. Why?

First, because when you work with coaching clients you love, you'll truly enjoy the work you're doing; you'll love every minute of it. (Well, almost every minute of it. It is work, after all.) And when you love the work you do, you'll do your *best* work, which is essential to booking yourself solid.

Second, because you *are* your clients. They are an expression and an extension of you. Do you remember when you were a teenager and your mother or father would give you a hard time about someone you were hanging out with? Your parents may have said that a particular kid was a bad influence. As a teen, you may have thought about how unfair that felt, but the truth is that you are the company you keep. The people you spend time with, make a significant impact on your state of mind and how you feel about yourself. Let this be the imperative of your business: choose your clients as carefully as you choose your friends. This is of critical importance in a coaching business because of the deep bond you will have with the clients you are serving.

The first step in building your foundation is to choose your ideal clients, the individuals or businesses with whom you do your best work, the people or environments that energize and inspire you. I'm going to help you identify specific characteristics of individuals or organizations that would make them ideal to work with. You will then develop a rigorous screening process to find more of them. I'm also going to help you prune your current client list of less-than-ideal clients.

When I began my coaching business I would work with anyone who had a pulse and a checkbook. Then I began to consider what it would mean to choose my clients. What it would mean to work only with clients who were ideal for me. And thank goodness I did. Now I live by what I call the Red Velvet Rope Policy of ideal clients. It increases my productivity and my happiness, it enables me to do my best work, and I have more clients and referrals than I can handle by myself. And so will you.

For maximum joy, prosperity, and abundance, think about the person you are when you are performing optimally, when you are with all the people who inspire and energize you. Now think about all of the frustration, tension, and anxiety you feel when you work with clients who are less than ideal—not so good, right?

Wouldn't it be great to spend every day working with clients who are ideal for you, clients whom you can hardly believe you get paid to work with? This ideal is completely possible once you identify with whom you want to work and determine with certainty that you will settle for nothing less. Once you do that, it's just a matter of knowing which of your existing clients qualify and how to acquire more just like them.

1.1.1 Written Exercise: To begin to identify the types of clients you don't want, consider which characteristics or behaviors you refuse to tolerate. What turns you off or shuts you down? What kinds of people should *not* be getting past the red velvet rope that protects you and your business?

Dump the Duds

Let's take this a step further. I suggest you dump your dud clients. I can just hear your shocked protestations and exclamations. "I thought this was a book about getting clients, not dumping them!" I'm referring to the *dud* clients—not all of your clients. It sounds harsh, but think about it. Your dud clients are those you dread interacting with, who drain the life out of you, bore you to tears, frustrate you, or worse, instill in you the desire to do them—or yourself—bodily harm, despite your loving nature.

You might think that because you're in the business of making people (and companies) better that you have an obligation to work with dud clients until they're not dud clients, but that's a fallacy. The best coaches in the world work with the most motivated clients. Think about highly paid sports coaches or million-dollar executive coaches. The higher the quality of the client (which is of course a subjective measure), the greater the impact the coach can achieve.

I'm well aware of the many reasons you *think* you can't dump your dud clients, and I know this can seem really scary early on, but hang in there with me. Embrace the concept and trust that this is sound advice from a loving teacher and a necessary step on the path to booking yourself solid.

Why have clients, or anyone for that matter, in your life who zap your energy and leave you feeling empty? In the first year of being in business on my own, I cut 10 clients in one week. It wasn't easy. It required a major leap of faith, but the emotional and financial rewards were astonishing. Within three months, I had replaced all 10 and added 6 more. Not only did I increase my revenue but I also felt more peaceful and calm than I ever had before, and I enjoyed my clients and my work more.

When I asked myself the question, "Would I rather spend my days working with incredibly amazing, exciting, super cool, awesome people who are both clients and friends, or spend one more agonizing, excruciating minute working with barely tolerable clients who suck the life out me?" I had no choice. I knew the temporary financial loss would be worth the payoff.

I know using the phrase "dump your dud clients" suggests that there is something wrong with them. But that's not necessarily the case. Well, in some cases you may have a real problem client on your hands, but most of the time, they're just not right for *you*. Clients who are not ideal for you could be ideal for someone else. I like using the phrase "dump your duds" because it might make you uncomfortable. It also trips nicely off the tongue.

Keep in mind that you don't need to create conflict and fire clients. You just need to help them find a better fit. You can be tactful, diplomatic, and loving. You can even attempt, when appropriate, to refer them to a colleague who might be a better fit. Whenever possible, keep it simple. Try, "I'm not the best person to serve you." Or "I don't think we'd be a good fit."

Are you always going to get a positive response when dumping your dud clients? Maybe not. If the first thing that comes to mind is, "I don't want anyone out there thinking badly of me," I'm with you. I want everyone to love me, too. But living life fully can require difficult conversations and you can't please everyone. To even try is an exercise in futility, as the following Aesop fable demonstrates.

The Old Man, the Little Boy, and the Donkey

An old man, a little boy, and a donkey were going to town. The little boy rode on the donkey and the old man walked beside him. As they went along, they passed some people who remarked it was a shame the old man was walking and the little boy was riding. The man and boy thought maybe the critics were right, so they changed positions.

Later, they passed some people who remarked, "What a shame! He makes that little boy walk." They then decided they both would walk.

Soon they passed some more people who thought they were stupid to walk when they had a decent donkey to ride. So they both rode the donkey. Later, they passed some people who shamed them by saying how awful to put such a load on a poor donkey. The boy and man said they were probably right, so they decided to carry the donkey. As they crossed the bridge, they lost their grip on the animal. He fell into the river and drowned.

The moral of the story? *If you try to please everyone, you might as well kiss your ass goodbye.*

When considering whom you want to work with, look for qualities in a person with whom you resonate, so don't limit yourself to just thinking about the clients you don't yet have. Your Red Velvet Rope Policy is a filtration system that lets in ideal clients. However, you can choose to loosen or tighten the rope at will. I'm not (necessarily) asking you to turn away your very first clients. I understand what you're up against. When you start your business, if you feel that you'd like to keep your red velvet rope a little looser so you can work with more clients, go right ahead.

Just make sure you know what is ideal and what isn't ideal about the people you're letting into the VIP room. As you become booked solid, you'll tighten your red velvet rope and become even more exclusive so as to work only with those who energize and inspire you—and most important— enable you to do your best work.

1.1.2 Written Exercise: Now take a good, hard look at your current clients. Be absolutely honest with yourself. Who among your current clients fits the profile you've just created of people who should *not* have gotten past the red velvet rope that protects you and your business?

1.1.3 Booked Solid Action Step: Dump the dud clients you've just listed in the preceding exercise. It may be just one client, or you may need another two pages to write them all down. Is your heart pounding? Is your stomach churning at just the thought? Have you broken out in a cold sweat? Or are you jumping up and down with excitement now that you've been given permission to dump your duds? Maybe you're experiencing both sensations at the same time; that's totally normal. Do it and you'll feel better.

Taking a Booked Solid Action Step is a bold action and requires courage. And courage is not about being fearless—it's about owning your fear and using it to move you forward, to give you strength. There is no more rewarding feeling than the pride you'll feel once you've moved past the fear to do what you set out to do. Maybe you'll find it easier to take it one step at a time. Start by dismissing just one of those dud clients. The feeling of empowerment you'll have once you've done it will motivate you to continue pruning your list of clients until the duds have all been removed.

What to Do When You Don't (Yet) Have Clients

But, Michael, what if I just started my business and don't yet have clients, let alone dud clients? Ah, yes, excellent point. Consider yourself lucky. You'll never have to worry about dud clients because you'll put your Red Velvet Rope Policy in place on day one.

In just a moment, you'll begin to create your Red Velvet Rope Policy. If you're starting from scratch, and don't yet have many, or any, clients to speak of at this point, as you're working through the exercises, think about current or former coworkers, friends, or even service providers that you've hired in the past. To create your future Red Velvet Rope Policy you'll be able to draw on your past experiences—who inspired you and who made you want to do them bodily harm. Refrain. Rewind. Remember: love and kindness. Love and kindness.

Pruning Your Client List

If you're struggling with the idea of pruning your client list, keep in mind that it's for your client's benefit as much as it is for yours. If you're feeling empty and drained, or frustrated and dreading the interaction with the client, you're giving that client far less than your best, and it's both of you who are suffering for it. You owe it to these clients to refer them to someone who can, and will, do their best work with them. If you are working with people with whom you do not do your best work, you are out of integrity. And as we discussed previously, you *are* your clients. When your clients go out into the world and speak of you to others, they are representing you.

With whom do you want to be associated—the duds or the ideal clients? It's also the ideal clients, those who are wildly happy with you and your services, who are most likely to go out and talk about you to others, to refer other clients like themselves, more ideal clients. The fewer duds you allow to hang around, the more ideal clients you have room for, the more referrals you'll get, and so on.

Clients are like family to me, so I know this can be hard. I lived through a period of intense and painful negative energy worrying about those challenging client relationships. It exhausted me and took me away from accomplishing the highest good for my clients. It was impossible for me to be productive, effective, or successful when working with less-than-ideal clients.

I must admit that I've been a less-than-ideal client myself. For a variety of reasons, my landscaper and I were just not a good fit for each other. One reason being that every so often I'd cut the grass on a whim and then his guys would show up with nothing to mow. Instead, I'd ask them to do other projects on the property, which I thought was reasonable. It turns out that he didn't like that. He knew I wasn't his ideal client, but rather than tell me so, he stayed with me while getting more and more annoyed until he blew up and acted like a jerk, forcing me to let him go. More than likely, he didn't feel comfortable dumping his dud clients, or the idea had never even crossed his mind. Granted, pruning his dud clients might not have been as easy as pruning his clients' trees, but had he not allowed the situation to deteriorate and end on such a bad note, I might have been able to refer other clients to him who would have been ideal for him. His inability to take the Booked Solid Action Step of letting his less-than-ideal clients go respectfully left both of us dissatisfied with the situation and jeopardized his reputation.

This is what can happen when you work with clients who are not ideal for you. At some point, you're going to create a conflict, whether intentionally or not, because you're going to be frustrated with those clients. Those clients will think you're not providing them with good service, and they'll be right. It doesn't serve you or the client when you stay in a less-than-ideal situation. Please don't make the same mistake my landscaper did. If you do, you'll have former clients going out into the world telling anyone who will listen that you're the worst person to work with.

And bear in mind that my relationship with my landscaper was rather transactional. We didn't spend a lot of time in each other's company. I wasn't relying on him for careful or sensitive guidance or problem-solving in the same way that your clients rely on you. The intimate and trusting nature of a coach-client relationship makes it even more critical that you work only with clients who are the greatest fit for you, and you for them.

Creating Your Red Velvet Rope Policy

The benefits of working with ideal clients are many and meaningful:

- You'll get to do your best work.
- You'll feel invigorated and inspired.

- You'll connect with clients on a deeper level.
- You'll feel successful and confident.
- You'll know your work matters and is changing lives.
- You'll feel fully self-expressed.

My ideal clients have these qualities:

- Bright (quick thinkers)
- Resilient (don't give up when it really matters)
- Courageous (face their fears)
- Think big (their projects benefit large groups of people)
- Value-oriented (they gain value from relationships)
- Naturally collaborative (they contribute to and focus on their solutions)
- Rapid responders (talk today, done tomorrow)
- Positive (naturally optimistic)

Your list might look completely different.

Take heed: how much money a client has or doesn't have is not what this is about. Your Red Velvet Rope Policy considers *what kind of person* you're dealing with, not how much this person has or doesn't have. People with fat wallets are often the primary consideration for many coaches who wind up working with clients who are less than ideal. Notice that my list considers the *qualities* of my ideal clients first—who they *are* rather than what they *have* or the circumstances they're in.

1.1.4 Written Exercise: Define your ideal client. What type of people do you love being around? What do they like to do? What do they talk about? With whom do they associate? What ethical standards do they follow? How do they learn? How do they contribute to society? Are they smiling, outgoing, or creative? What kind of environment do you want to create in your life? And who will get past the Red Velvet Rope Policy that protects you? List the *qualities, values,* or *personal characteristics* you'd like your ideal clients to possess.

1.1.5 Written Exercise: Now let's look at your current client base. Whom do you love interacting with the most? Whom do you look forward to seeing? Who are the clients who don't feel like work to you? *Who is it you sometimes just can't believe you get paid to work with?* Write down the names of clients, or people you've worked with, whom you love to be around.

1.1.6 Written Exercise: Get a clear picture of these people in your head. Write down the top five reasons that you love working with them. What about working with them turns you on?

1.1.7 Written Exercise: Now go deeper. If you were working only with ideal clients, what qualities would they absolutely *need* to possess for you to do your *best* work with them? Be honest and don't worry about excluding people. Be selfish. Think about yourself. For this exercise, assume you will work only with the best of the best. Be brave and bold and write without thinking or filtering your thoughts.

How different were the last two lists? You may have nailed it the first time. Maybe you're right on track, or maybe you have some perfect client opportunities to uncover.

By knowing who your ideal clients are and selecting only those who have at least 75% of the qualities you identified, you will have more fun, accomplish greater results, and experience incredible joy and fulfillment in your business.

This is beneficial because you'll be able to identify other ideal clients you'd love to work with. People enjoy knowing how important they are to you, and if they know you do your best work with, and for, people like them, they are much more inclined to work with you. It raises the stakes for them.

Look at these requirements and think about how you can start to turn them into filters. As for me, I'm like a giant generator—the more gas (meaning projects or clients) I take in, the more power I create. But the wrong kind of fuel causes me to sputter and conk out. Think about a hot sports car running on diesel fuel—not pretty. Neither is this roadster when he gets the wrong kind of energy. Every engine needs a filtration system to keep the system running smoothly and cleanly, just as you need a Red Velvet Rope Policy that will filter out the imperfections.

My client filters include these considerations:

- I feel more energized and excited after working with my clients.
- My clients seek open feedback, and better yet, they take action when they get it.
- My clients have faith that leaves some people bewildered and some astonished.
- My clients are not victims. They hold themselves accountable and think about the betterment of others.
- My clients continually seek out and develop valuable personal and professional relationships.
- My clients feel stimulated and energized by the input and collaborative efforts of others.
- My clients use anecdotes and colorful speech, and they share personal stories.
- My clients do not procrastinate. They respond quickly to new opportunities.
- My clients are naturally optimistic and do not complain (much).

1.1.8 Written Exercise: What filters do you want to run your perfect clients through?

Ideal Clients, the Duds, and Everyone Else

As you eliminate the duds, you'll open up room for ideal clients. As you use the Book Yourself Solid system to attract more and more ideal clients, you'll discover that you're happier, more vibrant, more energetic, and more productive. You'll be on fire. You'll be giving your clients the best of yourself and your services, and you'll love every minute of it.

1.1.9 Written Exercise: Draw a simple table with three columns: Label the first column "Ideal Clients," the second "Duds," and the third "Everyone Else." Now divide your clients into these three groups. Don't hold back or leave anyone out.

As if that weren't enough, you may begin to notice that many of your mid-range clients, those who made neither the ideal client nor the dud list, are undergoing a transformation. Why? While you were working with dud clients, you weren't performing at your best. If you think that that wasn't affecting your other clients, think again. The renewed energy and the more positive environment you'll create as a result of letting go of the duds will most likely rejuvenate the relationships between you and some of your mid-range clients, turning many of them into ideal clients.

1.1.10 Written Exercise: Brainstorm your own ideas for reigniting these mid-range clients. Contemplate the ways in which you may, even inadvertently, have contributed to some of your clients being less than ideal clients. Are there ways in which you can light a new fire or elicit greater passion for the work you do together? Do you need to set and manage expectations more clearly right from the beginning? Can you enrich the dynamics between you by challenging or inspiring your clients in new ways? Go ahead—turn off your left brain logical mind for a moment and let your right brain creativity go wild.

Carefully observe the ways in which your relationships with your clients begin to shift as you embrace the Book Yourself Solid way. Some of your mid-range clients may fall away. Others may step up their game and slide into the ideal client category.

When you're fully self-expressed, fully demonstrating your values and your views, you'll naturally attract and draw to yourself those you're best suited to work with, and you'll push away those you're not meant to work with.

A Perpetual Process

The process we've just worked through is one that you must do on a regular basis. Pruning your client list is a perpetual process because all relationships naturally cycle. The positive and dynamic relationships you have now with your ideal clients may at some point reach a plateau, and the time may come to go your separate ways. You'll get more comfortable with the process over time. It's one that has so many rewards that it's well worth the effort.

Let author Tom Peters (2006) sum it up for us: "This is your life. You *are* your clients. It is fair, sensible, and imperative to make these judgments. To dodge doing so shows a lack of integrity."

I'll go one step further and say that doing so is one of the best and smartest business and life decisions you can make. It's crucial to your success and your happiness. Prune regularly and before you know it, you'll be booked solid with clients you love working with.

2

Why People Buy What You're Selling

Before everything else, getting ready is the secret of success.
—Henry Ford

The next few steps we take down the Book Yourself Solid path will either feel like you're skipping over stepping stones or like you're taking giant leaps of faith. Either way, these few steps will be well worth the time spent. Stay by my side as we walk and work together on getting you booked solid.

Taking the following four steps will help you keenly understand why people buy what you're selling, an essential component in creating demand for your services.

Step 1: Identify your target market.

Step 2: Identify the urgent needs and compelling desires of your target market.

Step 3: Determine the number one biggest result your clients get.

Step 4: Uncover and demonstrate the benefits of your investable opportunities.

Step 1: Identify Your Target Market

Now that you've looked at the qualities of the people you want to work with, it's time to identify your target market, that is—the specific group of people or businesses you serve. For example, your target market might be seniors in Vancouver, British Columbia, or mothers who have their own home-based networking marketing business or orthopedic surgeons. Your ideal clients are a small subset of the target market you choose to serve. Remember, your ideal clients are those individuals who energize and inspire you. Your target market is the demographics of the group you're most passionate about serving. Your ideal clients are a small subset of your target market. Not all people in your target market are ideal clients for you. Nonetheless, it is just as important to identify the right target market as it is to identify the ideal clients.

It's also important to understand the difference between your target market and your niche. If you've done other research or reading on the subject of building your business, you may have heard both of these terms before, and you may have heard them used interchangeably. However, in the Book Yourself Solid system, they are *not* synonymous. There's an important distinction between the two: your target market is the group of people you serve, and your niche is the service you specialize in offering to your target market. For example, you and I may both serve the same target market, say, accountants or dentists, but offer them different services. I might specialize in marketing and you might help them create systems for their business. We'll get to your niche in Chapter 3. Before we can talk more about the services you offer, you've got to identify your target market.

Even if you believe you have identified and chosen a target market, please don't skip this section. I often see coaches who are struggling because either they've chosen a target market that isn't as specific as it needs to be, or they've chosen a target market based on what they think is the most logical and most lucrative choice, rather than one they feel passionate about serving. For the sake of your own success, read through this section, even if you don't think you need to. If your target market isn't specific enough or the right one for you, the rest of the book won't be as effective. And besides, you just might be surprised at what you discover.

There are three primary reasons to choose a target market:

- It helps you determine where to find potential clients who are looking for what you have to offer. If you have a target market, you know where to concentrate your marketing efforts. You know what associations to speak to, magazines and journals to write for, and influential people with whom to network—you know where your potential clients gather. You know where to show up.

- Virtually every target market already has some kind of network of communication established. For your marketing to work, your clients need to spread your messages for you. If they already have a network of communication set up, they can talk to each other about you, and your marketing messages can travel that much faster. What are networks of communication? Environments that are set up to help a group communicate—as I mentioned previously: associations, social networking sites, clubs, conferences, various publications, events, and more.

- And, finally, choosing a target market lets the people in that target market know that you're dedicated to them. You get them and their issues. You understand how they see the world. That means a lot to them.

Marketing and sales isn't about trying to persuade, coerce, or manipulate people into buying your services. It's about putting yourself out in front of, and offering your services to, those whom you are meant to serve—people who already need and are looking for your services.

To reach the people you're meant to serve, you've got to know where to find them. That's why an essential step is for you to identify a very specific target market to serve.

No matter how much you might like to be everything to everyone, it's just not possible. Even if you could be, you would be doing a disservice to yourself and your clients in the attempt. You can serve your clients much better, offer them much more of your time, energy, and expertise, if you narrow your market so that you're serving only those who most need your services and who can derive the greatest benefits from what you have to offer.

If you're just starting out in your business, or if you've been working in your business for a while but are not yet booked solid, you may be tempted to market to anyone and everyone with the assumption that the more people you market to, the more clients you'll get. Although narrowing your market to gain more clients may seem counterintuitive, that's exactly what you need to do to successfully book yourself solid.

Think of narrowing your market this way: which would you rather be—a small fish in a big pond or a big fish in a small pond? It's much easier to carve out a very lucrative domain for yourself once you've identified a specific target market. And once you're a big fish in a small pond, you'll get more invitations than you can handle to swim in other ponds. Remember that, as a consumer, especially when the stakes are high, you go narrow. All things being equal, you seek out the specialist, the provider who most narrowly focuses on your particular need.

There are two primary ways to grow a coaching business. You can choose a target market and, over time, continue to add new offers: new services and new products to this same target market. For example, if your target market is fitness professionals, and you're currently offering them private business coaching, as you grow, you might start offering them group masterminds and then digital products. Alternatively, once you get booked solid in one target market, you can begin to market and sell the same services in additional vertical target markets. So, if you currently help professional speakers with confidence issues, you might repackage the same offers to help authors who have similar issues. Once you get a foothold in that market, you might then begin to focus on sports professionals.

You might be thinking: "If I specialize and work only with a specific group of people, or specific types of companies within a specific industry, won't that limit my opportunities? And what if I get bored?" Let me answer the second question first. If you're someone who gets bored easily, you may have that problem no matter what you do. You may want to spend some time reflecting on why you're not able to stay focused on what you've chosen to do. Or it may be that you've chosen a target market that doesn't excite you, that you aren't passionate about, or interested in.

Over time, you can move into other areas if you so desire. When I started my coaching business, I helped fitness professionals get booked solid. Once I was fortunate enough to create demand for my services, I leveraged the reputation I built servicing the fitness industry as a springboard to other

service professionals of all kinds. As you establish your expertise and reputation, if you choose, you can broaden your target market. You can also, as
I mentioned previously, add other services to the same target market. After
almost 20 years of teaching people how to get booked solid, we built an
additional business called Heroic Public Speaking. At www.HeroicPublic
Speaking.com, we teach public speaking to the same target markets we've
been serving for decades. So if you want to increase your speed to getting
booked solid, choose a very specific target market and stay with that target
market until you are booked solid. Then you can move into other markets
if you like or stay with your original focus and grow your product and
service line.

Your Passions, Natural Talents, and Knowledge Are Key

If you haven't yet chosen a target market, let's do it now. Let's start with
some questions: What are you most passionate about? What excites you?
What do you enjoy doing so much that it feels more like play than work
and that will enable you to make the most of your natural talents and your
knowledge?

Why start by thinking of your own needs, desires, and passions rather
than those of your clients? For one very simple reason: if you are not
passionate about what you're doing, if your heart isn't in it, if it doesn't have
meaning to you, you are not going to devote the time and energy required
to be successful, then you'll never, in a million years, be able to convince
people in your target market that you're the best person to help them.

I've often found, when working with clients, that they've chosen a target market based on what they think makes sense or will earn them the
most money. The end result is that they're bored, frustrated, and struggling
to book themselves solid. Don't make that mistake. It is imperative that you
work with a target market that excites you, that you can feel passionate
about serving, and that you are confident that you can help. If you don't,
growing your business will quickly feel like drudgery, and you'll be miserable. When you choose a target market you're passionate about, growing
your business will feel like passionate play and will bring you joy.

That's not to say that you shouldn't also consider your clients. If
you've been in business for a while, even if you may not have as many

clients as you'd like, the clients you do have can help with this process. Look at the clients you're currently serving. Look for common elements among them—for example, a particular industry, geographic location, age, gender, or profession. If you find that most of your clients share one or more elements in common, it may be that you are naturally drawn to those elements or they are drawn to you. Perhaps your target market has already chosen you and you just haven't stopped to think about it long enough to realize it and then focus your marketing there.

1.2.1 Written Exercise: Take a few moments to think about the following questions and jot down whatever comes to you. Doing so will provide you with clues to the target market you're best suited to serve. Your passion, your natural talents, and what you already know and want to learn more about are key.

- Who are all the different groups of people who use your coaching services?
- Which of these groups do you most relate to or feel the most interest or excitement about working with?
- Which group(s) do you know people in or already have clients in?
- Which group(s) do you have the most knowledge about, or, on the flip side, would you find fascinating to learn more about?
- What are you most passionate about as it relates to your work?
- What natural talents and strengths do you bring to your work?
- What aspects of your field do you know the most about?

1.2.2 Written Exercise: Consider your life experience and interests. You'll be able to more sincerely identify and empathize with your target market if you share common life situations or interests.

- What life situations or roles do you identify with that might connect you to a particular target market?
- Do you have any interests or hobbies that might connect you with your target market?

Now that you've given some thought to these questions, are some new possibilities beginning to emerge? Let's take a look at a few examples that might help you see how you can incorporate some of your answers into serving a target market:

- If your whole family is in the construction industry, maybe you'd choose the construction industry as your target market because you know the sensibilities of the people in that industry, and you know a lot about its inner workings.
- Maybe you used to be a semipro athlete and you'd really enjoy working with athletes.
- If you've got a background in accountancy and you grew up in a family business that went bankrupt when you were a teen, you might like to work with family businesses to help them avoid what happened to your family.
- Perhaps you're fascinated by—and would like to learn more about—fashion, so you choose the fashion industry as your target market.
- If you're somebody who loves and naturally connects with artists, and you're very creative, imaginative, and patient, you might want to choose artists as your target market.

Let's take this last example and examine it more closely. Say this coach is booked solid. Chances are, their full roster isn't just because they studied to become a highly qualified expert on coaching artists, but because they have a natural affinity with creative types. This differentiator is what helped them book themself solid much more quickly than they would have if they focused on serving the general population.

Are you beginning to see the ways in which your passions, natural talents, knowledge, life experience, and even interests and hobbies might help you choose a more specific target market? Play, explore, and have fun with this process.

1.2.3 Written Exercise: For now, I just want you to answer this question: who is your target market? If you're not ready to make this choice, list the possibilities that appeal to you. Sit with them for a while (but not for too long) and then choose one. Even if you're not sure at this point, it will become clearer to you as you work through the next few chapters.

I've worked with many coaches who *knew* on some level the target market they most wanted to serve, and for one reason or another discounted it. Turn off your inner censor when doing this exercise and allow yourself to at least explore every possibility, no matter how wild, silly, or unrealistic it may seem on the surface.

If You Feel Stuck

For some, choosing a target market doesn't come easily. It can feel very challenging, and when you've been told how important it is to identify a target market and it doesn't come quickly and easily, the pressure to choose can feel overwhelming and uncomfortable.

Part of what keeps us stuck is that we take ourselves, and the process, too seriously. We turn it into a big deal and wind up getting increasingly frustrated with the whole thing, and with ourselves. Suddenly the process has become another thing to beat ourselves up about. Needless to say, the frustration and self-flagellation just further block our creativity and intuition, and the next thing we know, we're in this awful cycle, like a hamster on an exercise wheel, spinning around and around and getting nowhere.

Take a few deep breaths. Let yourself off the hook. See if you can approach the process with an attitude of play. Think of it as a jigsaw puzzle—challenging but fun. The point isn't to finish as quickly as possible. The point is to enjoy the journey and to find the target market that is right for you.

As with any jigsaw puzzle, first you sort through all the pieces to find the edges, the pieces easiest to identify and put together. Then you take your time sorting through the rest. You pick one piece up, you compare it to the bigger picture on the box, and you try to figure out where it might go. One piece at a time, the picture comes together. When you get tired, or bored, or frustrated, or you just feel drawn to do something else, get up and walk away, and as you go about the rest of your day, don't stress out about whether you'll ever get the puzzle finished.

Some days you might spend an hour or two with it, other times only minutes. Maybe every once in a while you stop for mere seconds, pick up a piece or two, and pop them right in where they fit as you pass by. Maybe a friend or family member stops by for a visit, picks up that piece that's been making you crazy for days, and pops it right into place for you.

Choosing a target market you can feel passionate about serving can be enjoyable and immensely rewarding if you approach the process with an open mind and an attitude of play, reaching out for help from family, friends, or a professional business coach to guide you.

Revisit the written exercises in step 1 and approach them with a spirit of play. Don't analyze; just jot down whatever answers come to you. Make it a game, listing as many ideas and possibilities as you can think of. If you're still having difficulty, ask someone to play with you. Someone outside your process can offer ideas and suggestions that occur to them, which you may not have the objectivity to consider. Remember to turn your inner censor off for this process. If you need to, let go of the process altogether for a while and move on. Releasing the pressure of having to choose sometimes enables ideas that were blocked to come racing through.

Step 2: Identify the Urgent Needs and Compelling Desires of Your Target Market

Your target market's urgent needs and compelling desires prompt them to go in search of you and your services, so it's critical to be able to identify and address them when they come looking or you'll miss your window of opportunity.

> *You must offer what your potential clients want to buy, not what you want to sell or think they should want to buy. You must be able to look at your services from your client's perspective—their urgent needs and compelling desires.*

Your clients' urgent needs are the things that they must have right away, usually pressing problems, and often the things they would like to move away from. Their compelling desires are the things that they want in the future. Sure, they'd like to have them right now but they may be part of a bigger picture dream, and they see themselves moving toward these desires.

1.2.4 Written Exercise: What are five of your clients' *urgent* needs? (What problems must they solve right away?)

Example: The urgent need that may have prompted you to buy this book might be a feeling of stress because you know you need more clients (and more money) but don't know where or how to begin marketing your coaching business. Maybe the bills are really starting to pile up and you're afraid. Or maybe you know what to do to market your services but just aren't doing it. You're procrastinating and your business is suffering as a result.

1.2.5 Written Exercise: What are five of your clients' *compelling desires*? (What would they like to move toward?)

Example: Let's use you as an example again. Your compelling desire might be to feel confident and in control as you get as many clients as you would like. Maybe you want financial freedom. Maybe you just want to be able to take a real vacation every year. Or maybe it's all about having a thriving coaching business that includes doing what you love and making oodles of money doing it.

Step 3: Determine the Biggest Result Your Clients Get

This simple step might be the most important step in understanding why people buy what you're selling. What is the number one result you help your clients achieve or get? And when I say, "number one result," I mean one big one. Of course, I know there are lots of things that you help your clients achieve, experience, or get. But, generally, when a client comes looking for you, they're looking to solve one big problem or achieve one big result. I mean, why did you buy this book? To get more clients. Period. End of story. Are there lots of other things you'll get from reading this book? No doubt—from more confidence to more accountability, and even more friends (we'll cover that in Chapter 11). But, bottom line, you want more coaching clients and the Book Yourself Solid system delivers on that promise. In fact, every product or service you offer must have one big promise. Your job is to fulfill that promise in the delivery of your service.

1.2.6 Written Exercise: Describe the biggest result you provide.

Step 4: Uncover and Demonstrate the Benefits of Your Investable Opportunities

Do potential clients within your target market see your services as opportunities that will give them a significant return on their investment?

They must. If your potential clients are going to purchase your services and products, they *must* see them as investable opportunities. They must feel that the return they receive is greater than the investment they made.

My rule of thumb is that your clients should be getting a return of at least 10 times their investment in your services. It's a big number but it's worth striving for. This return will come in different forms, depending on what you offer, but the return falls into four related categories: financial, emotional, physical, and spiritual, which I'll refer to by the acronym FEPS.

What kind of FEPS return on investment will your clients get from working with you? Will it be greater than their financial, emotional, physical, or spiritual investment in your services? If so, how much higher? Two times? Twenty times?

The secret to having a successful business is to know what your clients want and to deliver it to them.

To make it obvious that your solutions are investable opportunities for your potential clients, you need to uncover and demonstrate their benefits. The products and services that you sell are just the products and services you sell. Although they are *technically* what your clients buy, they are not what they *actually* buy. They actually buy the benefits of the results you produce or help them get—FEPS benefits.

For example, you might *technically* offers the following opportunities:

- An online course that helps your clients with time management
- A membership community to share productivity best practices with a group of peers

However, these are still only the offerings or opportunities. The core benefits of these offerings are much deeper. Benefits are sometimes tangible results, but more often they're intangible. They are the effects your services have on your clients' quality of life. They are what make your offer an investable opportunity—the FEPS that clients can experience because of your services. They are what people buy. Don't ever forget that.

To get a stronger sense of how this works, think about this. If I asked you what you wanted to accomplish in the next 90 days, you might say you'd like to get more clients or earn more money, but what is getting more clients really going to give you? Will it give you more than money in the bank or a wallet fat with $20, $50, and $100 bills?

The truth is that you don't ultimately want clients. What you really want is the financial, emotional, physical, and even spiritual benefits of having clients: financial freedom, peace of mind, time with your family, or reduced concerns about how you're going to make ends meet, and more. Am I right?

To accentuate this point, here are some more examples of the deeper benefits you'll get from reading this book:

- A paradigm shift in the way you look at marketing and sales so that you can forever create demand for your services in a way that feels authentic and comfortable to you
- Increased confidence in yourself and your capacity to handle any business challenge that you are faced with
- A feeling of pride and a sense of accomplishment as you take the actions you know you need to take and from which you see positive results
- Freedom from the physical and emotional stress and anxiety of not being able to cover the mortgage for the home you and your children live in
- A deep, spiritual connection to your purpose and the opportunity to be fully self-expressed
- And so much more

Do you see how identifying core FEPS benefits allows you to speak to and touch your target market on a much deeper and more personally and emotionally connected level? The more FEPS benefits you uncover, the quicker you will start to attract new clients. People buy results and the benefits of those results. So think about the results you offer and the subsequent benefits they provide.

1.2.7 Written Exercise: What are the deep-rooted benefits your clients will experience as a result of working with you?

Now do you see what clients are actually buying when they decide to work with you? Every time you communicate in person, by writing, on the internet, in an advertisement, in meetings, or on the phone, articulate and rearticulate these benefits. Use words that you hear your clients use and express very specific solutions to their very prominent problems.

Even if it seems simple, it's worth repeating. If you're a branding expert and you have a client who wants to establish their own personal brand and start earning money doing something they love, then every time you meet, remind them that their personal brand will offer them freedom so they won't ever have to *settle* again when it comes to the clients they work with. This is a compelling desire for them, so remind them how inspired they are going to feel once they work only with their ideal clients. Keeping the benefits on the top of their mind, they clearly see the fully realized vision of their business and stay focused on accomplishing their goals.

Relax, Be Playful, and Have Fun!

If some of these business concepts are getting heavy for you, remember to look for the lightness and humor in everything you do and think of ways you can have more fun and help your clients at the same time. I mean, we're just talking about getting clients, an important subject, no doubt, but not a heavy one. Start thinking about how you can incorporate more play into your life and work. Don't be afraid to do the following:

- Be playful and quirky—be yourself.
- Be full of energy—enthusiasm is contagious.
- Help others laugh a lot—it's the best sales technique in the world.

It's been said that children laugh an average of 450 times per day, while adults laugh an average of only 15 times a day. If that's true, and based on my experience with my beloved kids, Jake, Ruby and Leo, it is, how did we end up 435 laughs short of a good time? Embrace a childlike sense of play, and you'll be one step closer to booking yourself solid.

Clients Want You to Help Them

Don't forget: your clients come to you for help. It's critical that you view your role with your clients as that of a highly important and trusted advisor. To do anything other than counsel, advise, guide, and support your clients would be a huge disservice. Start to view yourself as a leader in their life. You are not a commodity.

We all want someone to believe in. Be that person and you can write your own ticket. If you view yourself as a trusted advisor, clients will never forget you. They will come back to you months or even years later. Trust is built over time, so a connection you make today may not develop until much later. Continue to share your vision, mission, and obligation to help people. Give clients benefit after benefit and show them exactly how they can fulfill the promise of your offerings.

There is an acronym that is often used in sales—A, B, C—*always be closing*. Yuck! Sounds like cheesy sales talk to me. Instead, I say—A, B, C—*always be communicating* the benefits you offer. But first:

1. Select a target market.
2. Identify your clients' urgent needs and compelling desires.
3. Determine the number one biggest result you will help them get.
4. Uncover the deep-rooted, core benefits of that big result (financial, emotional, physical, and spiritual).

Got it? Good.

3

Develop a Personal Brand

Every time you suppress some part of yourself or allow others to play you small, you are in essence ignoring the owner's manual your creator gave you and destroying your design.
—Oprah Winfrey

Having established your target market and identified their urgent needs and compelling desires, the big result you help them get, as well as the benefits of the investable opportunities you offer, you are ready to develop a plan for deciding how you want to be known in your market—in an irresistible and unforgettable way.

You will do this by developing a *personal* brand. Brands are not just for big corporations. In fact, a personal brand will serve as an important key to your success. A personal brand will help clearly and consistently define, express, and communicate who you are, whom you serve, and why you have chosen to dedicate your life and work to serving your target market so that you can attract your most ideal clients and not those who are less than ideal. Personal branding is far more than just what you do or what your logo and website look like. It *is* you—uniquely you. It enables you to distinguish yourself from everyone else: what is unique about who you are, what you stand for, and what you do.

Branding

Your brand is certainly about making yourself known for your skills and talents but more than that—your brand is about *what you stand for*. Successful coaches find their style, build a brand based on it, and boldly express themselves through that brand. To let the world see your true, authentic worth is powerful, and it makes you memorable.

Think about some of the most successful people you know, whom you might often see on television. Anybody who is invited to give their opinion on a morning news show, or their take on the latest celebrity gossip, or an insight into a hot political potato of the day had better have a strong, memorable take, or they'll never be invited back. The most popular entertainers, musicians, business icons, and politicians have as many haters as they have fans, precisely because they stand for something. They have clear opinions and they're not afraid to share them.

That's how a personal brand works—it defines you, but first you must define it. Your personal brand will give you the ability to attract fun and exciting clients who understand and *get* you. And you *get* them. But only if you show them what you stand for. Develop a personal brand that looks like you, thinks like you, and sounds and feels like you—one that is instantly recognizable as your essence:

- Clear
- Consistent
- Authentic
- Memorable
- Meaningful
- Soulful
- Personal

There are three components to your personal brand:

- The first is your who and do what statement, which is based on who you serve and what you help them do or get.
- The second is your why you do it statement, which is based on why you get up every day to do your work—what you stand for. Sure, you stand for lots of things but you're going to choose one big one to stake your name on.

- And the third is your personal tagline. More on these three components in a minute. But first . . .

Releasing Blocks

Before we begin to craft your personal brand, it's important to address any blocks you are inadvertently creating that may hold you back from fully expressing yourself. I know it can seem unusual to discuss personal blocks as it relates to branding, but this is *personal* branding, and this is your *life* we're talking about. You want to play the biggest game possible, don't you? The following questions can help you gain clarity about how you want to be known in the world. Consider them seriously.

> *The greatest strategy for personal and business development on the planet is bold self-expression.*

Are you fully self-expressed? I ask it because to create a gutsy, passionate, ardent, provocative, courageous, valiant, vibrant, dynamic, luminous, and respected personal brand, you must be fully self-expressed.

You can't hide behind the shingle that you've hung over your door and you can't water yourself down in any way, shape, or form. If you do, you won't be of interest to the people you're meant to serve.

As a coach, you probably already work *on* your business—such as setting up an automatic marketing system—and work *in* your business, serving your clients. How you brand yourself is equally critical and is a reflection of how you work *on yourself*.

Have you compromised yourself or watered yourself down in any area of your business? For example, have you been in a situation with a client or partner in which you walked away feeling like you settled for less or compromised your integrity? You may be thinking, "I don't sell out. I've never compromised or sold out." If you haven't, you are unique. It's completely normal to compromise yourself from time to time.

It's also completely normal, especially when you are starting out, to wonder whether you are "ready," whether you have enough training, or whether what you have to offer is of any value. The truth is that you may never feel completely "ready," and if you get stuck perseverating about these questions, you'll never go out and find those people you are meant to serve.

It will benefit you well to know exactly where you have run into trouble in the past. Because working independently and running a coaching business is challenging, you can eliminate a lot of pain and surprise right now by acknowledging the issues you may have buried or have had a difficult time confronting in the past.

1.3.1 Written Exercise: Even though it may be a bit unpleasant to think about, list the ways in which you've sold out, settled for less, or compromised your integrity in your business, either now or in the past.

1.3.2 Written Exercise: What about the flip side? Tap into instances in your business life when you've felt alive and vibrant—fully self-expressed. Everything you did just flowed. Draw on all of your senses. What was happening at that time that made you feel so alive?

1.3.3 Written Exercise: Now compare the two areas, the ones in which you sold out and the situations in which you felt most fully self-expressed. How can you change your behavior to speak boldly and from a place of free expression so that you're working in situations that make you feel fully self-expressed? How will you communicate to make sure you stop compromising or watering yourself down in the future?

1.3.4 Written Exercise: Start with a few situations (fairly comfortable ones) in which you could practice speaking from a bolder and more self-expressed place.

> **1.3.5 Written Exercise:** Write down a few more situations (that seem a little more difficult) that you'd like to work up to speaking more boldly about.

There are two reasons for the exercises you're doing. The first is so you can help clients understand how you can help them. The second is so you can make sure that your personal and professional intentions are clear. Clear intentions enable you to gracefully and confidently move toward your goals. Conflicting intentions will undermine your success without you even knowing it. They will hold you back from your dreams. They are the mother of energy drain and confusion. From a perspective of a personal brand identity, conflicting intentions will eventually lead to a bland message and a less successful you.

> **1.3.6 Written Exercise:** Identify one of your most important intentions as it relates to your business.
> *Example:* I intend to book myself solid.

> **1.3.7 Written Exercise:** Take a good hard look within to see if you can identify any potentially conflicting intentions for the intention you identified. These are likely to be subconscious and more difficult to identify, and they are nearly always based on fear.
> *Example:* If I book myself solid, I won't have time for myself. Or, to book myself solid, I'll have to promote myself, and self-promotion will make me feel pathetic and vulnerable. Or maybe you want to book yourself solid but you *think* self-promotion is unappealing.

> **1.3.8 Booked Solid Action Step:** Identifying and acknowledging your conflicting intentions is the first big step in releasing them. Awareness is key, but not always enough to prevent conflicting intentions from affecting and blocking your positive intentions. The next step in the process is to identify the underlying fears. Once you've identified them, you can begin to take steps to relieve them.

For this step, it's critical that you very carefully choose one or two sincerely and highly supportive friends to share your new insights with. They must be truly supportive and willing to help you change. Often, as we begin to make changes in our lives, whether business or personal, some of our most dearly beloved friends and family can feel threatened by the process of change. Although they may consciously want you to be successful, they may have their own subconscious conflicting intentions and be highly invested in wanting to maintain their own comfort zone by keeping you in yours. These are not the folks you want to ask for help from to do this exercise. In fact they're not people you want to spend much time with.

If you've got a coach of your own (which I hope you do!) then you may choose to work with them instead on this process.

Share the intentions and their conflicting counterparts with one or two others and ask your friends or coach to help you in recognizing whether these are genuine concerns or unfounded fears. Then brainstorm ways to address the problems.

Although you can take this step on your own, we're often too close to our own fears to see them clearly. Having a supportive friend, mentor, or coach of your own, who has a bit more objectivity than we do, can help put your fears into perspective.

You Are Uniquely You

It's often those qualities that make you uniquely you—the ones that come so naturally to you that you don't even think about them—that become the best personal brands.

A pleasant woman in her early 40s, Susan, came to me and asked me to help her discover "what she was born to do" so she could launch her own coaching business. It was a particularly tough time for her. She had recently been divorced and needed to support herself. As you might imagine, she was concerned about what she would do. Years earlier, she had been a successful trader on Wall Street. Yet it had now been over 20 years since what she referred to as her "glory days." I asked her, "What are your quirks?" "Quirks?" she replied. "I don't have any quirks." She sounded moderately offended. "Okay," I said. "Then tell me about your friendships. What are they based on?" Without a moment's hesitation she said, "My female friends are always asking me for advice on sex and intimacy." "Interesting. Now we're getting somewhere," I thought.

She told me about her unusual habit of giving scarlet-colored thongs (not the ones you wear on your feet at the beach) as gifts. This is the same woman who told me she didn't have any quirks. After more prompting and investigation into this unique, special, and entertaining quirk, it became clear that she was fully self-expressed when she was thinking and focusing on how women 40 and over can be, should be, and are, remarkable sexual beings (and more). She decided, even though she would have to resolve many conflicting intentions about doing so, that she was going to exploit her quirk and create the *Scarlet Thong Society*, an invitation-only social club for women over 40 who want to acknowledge their sexual prowess.

You may not have scarlet thongs to hand out, but chances are you do have something unique, maybe even quirky, that you really want to express and that others will notice and respond to.

1.3.9 Written Exercise: To know which secret quirk or natural talent is waiting in the wings to bring you wealth, happiness, and unbridled success in your business, answer the following questions:

- How are you unique?
- What are three things that make you memorable?
- What are the special talents that you are genetically coded to do? What have you been good at since you were a kid?
- What do people always compliment you on?
- What do you love or never grow tired of talking about in your personal life?
- What do you want to say that you would never grow tired of talking about when you are asked about your work?

Many times we are too close to see the qualities or quirks that stand out to others. Send a few of these questions to different people in your life to get their responses about you and your personality. Not only will you start to see some of the same truths about who you are but also you'll get back the most touching and warm emails. Give it a try.

<hr />

1.3.10 Booked Solid Action Step: Send an email to five or more people (include friends, family, clients, neighbors, and acquaintances from all the different aspects of your life).

- Ask them to provide you with your top three personality traits or quirks.
- Ask for fun or unique experiences they've had with you.
- Tell them to be brave and not to be shy.

<hr />

Remember that your work is likely to fail if you don't love it and share it with the world. And here's the biggie: *When you're fully self-expressed, you likely love marketing.* You won't have conflicting intentions about promoting yourself. You won't feel that the world is coming to an end when you get a rejection. You'll smile and move on to the next opportunity because your ability to express yourself is directly proportional to your level of confidence and vice versa.

With all of this new and insightful information about yourself, you should be thrilled that you've already made it through the challenge of choosing your path to becoming a coach. That's no easy task. Keep all of these insights in mind as you begin to craft your own personal brand.

The Three Components of Your Personal Brand

As I mentioned at the beginning of this chapter, there are three components to your personal brand:

- Your who and do what statement
- Your why you do it statement
- Your tagline

Laser-beam your focus on these three aspects of your personal brand until you feel totally and utterly fully expressed when you put words to your who and do what statement, your why you do it statement, and your tagline. The process may take a day or it may take a few months. It took me six months, but I didn't have this book to help me do it faster. The important thing is to give yourself the time to really give thought to it all.

Your Who and Do What Statement

Your who and do what statement lets others know exactly whom you help and what you can help them do. It is the first filter that people will put you through when considering hiring you. Your potential clients will look at it to see if you help people like them in their specific situation. But is it enough to hire you? Probably not. There are other people who offer the same or similar services that help them get what they want. So, once they are convinced that you help them get what they want, they consider . . .

Your Why You Do It Statement

After potential clients identify with your who and do what statement, they will want to know if they connect with you on personal, emotional, or philosophical level. They'll want to know if they connect with your why you do it statement—the reason you do what you do and what you stand for. The reason you get up every day to do the work that you do. It represents who you are. Those who resonate with your why you do it statement will feel it on a deep level and be strongly attracted to you. Your why you do it statement doesn't necessarily need to be wildly unique. Just deeply meaningful to you—and to the people you're *meant to serve.*

Your Tagline

Your tagline, based on your why you do it statement, is something you'll never get tired of hearing. And the first time you hear someone refer to you by it, you'll want to cry tears of joy. You'll formulate one simple sentence that enables people to define you in a manner of your own choosing. You'll never get tired of saying it or hearing it because it's based on what you stand for and what's important to you. And, most important, not only will it very deeply and truly mean something to you but also it will resonate with the people you're meant to serve. Reading or hearing your tagline will be the defining moment people need to decide whether to purchase your services, products, or programs.

Your tagline lets others know what it's like to be around you. It says something about who you are at your core, and it's the essence of what you want to achieve or experience in the world. Think of it as the bigger vision that is the inspiration for what you do in your business. Your why you do it statement and its associated tagline is the way in which you want to touch others' lives in a positive and meaningful way.

Your tagline is not necessarily specific to your target market. It may resonate with many people in your target market—your ideal clients, specifically—but your tagline is not necessarily about your target market; it's about the emotional connection you make with people in general *and* with your ideal clients in your target market. Many people serve the same target market you serve, but your tagline is what will resonate with some people and not with others. It will resonate with those you're meant to serve.

Why have you dedicated your life to serving others? How do you want to make a difference?

If you don't want to make a difference, consider making your living as something other than a coach, because a coach must stand in service for those around them, and the community as a whole.

Wrap-up review:

1. Who and do what statement (for example, I help coaches get booked solid)
2. Why you do it statement (for example, I want to help people think bigger about who they are and what they offer the world)
3. Tagline (for example, I'm the guy to call when you're tired of thinking small)

1.3.11 Written Exercise: Start with the basics. Keep it simple and straight-forward. What is your who and do what statement? Whom do you help and what do you help them do? Refer to your target market from Chapter 2. The first time around, just come up with something accurate and clear for now—make sure a five-year-old can understand it. List as many possibilities as come to mind. Finish this statement, "I help . . ."

Example: I help . . . coaches get booked solid. (Or, for the five-year-old, "I help people get more business.")

1.3.12 Written Exercise: Set aside your inner critic and give yourself permission to think big—I mean *really big,* bigger than you've ever dared to think or dream before. Be your most idealistic, inspired, creative, powerful you. What is your purpose? What is your vision of what you hope to achieve through your work? Remember, your work is an expression of who you are. List whatever comes to mind.

1.3.13 Written Exercise: Keeping the preceding in mind, craft a possible why you do it statement.

1.3.14 Booked Solid Action Step: If your why you do it statement is not immediately and easily identifiable, get together with a group of supportive friends or associates who know you well and ask them to brainstorm it with you. It's often the things about you that are most natural and that you don't even recognize that become key elements of your why you do it statement. Having some outside input and a few more objective perspectives can make all the difference.

1.3.15 Written Exercise: Craft a possible tagline that represents and demonstrates your why you do it statement.

Roma Non è Stata Costruita in un Giorno
(Rome Wasn't Built in a Day)

Neither was my personal brand. I went through many, many versions, even one a month, before I got to a why I do it statement and tagline that worked for me. I was getting caught up in trying to find the perfect brand message or positioning statement. I thought it had to be perfect because it couldn't be changed. Eventually, I recognized that creating a tagline that represented what I stood for was a process and that I'd just keep changing it until I got there. If I didn't start with something, though, what would I have had? Nothing. That's what.

First I got clear on my who and do what statement, that "I help professional service providers get more clients."

Then I got clear on my why I do it statement: "I want to help people think bigger about who they are and what they offer the world."

What took longer was nailing down my tagline. I worked really hard on trying to find it. It took about six months. I thought about it every day, but the amazing thing was that it came to me by accident. I was with a bunch of people, and we were masterminding and brainstorming about our businesses and everyone was talking about what they did. I was giving the others a hard time, teasing and questioning, asking, "Why would I hire you for that?" I was playing devil's advocate until finally, one of the women gave it right back to me and said, "Yeah, well, why would I hire you?" I blurted out, "Because I'm the guy to call when you're tired of thinking small." Suddenly the whole room went silent, as if everyone was holding their breath. After a few moments, the same woman shouted out "Yes! That is *so you!*" Everyone in the room was cheering and the air was charged with excitement.

Even so, I didn't really think much about it until a couple of weeks later as I was talking to a colleague about an idea I had for a social network in which people could come together to think bigger about who they are and what they offer the world. I was excited about it, but I questioned it: "I'm not sure about this *big* stuff. I came up with this tagline that I'm 'the guy to call when you're tired of thinking small,' but I'm not sure about it. A, because it's a little cheesy and B, do you think anyone will actually care about that?" She laughed and said, "Michael, are you dense?" I said, "Yes, but you're going to have to be more specific for me." She explained to me that she likes being around me because I help her think so much bigger about who she is and what she offers the world.

I realized then that because it was so natural to me to want to help people think bigger, it didn't seem like such a big deal. Actually, it can be a bit confronting to others because I'm pretty relentless about it. So, it can push people away if they want to keep playing small. It took discussing it with others who weren't as close to it as I was to get the perspective I needed. The exact thing that came most naturally to me was the thing that was drawing ideal clients to me.

As I began using my why I do it statement and tagline to let others know why I do what I do, I found that the people for whom it resonated would immediately comment on how much they connected with it. Those who didn't get it, wouldn't. That's okay. It's all about attracting those people who are meant to work with you.

The rest will be attracted to someone with whom they will resonate, and you won't end up with less-than-ideal clients.

Recall the story about the old man, the boy, and the donkey. The process of booking yourself solid isn't about how to please as many people as possible. It's about how to convey your own unique message to those who are waiting to hear it. That can't be achieved with personal branding that's been watered down in an attempt to appeal to everyone. It can be achieved only through bold, no-holds-barred self-expression. It's about being uniquely you and standing for something—in a big way.

4

How to Talk About What You Do

A conversation is a dialogue, not a monologue. That's why there are so few good conversations: due to scarcity, two intelligent talkers seldom meet.
—Truman Capote

A primary reason that many coaches fail to build thriving businesses is that they struggle to articulate in a clear and compelling way exactly what solutions and benefits they offer. They don't know how to talk about what they do without sounding confusing or bland or like everyone else—and without using an elevator speech. Yes, you heard me, *without* using an elevator speech.

The elevator speech (aka, the elevator pitch or 30-second commercial) reflects the idea that it should be possible to wow someone with what you do in the time it takes an elevator to go from the first to the fifth floor.

I've been polling audiences of thousands for years on this issue. During each speech I ask, "How many of you love, love, love *listening* to someone else's elevator speech?" Maybe two out of two thousand hands go up. I then ask, "How many of you love, love, love *giving* your elevator speech?"

Same thing. Only a few hands. So what gives? If we don't like listening to or giving the speech, why is it still being taught? Because, of course, we need to be able to talk about what we do—I get the concept. However, for coaches, not only does it not work well but also it makes us look foolish, or, worse yet, obnoxious.

The elevator pitch was born so that the inventor could pitch a product idea to a retailer or manufacturer or the *entrepreneur* could pitch a business idea to a venture capitalist or angel investor in the hopes of receiving funding, not for the coach to try to build a relationship of trust with a potential client over time. Venture capitalists often judge the quality of an idea on the basis of the quality of its elevator pitch. It makes perfect sense, in that situation. But this is not how a relationship develops between a client and a *coach*. You're trying to earn the status of a trusted advisor, not trying to raise money to create some new product like metal-detecting sandals. Totally different context. Totally different dynamic.

I'm on a mission to kill the elevator speech, to remove it from the business vernacular—for everybody except the few cases I just mentioned. I hope you'll join me on this mission and learn how to talk about what you do without ever resorting to an elevator speech. So, what do you do instead?

By using this crazy concept that I call a *conversation*. Weird, I know. Over the course of this chapter, I'm going to teach you a Book Yourself Solid Dialogue, a creative—but not scripted—conversation that will spark interest when appropriate about you and your coaching services, products, and programs. The Book Yourself Solid Dialogue will enable you to have a meaningful conversation (*conversation* being the operative word) with a potential client or referral source. The dialogue is a dynamic, lively description of the people you help, what challenges they face, how you help them, and the results and benefits they get from working with you. It is also intended to replace the static, boring, and usual response to the question, "What do you do?" "I'm a consultant," "I'm a coach," or "I'm a trainer"— answers that often elicit nothing more than a polite nod, comment, or awkward silence and a blank stare. Once you get that response, anything more you say about yourself or your services will sound pushy. Worse yet, you could supplement the rote answer with an overblown, high-highfalutin, hyperbole-laden elevator speech that's supposed to make you look like a rock star in 30 seconds. Unfortunately, I doubt the one-two punch of boring answer, followed by excessively exuberant elevator pitch is going to compel the listener to whip out their credit card right then and there.

Instead, how about a meaningful, connected *dialogue* with a potential client or referral source? Think of it as a conversation between two people, each of whom actually cares about what the other has to say.

The beautiful thing is that the interchange is based on successfully understanding why people buy what you're selling. And because of the work we did together in Chapter 2, you already know why people buy what you're selling.

You previously created your who and do what statement. That's a fantastic first step and an excellent tool for starting a conversation about what you do. Now you must be sure that you can captivate and actively engage the person you're talking to in a conversation that elicits questions rather than just polite acknowledgment. You must talk *with* people, not *at* them, which means listening to them, too, and really hearing what they're interested in, and what their needs are. After all, their needs may be exactly what you serve. Avoid giving a prepared script. Doing so is generally a train wreck waiting to happen. You'll see that you can have long, medium, or short conversations based on your Book Yourself Solid Dialogue that will enable you to connect with different people in different situations. You tell them about the people you work with and then you listen to their response. You build on their response, and before you know it, you are having a conversation that is informative and inspiring—and that's the key to talking about what you do without being bland or confusing or, worse yet, obnoxious, albeit unintended.

You are so much more than just your professional title: coach, advisor, trainer, consultant, mentor, aide, counselor, expert, instructor, teacher, or any other dictionary description that defines you as one of the masses.

Think about it for a moment. Let's say you're a personal trainer and you meet someone who really needs your help who would also be an ideal client. The only problem is that they have a preconceived notion of what fitness coaching is all about and what a personal trainer is like, and it's not a preconceived notion that sets you up for success.

Imagine this scenario: the potential client, let's call her Mary, asks you what you do. You say, "I'm a personal trainer." Before you know what's happened, you see the potential client's face contort, her left eyebrow lifts along with the left side of her upper lip, and her nostrils begin to flare. The potential client says, "Oh, yeah . . . I had a personal trainer as a neighbor once. She was really weird and made my life miserable. In fact, I had to move out of that apartment because of her and I loved that apartment! She had scores of people coming in and out at all hours of the day, blasting loud music and banging on the floor all day long. It was like the world was about to end! She was totally inconsiderate and the endless line of her sweaty clients really made me feel uncomfortable in my own home."

Uh-oh.

Would you like to get that kind of response when you tell someone what you do? And this can happen to anybody, not just to a personal trainer. Say a motivational sales coach meets someone whose only introduction to motivational sales meetings has been the movie *Boiler Room*, a movie about stockbrokers who try to swindle innocent people out of their life's savings. Or *Glengarry Glen Ross*, about dodgy real estate professionals. Or *The Wolf of Wall Street* in all its druggy dishonesty. Not a pretty picture.

How much more are you than your professional title? Your Book Yourself Solid Dialogue will enable you to set yourself apart from everyone else whose professional title is the same as yours. It provides you with the opportunity to highlight the ways in which you and your services, products, and programs are unique—and do so with passion.

If your Book Yourself Solid Dialogue reads like your résumé, you'll bore people to tears, and although they may not say it, they'll be thinking, "Who cares? So what? What has any of that got to do with me?" Your potential client wants to know, "What's in it for me?"

Developing Your Book Yourself Solid Dialogue

You're going to break this down into its smallest components and gather all the information you've worked hard to compile in the previous pages. You've chosen your target market and you've begun to develop your personal brand by crafting your who and do what statement, your why I do it statement, and your tagline. Now you're going to go back through all the exercises you've done and clean up your core message. If you've kept up on the exercises, mastering the ability to have a meaningful Book Yourself Solid Dialogue is a relatively simple process, and yet this powerful piece makes all the difference in your business and your message.

Five-Part Book Yourself Solid Dialogue Formula

Let's put it all together and create a few different versions of your dialogue: short, medium, and long. Please, please, bear in mind that we are not crafting a speech. I am just giving you some structure so that you can begin to imagine the possible content of the Book Yourself Solid Dialogue that is a *conversation*.

1.4.1 Written Exercise: Each of the following five parts has already been answered in previous exercises. All you need to do is pull the pieces into the following formula:

Part I: Introduce your target market.

Part II: Identify and summarize the three biggest and most critical problems that your target market faces.

Part III: List how you solve these problems and present clients with investable opportunities.

Part IV: Demonstrate the number-one most relevant result you help your clients achieve.

Part V: Reveal the deeper core benefits your clients experience.

You now have an outline that will help you clearly articulate what you do without sounding confusing and bland. In fact, you'll sound like a superstar because you can use this outline or framework to have a meaningful conversation with another human being. I know I'm being redundant here, but it's so important that I'm willing to. This is not an unchangeable script. Don't stay married to the format. Be sure to improvise. Using the structure can be helpful but you may not need to go through every element of this framework in every conversation. The person you're engaged with might end up doing all the talking and even supply your side of the dialogue accurately. Then you can just sit back and listen. The point is, if you're prepared with these five elements, you have the required ingredients for talking about what you do so you can cook up a sweet and tasty business, booked solid with high-paying, high-value clients. (Make note of how each part of the exercises you've just done fits into the conversations that follow, and note also how each part flows as the result of a natural conversation.)

Short and Sweet

Start by trying the short version, which is essentially an expanded who and do what statement.

- I help [Part I] . . . [insert Part V].

Example: Checkout line at the supermarket

BOBBY: Nice to meet you, Michael. What do you do?
MP: I'm a small-business advisor—I help [Part I] small-business owners [Part II] get more clients.
BOBBY: Oh, that's very interesting. My wife has a home-based business. Could you help her?
MP: Tell me a bit about what she does and what kind of support you think she needs.

Now, we're connecting.

The Mid-Length Version

You can easily adapt the Book Yourself Solid Dialogue as needed. Try a mid-length version and just tighten it up a bit.

- I help [Part I].
- You know how [insert Parts I and II]?
- Well, what I do is [insert Parts III and V].

Example: Industry conference

LISA: Nice to meet you, Michael. What do you do for a living?
MP: I'm a small-business advisor—I help [Part I] small-business owners [Part II] get more clients.
LISA: That's so important . . . getting more clients.
MP: Ain't that the truth. Business owners are always looking to find more clients but often complain that they hate marketing and selling [Parts I and more of II].

LISA: Can I confess something to you, Michael? I'm one of those business owners, and I always need new clients, but I really hate marketing and selling!

MP: I hear that! But it doesn't have to be that way. In fact, I teach people just like you how to *love* marketing and selling, and at the same time, get all the clients they want (More of Part II, Part III, and V).

LISA: Tell me more!

And now we're connecting.

The Long Version

Easy-peasy-lemon-squeezy. All you need to do is insert Parts I through V as appropriate.

- You know how [drop in Part I] do, are, or feel [include some of Part II]?
- Well, what I do is [articulate Part III].
- The result is [reveal Part IV].
- The benefits are [insert lots of Part V].

Example: Casual conversation at a cocktail party

JOE: Hey, Michael, what is it that you do?

MP: Thanks for asking, Joe. You know how many self-employed professionals (Part I) go out on their own looking for the freedom that working independently promises but they wind up isolated, frustrated, and often struggle financially? (Part II) Do you know people like that?

JOE: Oh, yeah, I definitely do. Actually, that sounds exactly like my sister, Jane.

MP: Oh, no kidding . . . is she working more hours than she should or wants to, never seems to be able to relax, and is constantly stressed about money? Or worse . . . has she become disillusioned about working for herself (more of Part II)?

JOE: Yeah, that's exactly right! I've been trying to encourage her, but frankly I'm all out of ideas as to how to help her.

MP: I hear you. Please tell her that she's not alone. Her situation is remarkably common. So common, in fact, that I teach a process for people like her to book themselves solid in my seminars and coaching programs (Part III). Fortunately, over 90% of the people who have gone through my programs increase the number of clients they serve by over 30% and improve their revenues by over 40% within a year of taking the program (Part IV). So, there's hope!

JOE: Oh, wow! That's pretty cool. I just wish Jane could have the clients she wants.

MP: Well, yeah, it's very cool, but it's about more than just getting clients and making money. Jane would begin to think a heck of a lot bigger about who she is and what she offers the world so she won't have to worry so much anymore. She'll be able to passionately share her work with the people she's meant to serve (Part V).

Joe sighs, takes a meaningful pause, then says . . .

JOE: I'm so glad I asked you what you did. How can I get my sister in touch with you? She could really use your help.

MP: Would you like to give me your card and I'll follow up with you on Monday so you can introduce me to your sister?

JOE: That would be great, Michael. This way, I don't have to put it on my already overly long to-do list.

MP: You know . . . I wrote a book based on my process called *Book Yourself Solid*. Why don't I send a signed copy to your sister as a gift from you?

JOE: That would be great. Thank you. When you email me, I'll give you her address so you can mail it to her.

That's a pretty good way to have a real conversation with someone about what you do. Of course, I've written this scene, so it works perfectly. And, when it's in written form like this, it can feel like a script. It's not, though. In real life, it won't always be this smooth or successful. But, if you listen well, are flexible, and can adapt to the dynamic and specifics at hand, more often than not, you'll knock it out of the park.

Or I could start by saying, "I'm a *New York Times, Wall Street Journal, USA Today,* and *Publisher's Weekly* best-selling author of six books, including my most recent, called *Steal the Show,* and *Book Yourself Solid,* which is one of the most popular books in the world on marketing for service professionals and has been translated into 21 languages and is in five editions and counting, along with a separate illustrated edition, who appears regularly on network and cable TV shows as an expert on business and communication. I am one of the most sought-after professional speakers in the business, and have certified over 500 coaches to teach Book Yourself Solid around the world in our Book Yourself Solid School of Coach Training. Oh, and let's not forget my other business, called Heroic Public Speaking, which is widely considered the most effective and unique public speaking school in the world. It's like Hogwarts for speakers." But then I'd sound like an arrogant, self-important jerk with a narcissistic personality disorder. These kinds of credentials and information should come out over time, when appropriate, not three seconds after someone says, "What do you do?"

Once you've clearly identified your target market, understand their needs and desires, and can articulate how you help them by identifying the core benefits associated with the results of your services, you'll never be caught off guard again. I suggest you continue to hone and refine your message and then practice it over and over. I do.

Getting into a Book Yourself Solid Dialogue with Ease

Start in the comfortable confines of your home. It may take some time for your Book Yourself Solid Dialogue to feel natural. Although you don't want your dialogue to sound stiff and rehearsed, you do want to practice it. The more you practice it, the more comfortable you'll get with it, the less rehearsed it will sound, and the more improvisational you will be. You get only one chance to make a first impression. Present yourself and your business in a powerful and compelling way.

Practicing in this way will help you to become comfortable with the multitude of ways in which your Book Yourself Dialogue will unfold when you're speaking with a variety of people. It is truly a dialogue, not a speech or a script, so every time you have a dialogue with someone about what you do, it will be unique. Because the people you'll be speaking with won't be reading a script, they may or may not respond in similar ways to what I outlined here, but you'll soon discover that when you know your Book Yourself Solid Dialogue well, it won't matter. You'll easily and effortlessly respond in the most appropriate way.

1.4.2 Booked Solid Action Step: Practice with a colleague or two. Call each other spontaneously to ask, "What is it that you do?" The most important principle of the Book Yourself Solid system is actually using what I teach you. Learning it is only a means to an end. Taking action will get you booked solid.

After you've practiced with your colleague, answer these questions for each other:

- Did I sound relaxed and comfortable?
- Could you sense my passion and excitement for what I do?
- What really grabbed your attention?
- What did you like best or least about my Book Yourself Solid Dialogue?

Use this exercise as the great opportunity it is to get honest, open feedback so that you can fine-tune your Book Yourself Solid Dialogue and make it the best it can be.

Be sure to speak with lots of expression. Get excited and show the passion you have for the problems you solve and what you do in the world. If you're not very interested in what you do, no one else will be, either.

When you're passionate and excited about what you do and you let it show, it's attractive. Real passion can't be faked and there's nothing more appealing and convincing than knowing someone is speaking from the heart.

And don't forget to do the following:

- *Smile:* I mean really smile—a big, bold, friendly smile.
- *Make eye contact:* You probably won't connect with others on a deep level if you aren't making eye contact.
- *Be confident:* Use confident, open body language. Stand up straight, yet be relaxed.
- *Listen!* Stop and listen intently to the needs and desires of the person you're speaking to so that you can address whatever is most important and relevant to her. Stay in the moment and avoid anticipating where the conversation is going to go and what you plan on saying.

A well-crafted Book Yourself Solid Dialogue that is infused with your own unique brilliance and passion is incredibly powerful. Claim your passion, claim your voice, and share it with the world one person at a time.

Building Trust and Credibility

To be booked solid requires that you are considered credible within your marketplace, that you be perceived as likeable, and that you earn the trust of the people you'd like to serve. Now that you've got a solid foundation, it's time to look at how to develop a strategy for creating trust and credibility so that you stand out from the crowd and begin to build relationships with your potential clients. Your strategy will be based on the following actions:

- Becoming and establishing yourself as a likeable expert in your field
- Building relationships of trust over time through your sales cycle
- Keeping in touch with clients, potential clients, and referral partners
- Developing brand-building services, products and programs

In the first module, you spent time contemplating the people you want to serve, how best to serve them, how to express yourself uniquely through the services you offer, and how to talk to people you hope to serve about how you can help them. Now it's time to step things up a notch and look at what you have to do to earn the trust of the people you're meant to serve.

As before, I walk you step-by-step through the process, and you'll begin to see that marketing and sales doesn't have to be so hard after all. In fact, I think you'll find that it can even be exciting and fun.

CHAPTER 5

Becoming a Likeable Expert in Your Field

All credibility, all good conscience, all evidence of truth comes only from the senses.
—Friedrich Nietzsche

Have you heard the expression, "It's not what you know that's important but who you know"? There's some truth to it but, if you're a working coach, consider the importance of "Who knows *what* you know and do they *like* you?" If you want to establish yourself as an expert in your field, a "category authority," potential clients as well as marketing and referral partners need to know that you know what you know . . . and they need to like you.

Even before we discuss how to position yourself as an expert within your field, let's get down to the nitty-gritty—the standard credibility builders. The standard credibility builders are the things that you need to do and have in place to appear credible and professional. Once you have all your basics covered, then and only then can we discuss how to establish your reputation as an authority in your field and look at how your likeability influences your ability to get booked solid.

The Standard Credibility Builders

The standard credibility builders may seem obvious, but without them you won't be taken seriously, so they're worth reviewing:

- *You must have a professional email address:* Preferably one that includes your domain name. juicytushy@aol.com doesn't qualify. Neither does 175bb3c@yahoo.com. Either yourfirstname@yourfullname .com or yourfirstname@yourbusinessname.com or similar variation is more appropriate. And, even if you don't have a website built yet, you can still purchase a domain name and use an email address associated with that domain in the meantime.

- *Invest in quality business cards:* There's an argument that you don't need business cards at all any more. And it's far more useful to collect them than to hand them out, because that way you're in control of the follow-up. But if you are collecting them, then you're probably judging them. And if you are handing them out, then you will, in turn, be judged. Business cards with perforated edges that you've printed at home, or the free cards with the printing company's name on the back, will undermine your credibility. On the flipside, over-produced cards with hyped-up text or a highly stylized headshot can also undermine your credibility. Only do something unusual with things like business cards if you're an expert at that kind of differentiation, like a branding coach. Otherwise, keep it simple.

- *If you don't have a website, get one now!* Actually, wait until you read Chapter 16 of this book, the Book Yourself Solid Web Strategy. If you do have a website and it's out of date or nonfunctional, build a new one. Please don't design your site yourself unless you're a professional or an exceptionally skilled amateur. Have a site that looks professionally designed. It can be a super simple one page website that showcases to the world exactly how you want to be seen. Again, more on this in Chapter 16.

- *Make sure your social profiles represent you professionally:* Think about how a potential client perceives you. What do you want them to know and what might turn them off? Learn more about social media profiles in Chapter 16.

- *Have professionally produced photographs taken:* Display them on your website, on your social media profiles and in promotional materials. A photo of you in your pajamas with your cat is not going to inspire a lot of confidence (unless, of course, you're a cat coach who dabbles in sleep hygiene advice). Find any way you can to use pictures or video to demonstrate your professionalism on all promotional materials both online and off. And certainly display photographs of yourself speaking to groups of people or engaged with your clients. Not having photographs readily available on your website or other marketing materials leaves your potential clients wondering what you have to hide. And it doesn't give them the opportunity to connect with you. Interestingly, there is some social science that suggests when people don't know you, if they see lots of photos of you in different environments, then they begin to feel that they do, in fact, know you.

- *Obtain and showcase specific testimonials rather than general testimonials:* A comment from a client named H. G. that says, "Pam was great. She really helped" is not going to hold a lot of weight and it's certainly not going to get you booked solid. However, a very specific testimonial from a person with a name, a company, and maybe even a website address, if applicable, that says, "In two months, Pam helped me lose 15 pounds. I could not have done it without her!" will carry more weight (no pun intended). The testimonial is results oriented. If Pam is a health coach, the client's satisfaction represents the results that many of her clients want to achieve. Even better is a testimonial from a well-known person. For example, if Cindy Crawford was a client of Pam's, and she offered the same testimonial, wouldn't you want to work with Pam? You'd figure if she's good enough for Cindy, she's good enough for me. I would. This is important because testimonials can come off as mundane and may not serve as true differentiators unless they are from people recognizable to the potential client. So, ask everybody you work with to offer specific, positive praise of you and your work and reach out to people you respect. Connect with them, and when the time is right, ask them to supply you with a testimonial of your work.

- Bonus: *Establish an advisory board:* If well-known individuals lend you their names, it will help you establish credibility within your target market. Just your association with other recognized experts—not necessarily coaches but other professionals who will be familiar to your target market—will do wonders for establishing your credibility.

Standards of Service

Listed here are the basic standards of service that are essential for any decent coach to adhere to and that your clients expect. They help establish your credibility. The mistake that many coaches make is thinking that these standards of service are all that is necessary to help them stand out from the crowd.

- *Quality of service:* Of course you should have a high quality of service. A potential client expects that you offer a high quality of service. The barriers to entry for the coaching industry aren't high and there are many mediocre coaches. Don't be one of those.
- *Methods and tools:* It's expected that you have the best methods and tools.
- *Responsiveness:* Your clients expect you to be responsive. They may not expect you to go to their house on a whim at 3 a.m. on a Sunday for an urgent mindset reset (unless that's what they paid for) but they do expect you or your team to respond to their calls and emails quickly, whether they're a prospective client or an existing client.
- *Credentials:* For most coaches, clients don't care as much about credentials as you might think. At the time of writing there is no universally recognized governing body for the coaching profession. However there are many excellent training institutions and if you have benefited from studying coaching under their guidance and have the certificates to prove it, let the world know.
- *Client importance:* Your clients expect to be considered important. It's essential to always make your clients feel important—more than important, in fact. You want to make your clients feel like the sun

rises and shines just for them, because it does, if you want to book yourself solid. Making clients feel as important as they truly are builds your credibility, and it should be a given. Although your clients may well be looking to you as a leader, that doesn't mean you get to treat them like you're a drill sergeant and they're a new recruit (again, unless that's what they've paid for).

- *Appropriate price:* People don't generally buy on price (even though they say they do) and certainly not when it comes to their personal satisfaction, family, or their business, which I guess is almost everything. Offering the lowest price is not necessarily going to help you establish credibility. In fact, many potential clients may be leery if your prices are significantly below market value. More on pricing in Chapter 9.
- *Confidentiality:* You're in a very privileged position the moment that a client entrusts you with their problems, dreams, aspirations, and motivations. You destroy all trust, irrevocably and immediately, if they even suspect that you have betrayed the bounds of confidence that came as part of hiring you. This is true even if you're facilitating masterminds or group programs: your participants must be clear on their responsibilities and see you as upholding the standards that you enforce.

Please do not assume that these standards of service will set you apart. They won't. They're a baseline. They're what every savvy consumer will expect. However, there is something very special that will make you stand out from the crowd every day of the week.

Becoming and Establishing Yourself as a Category Authority

Although being a category authority and establishing yourself as one may, at first glance, appear to be the same thing, they're not. This isn't about faking it until you make it. Anybody can hang a shingle and claim to be a coach. But you're going to do it differently. Before you can establish yourself as a category authority, you must *be* one. How do you do that? You truly become a category authority by learning everything you possibly can about the one thing you've decided you want to become known for.

For many of us, the leap into learning all we can about our field can be immediately overwhelming, as the first thing we often learn is just how much we don't know. But this is a good thing. You can't seek knowledge that you don't know you need, so it is much better to first study what you didn't realize previously that you didn't know, even if it deflates your ego.

If the thought of becoming and establishing yourself as a category authority immediately induces a sense of panic at the thought of all you'd have to learn and do, you're not alone. Or maybe you feel you already know enough to be an expert, but the thought of having to put yourself so boldly—and publicly—front and center of your target market makes you want to run home for Mom's homemade chicken soup.

For some, the idea of putting yourself out in front of the people you'd like to serve in a big, bold, public way, where you'll be subject to public scrutiny, can trigger a multitude of insecurities. You'll know your dark side has taken over when thoughts start racing round and round inside your head like, "Who am I to call myself an expert? What do I know? I'm such a fraud. I don't know enough yet. Maybe I'll never learn enough to be an expert. I don't even know where to begin." Or worse yet, "What if I put myself out there and fall flat on my face? What if I look silly and embarrass myself? What if everyone hates me? What if I get made fun of or criticized?" Does this sound familiar? I'll bet it does. Again, you're not alone. If your dark side is running rampant, lock it in a soundproof closet and give control back to the bold and brilliant person you know you really are, and keep reading.

There's a big difference between being an expert in your field and being *the* expert in your field. I'm not asking you to hold yourself out as better than everyone else or as the absolutely best in your field. If you do, you'll seem phony, like someone who appoints themselves "America's sales coach" or "The number one holistic health coach in Timbuktu," when they are actually the *only* holistic health coach in Timbuktu. I always wonder, "By whose standards? On what metrics is the statement based?" Those kinds of claims are over-the-top and likely false. I'm simply asking you to be comfortable stating and demonstrating your expertise.

Do I Have To?

If now that you've avoided the dark side, some other side of you has taken over and is whining, "Do I have to?" the answer is a firm and resounding,

"Yes, you do." Like it or not, becoming a category authority, an expert in your field, isn't optional if you want your business to be as successful as it can be. It's a must. Becoming and establishing yourself as a category authority will have such a powerful effect on the success of your business, and will be so incredibly rewarding, that it's well worth the effort and *perceived* risk (which means no real risk at all).

Becoming a category authority will accomplish the following:

- Create the credibility and trust necessary for potential clients to feel comfortable and confident about purchasing your services, products, and programs.
- Gain you the visibility you'll need to reach all of your target market.
- Enable you to get your message out to the world in a big way as it raises awareness of yourself and your business within your target market. The idea is to be the first to come to mind when someone needs the kind of services, products, and programs that you offer.
- Help you gain clients and increase sales more easily and effortlessly while also enabling you to earn higher fees. It will give you the edge you need to stand out from the crowd of others who offer similar services, products, and programs. Suddenly, you'll no longer be just one of the masses.
- Make it much easier to move and expand into new markets of your choosing.
- Increase your own confidence in your ability to provide the best possible services, products, and programs to those who most need and want them.

Where to Begin

Do you remember that, in Chapter 2, I said that there is a difference between your target market and niche? Your target market is the group of people or businesses that you serve, and your area of specialty, what you become known for, is your niche.

You clarify this by first identifying what you'd like to become known for within your target market. If what you want to be known for is too broad or you try to become a category authority on too many topics, you'll overwhelm yourself and confuse your target market. A niche is focused, precise, and easy to demonstrate and articulate.

By identifying and focusing on the one thing you most want to become known for, you simplify and speed up the process, leaving no question in the minds of those in your target market about your area of expertise. This will enable you to create a synergy, not only among your services, products, and programs but also among all the techniques you'll use to establish yourself as a category authority.

When it comes time to powerfully establish yourself as a category authority, you're going to saturate your target market using a variety of techniques that we'll discuss in Module Four, such as networking, direct outreach, referral strategies, speaking, writing, and web strategies. To do that later, it helps to focus, focus, focus now.

It's very difficult to become *the* category authority or even a category authority in a target market that's too broad. "The World's Number One Marketing Coach" is aspirational but unwieldy. "The Number One Marketing Coach for Real Estate Professionals in Smallville, Ohio" is a much better place to start. Remember, you will grow your target market as your credibility and reputation grows.

2.5.1 Written Exercise: Please answer the following questions:

1. In what areas are you currently an expert?
2. In what areas do you need to develop your expertise?
3. What promises can you make and deliver to your target market that will position you as an expert?
4. What promises would you like to make and deliver to your target market but don't yet feel comfortable with?
5. What do you need to do to become comfortable at making and delivering these promises?

2.5.2 Written Exercise: Keeping the answers from the previous written exercise in mind, if there was *one thing* you could be known for within your target market, what would it be?

2.5.3 Written Exercise: What do you need to *learn* to become a category authority in the area you'd like to be known for?

2.5.4 Written Exercise: List the ways in which you could learn the things you identified in the preceding written exercise.

Example: Books, internet research, training programs, apprenticing with a mentor who is already a category authority

Even if you're already very knowledgeable about whatever it is you want to become known for, continuing to learn and staying up-to-date with the latest information in your field is not only a good idea but also is required to remain booked solid. I recommend that you read at least one book a month, if not more, on your chosen subject, which will increase your knowledge, challenge you to see a different perspective, or spark new ideas and thoughts, all of which will enhance the value you provide to your clients.

2.5.5 Written Exercise: Research and list three books that meet the preceding criteria.

2.5.6 Booked Solid Action Step: Buy these three books.

Making the Mental Shift

We've discussed what you need to have and do to be credible, and by now you understand the importance of becoming and establishing yourself as a category authority in a particular niche. I hope it's clear that it really helps to actually *be* an expert. You might think the logical next step would be to implement a plan to establish yourself as a category authority within your target market, but it's not. There's a critical mental shift that must take place first.

All of the Book Yourself Solid marketing strategies that you're going to learn in Module Four will put you out in front of your target market in such a big way that you will establish yourself as a category authority. First consider what you need to learn and what you need to do to establish your expertise so that when the time comes to implement the Book Yourself Solid Six Core Self-Promotion Strategies, you will *be* an expert. You will make the crucial mental shift of thinking of yourself as an expert. If *you* don't believe it, you'll have a hard time persuading anyone else to believe it.

Begin to think of and refer to yourself as a category authority—an expert in your field.

When the time comes to establish yourself as a category authority within your target market, you'll be comfortable with, and confident of, your expertise. If you already consider yourself an expert, then by all means begin including that in your current marketing materials.

Just remember—when communicating with your potential clients, be clear about what you know and clear about what you don't. People who are credible don't actually know everything, and they are just as comfortable saying that they don't know something as they are saying that they do. Remember: specialists get paid more and get more referrals.

There is one other very powerful mental and emotional factor that has a profound impact on your efforts to establish yourself as a category authority, one that may surprise you. I urge you not to discount or underestimate it.

The Power of Likeability

Now that you know what you need to do to become and establish yourself as a category authority, we're going to look at an even more important factor to consider: Do your potential clients like you? Do they perceive you as likeable? And I mean *really* likeable.

The fact is that if they don't, none of the rest of your efforts to establish yourself as a category authority will matter very much. That's a pretty bold statement, and it may come as a surprise to you, but bear with me as I shine some light on the subject, with the help of Tim Sanders (2005) and a few concepts from his book, *The Likeability Factor: How to Boost Your L-Factor and Achieve Your Life's Dreams.*

When you get right down to it, Sanders points out, "Life is a series of popularity contests." We don't want to admit it, we don't want to believe it, we've been told it ain't necessarily so, but ultimately, if you're well liked, if your likeability factor is high, you're more likely to be chosen and to get booked solid.

Mark McCormack, the founder of International Management Group (IMG), the most powerful sports management and marketing company, agrees: "All things being equal, people will do business with a friend. All things being unequal, people will still do business with a friend." (Mitchell, 2017). If a potential client perceives you as the most credible and likeable, you're probably the one they'll hire. And even if all things are *not* equal, even if you aren't the candidate with the most experience or expertise, if your potential client likes you, it's your likeability that will win the day and the client.

To make choices, we go through a three-step process. First, we *listen* to something out of a field of opportunities. Then we either do or do not *believe* what we've heard. Finally, we put a *value* on what we've heard. Then, we make our choice.

With so many demands on our attention these days, we have to filter and carefully select what we give our attention to. This is why becoming and establishing yourself as a category authority is so important. Your target market and your potential clients need a reason to deem your message important enough to sit up and pay attention, to *listen* to it. If you're likeable, they're much more likely to do so and to remember what they've heard.

Once you've got their attention, they're listening, but will they *believe* what they're hearing? This is where your credibility comes into play. With so many advertising messages coming at us from every direction each day—through spam email, social media, radio and TV commercials, and infomercials, to name a few—we've become highly skeptical of much of what we hear. If you're credible, you're much more likely to be believed.

But wait, that's not the only factor that comes into play when someone is determining whether to believe you. Again, your likeability is a critical factor in establishing trust. Think about it for a moment. You're much more likely to trust, and to *believe,* someone you like. Sanders says, "When people like the source of a message, they tend to trust the message or, at least, try to find a way to believe it."

Let's suppose that you've made it through the first two steps of this process. Your potential client has listened to you and believes you. Now they must determine the value of you and your message. Consider this example.

Susan owns a gym and is interviewing two personal trainers (PTs). The first candidate has been a professional for 12 years, is certified in nutrition, Pilates, CrossFit, yoga, and Olympic weightlifting. The second candidate has only recently completed a basic personal training program and has minimal experience but comes with good references. They both expect to earn approximately the same amount per session.

The first trainer walks into the interview 10 minutes late, frowning and obviously agitated. She then launches into a litany of complaints about her day to explain her delayed arrival. This candidate leaves Susan feeling on edge and irritated. Susan realizes very quickly that her clients and staff are likely to have a similar negative reaction to this PT's demeanor.

The second PT, the one who has just received her certification, is waiting patiently for her interview when Susan finishes with the first. She beams a radiant smile at Susan as she enters the office. Her upbeat temperament has a profound and immediate effect on Susan, and she feels herself relax as she smiles back. She already knows that her clients and staff will love her.

Who do you think is hired? Likely, it's the less experienced but highly likeable trainer who gets the nod.

Your likeability factor has an enormous impact on your perceived value. Develop your credibility; establish yourself as an expert; strive to be your best, most likeable self; and you'll quickly become the best and most obvious choice for your potential clients.

CHAPTER

6

The Book Yourself Solid Sales Cycle Process

> *It is a mistake to look too far ahead. Only one link in*
> *the chain of destiny can be handled at a time.*
> —Sir Winston Churchill

Building Relationships of Trust

Sales start with a simple conversation. It may be a conversation between you and a potential client, between one of your clients and a potential referral, between one of your peers and a potential referral, or between your website and a potential client. An effective sales cycle is based on turning these simple conversations into relationships of trust with your potential clients over time. We know that people buy from those they like and trust. This is never truer than for the coach. We've covered likeability. Now, let's address the trust factor.

If you don't have trust, then it doesn't matter how well you've planned, what you're offering, or whether you've created a wide variety of offers to meet varying budgets. If a potential client doesn't trust you, nothing else matters. They aren't going to buy from you—period. If you think about it, this may be one of the main reasons you say you hate marketing and selling. You may be trying to sell to people with whom you have not yet built enough trust. All sales offers must be proportionate to the amount of trust that you've earned.

What are your potential clients thinking?

- Do they really believe you can deliver what you say you can?
- Do they like you or the coaches who work for you?
- Do they feel safe with you?
- Do they believe hiring you will give them a significant return on their investment?

If you want a perpetual stream of inspiring and life-fulfilling ideal clients clamoring for your services and products, then just remember—all sales start with a simple conversation and are executed when a need is met and the appropriate amount of trust is ensured.

Turn Strangers into Friends and Friends into Clients

Seth Godin (1999), author of *Permission Marketing*, implores us to stop interrupting people with our marketing messages and instead turn strangers into friends by adding value and friends into customers by getting permission from them to offer your products and services. In its most effective form, the Book Yourself Solid Sales Cycle not only turns strangers into friends and friends into potential clients but also potential clients into current clients and past clients into current clients.

To design a sales cycle for your business, you must first understand how you're going to lead people into your sales cycle. Then we can actually build out a sales cycle process that will attract more clients than you can handle and do so with the utmost integrity.

The Book Yourself Solid Six Keys to Creating Connection: Who, What, Where, When, Why, and How

The Book Yourself Solid Sales Cycle works when you know the following:

1. *Who* your target clients are
2. *What* they are looking for
3. *Where* they look for you
4. *When* they look for you

5. *Why* they should choose you
6. *How* you want them to engage with you

Know your responses to these six keys and you will ensure that the offers you are making in your sales cycle process are right on target.

Key Number One: Who Is Your Target Client or Customer?

We've covered in depth how to choose a target market, but I'm going to reiterate it here because of its importance. You need to choose whom you'd like to bring into your cycle. The more specific you are the better. Choose one person (or organization) within your target market to focus on.

Identifying and gearing your marketing to a specific individual or organization enables you to make the important emotional connection that is the first step in developing a relationship with your potential client. When you have made the effort to speak and write directly to your ideal client in your target market, they'll feel it. They will feel as though you truly know and understand their needs and desires—because you will. That task alone will go a long way toward building the trust you desire with the clients you seek.

If you're not super clear on whom specifically you're targeting, whom you want to reach out to and attract, it's going to be hard to develop a sales cycle that works because you'll be chasing after every potential opportunity and you won't be making a strong connection with anyone.

2.6.1 Written Exercise: *Who* is your target client or customer? Describe what they are like. Get really creative with this one. List as many specific details as you can.

Example: My friend Lorrie Morgan Ferrero, an excellent copywriter, describes her target customer like this: "Nikki Stanton, a 37-year-old divorced entrepreneur with a web conferencing business. She's internet and business savvy. Invests most of her profit back into the business. Lives in San Diego in a gated community with her 10-year-old daughter, Madison. She's involved in her daughter's school and drives her to dance classes. Has a home office and makes approximately $117,000 a year. Jogs three times a week in the neighborhood. She loves to find bargains on designer clothes and dreams of visiting Italy with her daughter someday."

Your turn. Describe whom you'd like to attract into your sales cycle.

Key Number Two: What Are They Looking For?

It's important to understand what your ideal clients or customers are looking for—the kinds of products or services they think will solve their problems or help them reach their goals. It's very important to be clear on your answers because if you don't know what your potential clients are looking for, you won't know what kind of product and service offers to make in your sales cycle. We usually make offers that *we think* are relevant. It's time to put your target market first and work to truly understand what *they know* is relevant, what they actually say they *want*. Then you can decide on what you're going to offer them that will meet their needs according to the amount of trust that you've earned at various stages in your sales cycle.

2.6.2 Written Exercise: *What* are your potential clients looking for?
   Examples: In my case, they want a book that can help them get clients. They want to read an article or report on how to use social media. They want private coaching. They want to attend a marketing seminar. And so on.

Key Number Three: Where Do They Look for You?

Do you know where your target market looks for you? Do they search online? Are they in peer groups on social media? Do they read magazines? Do they call their friends for referrals for the kind of service that you're providing? What other types of business professionals do they trust to get their referrals from? If you don't know, survey your current clients. Always ask, "How did you come to find me?" If you don't have any clients of your own yet, ask a colleague who serves the same target market how their clients found them.

2.6.3 Written Exercise: *Where* do your ideal clients look for you?

Key Number Four: When Do They Look for You?

When do the people or organizations in your target market look for the services you offer? What needs to happen in their personal life or work life for them to purchase your coaching services? How high do the stakes need to be before they decide to buy what you're selling? They may be interested in what you do, and your offerings may resonate with them, but they might not need you at the moment they find you.

This is why the Book Yourself Solid Sales Cycle is so important. You'll want to make it easy for them to step into your environment and move closer to your core offers over time. When their stakes rise, they'll reach out to you and ask for you. But you've got to keep the conversation going.

2.6.4 Written Exercise: Describe the situations that are likely to drive potential clients to seek your services, products, and programs. *When* do they look for you?

Examples: They've lost their job. They're starting their own business. They're so disorganized that they're losing business. They are experiencing extreme discord in their relationship. They've just had a baby.

Key Number Five: Why Should They Choose You?

That's a big question. Why are they going to choose you? Are you a credible authority in your field? What makes you the best choice for them? What is unique about you or the solutions you offer?

For this exercise, it's crucial that you set your modesty aside and express yourself clearly and with confidence—no wishy-washy answers to these questions. Most coaches have had coaches of their own. Think back to the last time you went in search of a coach. When you first spoke to them to inquire about their services, their expertise, and whether they could help you, the *last* thing you wanted to hear was, "Well, I kinda know what I'm doing. I might be able to help you. I'll give it a shot."

Although it may feel uncomfortable at first, you've got to get comfortable saying, "The best thing for you is me!"

Granted, saying you are the best may be a bit too bold for you, but at the least you've got to be able to say, "You've come to the right person. Yes, absolutely, I *can* help you. I'm an expert at what I do and this is how I can help."

Bragging is about comparing yourself to others and proclaiming your superiority. Declaring your strengths, your skills, your expertise, and your ability to help is not bragging but expressing confidence in what your potential clients expect, want, and need to hear from you.

2.6.5 Written Exercise: *Why* should your potential clients choose you? Be bold! Express yourself fully. This is not the time for modesty.

Key Number Six: How Do You Want Them to Engage with You?

Once potential clients have learned about you, how would you like them to interact or engage with you? Do you want them to call your office? Do you want them to sign up for your newsletter? Send you a private message? What is it that you want potential clients to *do?*

Naturally, we'd love for them to immediately purchase our highest-priced product, program, or service, but this is rare. Most of your potential clients need to get to know you and trust you over time. They need to be eased gradually toward what they may perceive to be your high-risk offerings. It's often said that, on average, you will need to connect with a potential client seven times before they'll purchase from you. Not always, but if you understand this principle, you will be on the road to booking yourself solid a lot faster than if you try to engage in one-step selling. "Hi, I'm a coach, wanna hire me today?" isn't going to be effective. That's definitely not the Book Yourself Solid way. Maybe we should call one-step selling one-*stop* selling because that's what it'll do—stop your sales process dead in its tracks.

Clearly defining these six keys will help you to determine what you want to offer your potential clients in each stage of your sales cycle and will help you craft the most effective sales cycle possible. Moreover, defining these six keys will also help you tremendously when implementing the Book Yourself Solid Six Core Self-Promotion Strategies.

2.6.6 Written Exercise: *How* do you want your potential clients to interact or engage with you? (Note: establishing a line of communication is the first step in developing a relationship of trust.)

The Book Yourself Solid Sales Cycle Process

Your services may have a high barrier to entry. To potential new clients, your services are intangible and expensive—whether you think they are or not—especially to those who have not worked with a coach or bought an online product or who have not had good results with their previous coaches.

The Book Yourself Solid Sales Cycle is a sequence of phases that a client moves through when deciding whether to work with you. You begin your sales cycle by making no-barrier-to-entry offers to potential clients. A no-barrier-to-entry offer is one that has no risk whatsoever for a potential client so that they can *sample* your services. I'm not talking just about offering a free coaching session, which is still common practice. I take this concept much further with much more success.

No doubt you've heard the term *sales funnel*. A sales funnel and the Book Yourself Solid Sales Cycle are different. A sales funnel drives people through a strategically designed campaign window to buy a particular product at a particular time. Sales funnels can be powerfully effective when launching coaching products or live events or group programs with a fixed start date. The Book Yourself Solid Sales Cycle process is different in that it respects the fundamental truism that clients buy services when they are ready to buy (and not necessarily when you want them to), and that clients buy in proportion to the trust and credibility that you have created with them over time.

The Many Stages of a Sales Cycle

In Module Four, you'll learn how to use the Book Yourself Solid Six Core Self-Promotion Strategies, including networking, direct outreach, referral, speaking, writing, and using the web to create awareness for the solutions you offer. However, rather than attempting to *sell* to a client, you will simply offer them an invitation that has no barrier to entry.

You already know that "who knows what you know" is important when working toward booking yourself solid. Do you realize how many more clients you could be serving if they just knew what you had to offer? The best way to inform them is to have at least one, if not a few, compelling offers that have no barrier to entry.

The Book Yourself Solid Sales Cycle works in a way that allows buyers to enter at any point in the process, depending on their situation. A client hires you when the circumstances in their life or work match the offers that you make. If you're a communications coach who specializes in raising funding, they might not need your services right now. But perhaps, six months from now, they get an opportunity to pitch their business to one of the country's biggest venture capital firms. You can bet that they'll not only want your services but also they'll need them immediately. Do you see how the stakes have changed? Chances are that if you haven't built trust with this client over the past six months by offering great value along the way (without expecting anything in return, mind you), it's unlikely you'll cross their mind when they look to deliver the most important pitch of their life.

The following example will give you a framework for the process. Your sales cycle may include 3, 10, or even 15 stages, depending on your particular business and the different services and products you offer. If you're just starting out, I recommend not implementing more than four or five stages. I'm going to teach you the principles that govern an effective sales cycle so that you can craft one that serves your particular coaching business and meets the individual needs and tastes of your clients.

I will explain each stage and give you a real example from my own public speaking coaching business, HeroicPublicSpeaking.com, to help you visualize exactly how each stage works. I'm going to also ask you to write out your objective for each stage and how you're going to achieve your objective. This way, by the end of the chapter, you'll have completed your very own Book Yourself Solid Sales Cycle. I'll do my best to make it as easy as possible to absorb and implement the information. If you do get a bit overwhelmed, please stay with it. This is an important part of the Book Yourself Solid system, and understanding the principles behind these techniques will ensure that you're well on your way to being booked solid. In fact, I'd say it's the linchpin of the Book Yourself Solid system.

As you work through this process, remember all that you are doing is having a simple conversation with someone. You are making a connection that will build trust so that you will then be able to share your services with another person. How cool is that?

Book Yourself Solid Sales Cycle Stage One

To book yourself solid, perform daily tasks that will keep your name in front of potential clients. In stage one, your objective is to get a potential client to do something – go to your website, call a number, fill out a form, or another action that begins to affiliate them to you. To best do this, you need to create awareness for the services, products, and programs you offer using one or all of the Book Yourself Solid Six Core Self-Promotion Strategies. You will have your choice of the Book Yourself Solid strategies:

1. Networking
2. Direct outreach
3. Referral
4. Speaking
5. Writing
6. Web

Your objective for stage one of the sales cycle should be simple and measurable, like driving prospective clients to your website. Or maybe you want them to call your office directly. It's up to you. But once you've chosen an objective, you'll choose the strategies you would like to use to achieve it.

The sales cycle is most effective when used in conjunction with a keep-in-touch plan. I'll show you how to do that in the next chapter.

Stage one example: My stage one objective is to drive potential clients to our HEROIC Insights at HeroicPublicSpeaking.com. (This is the answer to the sixth key to creating connection, "How do you want your potential clients to engage with you?").

2.6.7 Written Exercise: Book Yourself Solid Sales Cycle stage one:

- What is your objective in stage one of the sales cycle?
- How are you going to achieve it?

Book Yourself Solid Sales Cycle Stage Two

In this stage you will demonstrate your knowledge, solutions, and sincere desire to provide value to your target market free of charge, with no barrier to entry, and at no risk to them. The benefits include increased trust—they will feel as though they know you somewhat better.

To familiarize your prospective clients with your services, you need to offer them solutions, opportunities, and relevant information in exchange for their contact information and permission to continue communicating with them over time. What does that communication look like? You may provide a tip sheet, special report, or white paper that addresses their urgent needs and compelling desires. It could be your always-have-something-to-invite-people-to offer, which I discuss in detail at the end of this chapter. No matter what you select, it should be something that speaks not only to their needs but also what you want them to know about how you can serve them.

Stage two example: My stage two objective is to encourage my website visitors to sign up for a free membership to HEROIC Insights by entering their name and email address. If they do, they will get a weekly email with links to two new articles. Each article is written in two parts:

- Part one contains the what, why, and why now aspects. This is where we challenge conventional wisdom and help them embrace the idea that there might be a better way. A better way they should consider embracing today. This is *visionary* content.
- Part two contains the how-to content. This is where we teach our premium paid members how to turn the idea we exposed in part one into action. We teach them exactly how to do it.

2.6.8 Written Exercise: Book Yourself Solid Sales Cycle stage two:

- What is your objective in stage two of the cycle?
- How are you going to achieve it?

Book Yourself Solid Sales Cycle Stage Three

Now that you've started building trust between you and your potential clients, you're going to work on developing and enhancing that trust and cultivating the relationship.

In stage three of the sales cycle your objective is twofold: to continue to add value by helping your potential clients incorporate the information that you gave them in stage two of the cycle and to make a sale. If you gave them a free report, you should follow up with emails that help them use the content in the report to create value. Or if you invited them to your always-have-something-to-invite-people-to offer, you'll tell them more about it, make sure they know how to take advantage of it, and of course, what the benefits of participating in it will be. You should also offer them something that will surprise them. It could be a complimentary pass to a workshop you're doing or a personal note on your stationery or branded postcard with a list of books on your area of expertise that you know will speak to their urgent needs. Remember, the value you add doesn't have to be all about you. If you recommend a resource to your potential clients, they will very likely associate the value they received from that resource with you.

This is the first time in the sales cycle where you might also offer your potential clients a service or product that will cost them money, for example, an in-person seminar or intake session. It might be one of your information products: e-book, regular book, workbook, manual, guidebook, mini-course, challenge, or webinar, all of which we'll get to in later in this book. When you send your follow-up emails, you will let your potential clients know of the opportunities you have for them that speak directly to their urgent needs and compelling desires, and you'll continue to add value without expecting anything in return.

What's important to understand is that the monetized offer you are making should not have a very high barrier to entry. You're not going to rush out of the gate and surprise potential clients with your highest-priced offer, just as you wouldn't propose marriage on a first date, no matter how smitten you are. You want to offer them something they are ready for, and if they're ready for more at that moment, they'll ask for it. Of course, you'll happily speak to any potential client who asks you about other ways of working with you just in case they are ready to walk down the aisle.

Stage three example: My stage three objective is to introduce those who opted in for my newsletter to one of the books I have written on public speaking, *Steal the Show,* or *The Referable Speaker,* which I cowrote with Andrew Davis.

2.6.9 Written Exercise: Book Yourself Solid Sales Cycle stage three:

- What is your objective in stage three of the cycle?
- How are you going to achieve it?

Book Yourself Solid Sales Cycle Stage Four

Your focus now is to help your potential clients move to the next level of your sales cycle. Let's say a potential client bought your low-barrier-to-entry product or service, thanks to your efforts in stage three of the sales cycle. Now is the time to offer your next level of product or service, something that requires more of an investment than the previous product or service they purchased. Notice how this client is moving closer and closer to your core offerings and your higher-priced offerings. This is usually the case but only after you've earned more trust, proven that your solutions work, and that you deliver on the promises you make.

If the potential client does not engage in one of your stage three offerings right away, don't despair. Just remember that you are building relationships of trust that will grow and, you hope, last a lifetime. When the time is right, a potential client will become a current client.

Stage four example: My stage four objective is to have HEROIC Insights members to attend CORE | The Breakthrough Experience, a celebrated two-day in-person training event at our campus in Lambertville, New Jersey.

Each stage of this cycle applies to you regardless of whether you're holding live events for 500 people or you have a solo coaching practice. To do these exercises, simply replace my offerings with the appropriate offerings for you and your clients. Remember, your sales cycle will have as many stages as is appropriate for you and your business right now. You might have only three stages in your sales cycle at present. It may evolve and grow as your business evolves and grows.

2.6.10 Written Exercise: Book Yourself Solid Sales Cycle stage four:

- What is your objective in stage four of the cycle?
- How are you going to achieve it?

Book Yourself Solid Sales Cycle Stage Five

Your objective in stage five is similar to the previous one: to help potential clients move to the next level of your sales cycle by offering them a higher-level product or service. What's important to understand about this process is that not every person or organization who enters into your sales cycle will move all the way through it, and the time that each potential client takes to do so will be different as well.

Stage five example: My stage five objective is to enroll ideal clients into one of our mastery-level training programs. Again, there are many people who join one of these programs, or attend an event, right after they read one of my books, or even before they do, simply because they were referred to me by a person they trust. But you can't count on that. You'll have better success if you lay out a plan for how you introduce people to your offerings.

The in-person small-group training programs we offer require more of a financial investment than our other programs. That's why it's very important to me that those who join these programs know that it is the right place for them to continue their development and trust that my team and I will over-deliver on our promises. I imagine you would want the same thing. This is why the Book Yourself Solid Sales Cycle is so effective. You're building trust with people over time, trust that is proportionate to the size of the offer you're making to them.

I don't want to try to sell them this high-commitment coaching course until they've had the opportunity to read one of my books or attended one of our smaller events. I want them to know that we can serve them before they enroll in a coaching course. That one factor, knowing that we can serve them, will give our participants better results, and that's our goal—to help our clients get the results they want. Your goal throughout the sales cycle is to help people move closer and closer to your core offerings by ensuring that they are getting the results they need at each stage of the cycle.

All of your sales offers should be proportionate to the amount of trust that you've earned.

As a professional coach you don't want to try to convince people that what you're offering is right for them. You want to provide value on value until they believe that your services are right for them. They will get better results that way and be more satisfied with your services, a factor that is way too important to forget about.

2.6.11 Written Exercise: Book Yourself Solid Sales Cycle stage five:

- What is your objective in stage five of the cycle?
- How are you going to achieve it?

The Book Yourself Solid Always-Have-Something-to-Invite-People-to Offer

This strategy might just be the most effective marketing and trust-building strategy on the planet for the professional service provider. You'll want to consider your own always-have-something-to-invite-people-to offer as you design the first few stages of your Book Yourself Solid Sales Cycle. It might be what you choose to direct potential clients to when you use the Book Yourself Solid Six Core Self-Promotion Strategies in stage one of the sales cycle.

People generally hate to be sold, but they love to be invited—as long as the invitations are relevant and anticipated, meaning, they've given you permission to make an invitation. By my second year in business, this one strategy actually doubled my income.

When I started my business, I offered a complimentary teleseminar (this was before the days of webinars and live streaming) that I called the "Think Big Revolution." I offered it on a weekly basis, and it was designed to help people think bigger about who they are and what they offer the world. Sometimes I would discuss a topic that was specifically related to getting more clients, and other times I discussed different principles and strategies that would help the participants be more successful in business and in life.

Note that it was free to participate. If I met someone I thought would benefit from membership, I'd invite them to join.

There are many ways you can set up this kind of always-have-something-to-invite-people-to self-promotion strategy. You are limited only by the scope of your imagination. If ideas for your own always-have-something-to-invite-people-to offer are just not springing to life for you right now, don't fret. I'm going to give you plenty of specific ideas and ways of brainstorming your own.

There is another added benefit of this kind of always-have-something-to-invite-people-to offer. It can serve as one of the most effective ways of establishing your personal brand. Notice how the Think Big Revolution is an extension of my why I do it statement. Your always-have-something-to-invite-people-to offer is the perfect way to integrate and align your who and do what statement (whom you help and what you help them do) and your why you do it statement (the reason you do what you do).

Consider another example: early in my business, I worked with a man who is a personal trainer and a healthy-eating chef. When he came to me, he was facing two challenges that he needed my help with. He was not living up to his full income potential because of working with clients on just a one-on-one basis, and he hadn't created a real demand for his services. Both of these concerns caused him to be anxious over what his future held.

I first asked him to look at how we could adapt his services from just offering one-on-one training to group programs. Then we created his always-have-something-to-invite-people-to offer: the *Fitness Fiesta for Foodies*. One Sunday evening a month, he would host a party at which he would teach his guests how to prepare healthful meals that help them stay fit. There were two requirements for attendance, however. He would put that month's menu on his website and each guest was required to bring one item off the menu. Each guest was also asked to bring someone new to the event, thus creating a new audience for his work. He barely had to market himself. It was magical. People loved it and they loved him for doing it. And they joined his programs because of it.

A money mindset coach could do something similar either through a webinar or in person. Even a simple Q&A about building wealth would do the trick. Are you beginning to get your own ideas on how this could work for you? The value you add in your offer meets the needs and desires of the people you serve. This no-barrier-to-entry offer is a helpful component of the Book Yourself Solid Sales Cycle. Then as you continue to build trust over time by offering additional value and creating awareness for the services you provide, you'll attract potential clients deeper into the sales cycle, moving them closer to your core offerings.

You'll notice that the two always-have-something-to-invite-people-to examples I offered are done in a group format. There are three important reasons for this:

- You'll leverage your time so you're connecting with as many potential clients as possible in the shortest amount of time.
- You'll leverage the power of communities. When you bring people together, they create far more energy and excitement than you can on your own. Your guests will also see other people interested in what you have to offer, and that's the best way to build credibility.
- You'll be viewed as a really cool person. Seriously, if you're known in your marketplace as someone who brings people together, that will help you build your reputation and increase your likeability.

Please give away so much value that you think you've given too much, and then give more. I had a friend in college who, when he ordered his hero sandwiches, would say, "Put so much mayonnaise on it that you think you've ruined it, and then put more." Gross, I know (I believe that he has since stopped eating his sandwiches that way and his arteries have thanked him), but adding value is similar. Remember, your potential clients must know *what* you know. They must really like you and believe that you have the solutions to their very personal, specific, and urgent problems. The single best way to do that is to invite them to experience what it's like to be around you and the people you serve.

Use the Book Yourself Solid Sales Cycle to Unconditionally Serve Your Clients

You can have as many stages in your sales cycle as you need to build trust with potential clients for the kinds of offers you make. Just thinking about your sales cycle will help you clarify and expand your offerings. If you're not already established, the days of offering only one type of offer may be coming to an end. The marketplace is too competitive and diverse. Every day a new coach enters the marketplace, and some days, many more than one! There are coach training institutions in almost every country in the world that cater to more and more people feeling the call to stand in the service of others.

Expanding your offerings to create a Book Yourself Solid Sales Cycle may just enhance your business model—the mechanism by which you generate revenue—from only one offering with one stream of revenue to multiple offerings with multiple streams of revenue.

The Book Yourself Solid Sales Cycle is not just about getting new clients to hire you. It is designed to unconditionally serve your current clients as well. It is much harder to sell your services, products, and programs to a new client than to those who have already received value from you as a client. The most successful businesses, both large and small, know this. It's one of the reasons Amazon.com is so successful. Once you've become a customer, they know you, they know what you need, what you read, and they work to continue to serve you. The typical client-snagging mentality suggests that you make a sale and move on. The Book Yourself Solid way requires that you make a sale and ask, "How can I over-deliver and continue to serve this person or organization?" This is not a small thing.

Now it's your turn to develop your own unique sales cycle. Don't limit yourself to just the few examples I've already touched on. There are a multitude of ways to build trust with your potential clients and to ease them toward purchasing your higher price point offerings. Use your imagination and creativity to tailor your sales cycle to what works best, feels most natural, and resonates most with you.

7

The Book Yourself Solid Keep-in-Touch Strategy

Be well, do good work, and keep in touch.
—Garrison Keillor

You already know that, generally, you need to connect with potential clients many times before they feel comfortable hiring you or purchasing your products. If you don't have a systematized and sometimes automated keep-in-touch strategy in place to support your sales cycle process, you may, as the saying goes, leave a lot of business on the table.

Many businesses fail for lack of a solid keep-in-touch marketing strategy. Either they bombard you with too much information and too many offers that turn you off, or you never hear from them at all, which leaves you feeling unimportant and irrelevant.

Consider the experience of one of our clients, Barbara. Within a few short years she had compiled more than 5,000 subscribers.

The names were captured, but Barbara never really followed up with any of them until one day when she created a promotional offer to send to her list, and she eagerly clicked *send*. What came back were mostly emails from recipients inquiring as to who she was and how she got their email address. Barbara learned a valuable lesson that day: determine the best approach for using this strategy and build it into your keep-in-touch plans.

There is an important distinction to be made between following up with potential clients, colleagues, and others on a personal (one-to-one) level, and developing an automated keep-in-touch strategy through which you broadcast electronic newsletters, send direct mail campaigns, or use other publishing platforms like social media (one-to-many).

When you've met someone and exchanged contact information, you have permission to communicate, and to start or continue a dialogue that is valuable to both of you. However, this does not equate to having permission to add that person to your mailing list so you can send them your newsletter or other automated or broadcast messages.

All of the broadcast follow-up that you do to groups must be based on the principles of permission marketing, offering a potential client the opportunity to volunteer to be marketed to. According to Seth Godin (1999), in his book *Permission Marketing,* "By only talking to volunteers, permission marketing guarantees that consumers pay more attention to the marketing message. It allows marketers to calmly and succinctly tell their story. It serves both consumers and marketers in a symbiotic exchange." Permission marketing is anticipated, personal, and relevant to the potential client.

- *Anticipated:* people look forward to hearing from you.
- *Personal:* the messages are directly related to the individual.
- *Relevant:* the marketing is about something the prospect is interested in.

This is essential because you want to communicate only with someone who is looking forward to hearing from you. When potential customers anticipate your marketing messages, they're more open to them. And, of course, when they have not explicitly asked you to send them things like a newsletter, and you do, it's not just possible spam, it is 100% pure spam, no matter how much you think they'll enjoy it.

With that said, once you get to know people, you should ask them if they'd like you to subscribe them to your newsletter. Tell them about it, what's valuable about it, when it's delivered, and any other relevant information. Then, if they accept your invitation to be on your mailing list, you have permission to send it to them along with special offers and other promotions.

Relevant, Interesting, Current, and Valuable Content

It's up to you to ensure that the content you share with your potential clients through your leveraged (one-to-many) keep-in-touch strategy is relevant, interesting, current, and valuable. There are six basic categories of content that meet those criteria:

- Industry information
- Strategies, tips, and techniques
- Content from other sources
- Product and service offerings
- Cool keep-in-touch
- Special announcements

Industry Information

Industry information that is relevant to your target market and that may or may not be widely known is excellent content to share. You'll position yourself as an expert within your industry while providing constant value to your current and potential clients. What's more, they will appreciate the information and your generosity for sharing it.

Let's say that you coach yoga teachers. Information regarding industry standards, regulations, and laws would be helpful to your target market. Perhaps if you coach clients in the construction industry, the latest findings and announcements from OSHA would be meaningful, as would information about safety issues.

Including important information in your keep-in-touch strategy also makes it more likely that your potential clients will keep the information and refer back to it, keeping you at the top of their mind for future support.

Strategies, Tips, and Techniques

Strategies, tips, and techniques are probably the most common type of content shared by service professionals.

Despite the appeal of this content-rich approach, many coaches fear they will give away too much of their material. "If I provide all these great tips and strategies for free, then why would anyone ever hire me?" they wonder. Of course there are some who will take everything you offer and never hire you or purchase a product, but they wouldn't be hiring you anyway, and you never know—they may be out in the world talking about what you do and how you help. Over the years, I've received millions of dollars' worth of referrals from people who are not clients just because I've helped them for *free*. Most people who eventually do hire you or buy your products will need to receive free advice and support to build the trust they need for them to believe that you can really help them. Furthermore, most people will assume that you know a lot more than what you are giving away. They'll think, "Wow! If he gives away this much great stuff, can you imagine what I'll get if I actually pay him?"

Content from Other Sources

I often provide my current and potential clients with relevant content from other people so that I can over-deliver as much as possible. This gives me a break from continuously creating content. It also enables me to offer our subscribers more than we can offer ourselves and at the same time position other professionals as experts in their field; they appreciate the promotion. There is a bonus as well: the experts featured often return the favor by promoting my work to the people *they* serve. Isn't that a win for everybody? It's also an easy way to create great value for the people who have given you permission to serve them when you're first starting out.

For example, read anything these authors have written:

- John Jantsch and his Duct Tape Marketing books
- Bob Burg and his Go-Giver books
- Scott Stratten and his UnMarketing books
- And anything by Chris Brogan, Seth Godin, Tim Sanders, Jim Collins, Marcus Buckingham, and Jay Baer

If you're concerned that you'll lose clients because you highlight other experts, please recall the following Book Yourself Solid principle.

> *There are certain people you're meant to serve and others you're not. If you can help other coaches attract business through you, you're creating more abundance for everyone involved.*

Product and Service Offerings

You must make offers when keeping in touch. I generally try not to say, "You must" or "You have to" because you don't have to do anything. You certainly don't have to do what I tell you to do. But, in this case, I feel comfortable saying you must make offers. Make offers that are proportional to the amount of trust you've earned but make offers. Or, don't, but if you don't, it's unlikely your business will be around for too long. With that said, making only product and service offerings to your potential clients may not be appreciated very much. Your offers must be accompanied by an over-delivery of free value. My personal goal is to subscribe to the 80/20 rule when it comes to keeping in touch. That means 80% of our keep-in-touch marketing is based on giving away free content, opportunities, and resources that will help the people we serve, and 20% is made up of offers to purchase services, products, and programs that will also help the people we serve. Remember, the people who have expressed interest in your services want to know how they can work with you. Show them their options.

Cool Keep-in-Touch

I love it when you express yourself. By now you know that you will more easily and quickly attract your ideal clients when you do. This category is the cool keep-in-touch category because it can include any fun, different, unique, or exotic method of keeping in touch, some of which may expose your quirks. Please remember that quirky does not mean scary or bizarre. It means unusual, unique, and special. So get creative. Be bold. Dare to stand out from the crowd.

Tell jokes, let your prospective clients behind the scenes of your day-to-day life. Don't take yourself too seriously. Introduce them to your pets and send them photos from your vacation. Have fun; it's contagious!

What is your special, unique, and entertaining quirk that can be turned into a cool keep-in-touch strategy?

Special Announcements

This is a valuable method of keeping in touch if the special announcement is relevant, important, and presented as a learning tool to your target market. For example, when we built a new 5,300-square-foot headquarters and launched it with parties honoring some of our best clients, we told the world about it. It was a major milestone for us and our clients were part of it. Sure, some of my readers couldn't care less, but our long-term clients, our best clients—our community—they loved being a part of it. But be careful—it's often an overused category and can be irrelevant and annoying when it comes in the *all-about-me* form, like news about your company that is irrelevant to your contacts. They don't really care that you have a new logo or built a new website. How many times have you received announcements telling you about a new development in a company or about a change in management that you really cared about?

2.7.1 Written Exercise: What is the best kind of content to include in your keep-in-touch strategy based on your interests and the needs and desires of your target market?

Choosing Your Keep-in-Touch Tools

Once you've got great content to share with your clients and potential clients, you've got to choose how best to deliver that content to them. These are the most common methods:

- Electronic newsletters
- Printed newsletters
- Phone
- Postcards and mailers
- Social media

Historically, email newsletters were the easiest and most cost-effective way to keep in touch with large numbers of people. That's been changing, in large part because of consumer behavior—most of us ignore as much email as we possibly can because of the never-ending, mass proliferation of spam and, to a lesser degree, because of the advent and rise of social media as an alternative keep-in-touch tool. Paper newsletters might have some value as a marketing tool—the kind you get from your alma mater—but they can be costly to print and mail. The phone is a wonderful direct outreach tool but often the most anxiety provoking of them all, so I say stay away from cold-calling and wait to get on the phone until you've had at least one positive interaction with your direct outreach subject.

We'll talk about how to use social media to keep in touch with large groups of people in Chapter 16. For now, let's focus on email newsletters, which are still an effective marketing tool for these situations:

- Building your mailing list, adding value, and marketing to your subscribers over and over again
- Selling your products and services while you're delivering great content and adding value
- Positioning yourself as an expert within your industry or field
- Keeping in touch with all the people who've expressed interest in your products or services, and reaching them all with the click of a button
- Creating a viral marketing campaign (it grows exponentially as it's passed along to others) because your subscribers will send it to their friends when they think it will help them
- Creating ongoing marketing campaigns that cost virtually nothing and reap great rewards

In the early days of Heroic Public Speaking, 90% of our product and service sales were generated from 20% of the space in our monthly email newsletter as well as through other direct email promotions. Let me be clear about this because it's so important.

Of course we track all of our sales and where they come from and know that 90% of our online sales were in direct response to the monthly email newsletter, not from a new visitor landing on one of our websites. As you'll learn when we discuss your web strategy, your website is used most effectively as a vehicle for enticing people to opt in to your subscriber list so that you deliver value and build trust over time. Your follow-up is where you reap the financial and personal rewards of your marketing efforts.

Email Newsletter Format

There are many ways to format an email newsletter. For starters, start with whatever is easiest, most cost-effective, and aligned with your strengths. Almost every email marketing platform offers simple templates. Keep it straightforward. Go light on the graphics (if you have to use graphics at all) and focus on a clean, well-written message.

You don't need a fancy layout or multiple social media links. You don't need to get a new headshot for every email you send. In fact, some of the most successful effective email newsletters are plain text only, in part, because they can feel more personal to the reader.

The layout of the text in your email newsletter is just as important as what you have to say. Most of your readers will not actually be reading the email. First, they'll scan it. Then, if the issue seems relevant and interesting, they'll read it more carefully. Note, however, that many, if not most of your readers are viewing your email on their mobile device. So, whatever format you use will need to be responsive to whichever platform the reader is using.

Keep your paragraphs short. Large blocks of text are harder to scan. And finally, to make the layout support your content, consider the following criteria when writing any kind of keep-in-touch or promotional content:

- Write compelling headlines to get your readers interested.
- Use case studies and testimonials to add credibility to your claims.
- Write from your reader's point of view.
- Write about benefits, not just features.
- Read your text out loud to make sure it sounds conversational.
- Get a colleague or client to review your copy and make suggestions.
- Write as if you're speaking to one person—the person who's reading the email, not a group of people. You don't say, "Hey guys, you all have been asking for . . ." You say, "Hey, you've been asking for . . ."
- Be specific.
- Be concise.
- Keep it simple.

Email Frequency

Frequency depends on a lot of factors but should be mostly based on what you're trying to accomplish and to whom you're sending the email. Some people send out weekly email newsletters, some twice a month, and others monthly or quarterly. I've even seen some daily email newsletters.

If you're going to commit to a weekly newsletter, make sure you let your readers know what to expect. If you're not sure you're going to be able to write a weekly email, then don't call it a "weekly newsletter," so as to manage your readers' expectations.

To see firsthand how we create connections with—and value for—our newsletter subscribers, go to www.BookYourselfSolid.com or www .HeroicPublicSpeaking.com and subscribe now. Not only will you see how we do it but we'll also be able to continue to help you book yourself solid and present yourself in the most compelling way possible.

Automating Your Keep-in-Touch Strategy

Creating a monthly email newsletter, and whatever other content and offers you plan to provide to those you are keeping in touch with is only the beginning of implementing the strategy. It's time to do the following:

- Build and manage your database.
- Follow up with prospects and professional opportunities.

Building and Managing Your Database

I'm sure you've met hundreds, if not thousands of people over your professional life you've not kept in touch with. Now that you're a coach wanting to attract more clients than you can handle, I'll bet you wish you had kept in touch with all those folks. Well, no matter. You will keep in touch with everyone you meet from this point forward. Well, only the people you like and want to keep in touch with. It is encouraging, however, to reflect on all of the people you have met with whom you did not keep in touch because it shows you how easy it can be to build a database of potential clients and networking contacts if you do keep in touch.

Choosing a Database Program   To have an effective keep-in-touch strategy, you'll need a reliable and comprehensive database program. There are many database programs from which you can choose, and more than I can list here, but I'll give you a few examples and important criteria to consider as you make your choice.

There are two important differentiators that I want you to consider: sales management versus contact management. Customer relationship management (CRM) systems like Infusionsoft, Salesforce, Aweber, and MailChimp are all designed to manage not only contacts but also the sales process, to turn leads into opportunities and opportunities into clients.

Contact management systems like Microsoft Outlook and Google Contacts typically provide a way to organize your contacts. Contact management systems may provide a way to take notes on a record, but they don't provide a good way to track the sales process, which might be the most critical process in your business.

Frankly, this stuff is kind of boring on the surface but because you're still reading and engaged, you understand the importance of it. There are some things that we need to do in business that aren't particularly fun but are wonderfully exciting when you see them working in your favor to produce sales. So, with that said, it's time to start using a real CRM system to manage your sales process, from lead generation to opportunity management to sales conversion.

Using a CRM system you'll be able to do the following:

- Track performance of lead sources: it's likely that a small amount of lead generation efforts will drive the bulk of your sales.
- Create a consistent sales process even if you work alone. It will help you see what is driving results.
- Increase the speed of your sales conversion: respond to new leads quickly, follow up frequently with emails and calls, and nurture leads that don't convert immediately.
- Keep track of activities: get things done when you need to and when you say you will.

- Report on past performance: if you don't know what you've done, how are you going to know what you need to do?
- Forecast future sales: if you don't know where you're going, how will you know when you're there?

The key isn't purchasing the program to help you manage your keep-in-touch strategy, it's actually using the program to keep in touch with potential clients, current clients, and past clients. Bottom line: CRM is about managing these relationships better.

Entering Data You certainly have to get a new lead's contact information, but that's not where most people fall short. It's that they don't actually do anything with it. It must be entered and stored in the system so that you can continue to connect with the lead, building trust over time. The size of your database, but most importantly the *quality* of the relationships you have with the people in your database, is directly proportional to the financial health of your business.

Getting and Following Up with Prospects and Professional Opportunities

Following up with prospects and professional opportunities is a major key to your success. It's an investment that will deliver huge returns. Your Book Yourself Solid Sales Cycle is based on the success of your keep-in-touch strategy and requires you to deliver great value. Please, I implore you to make this a top priority.

> **2.7.2 Written Exercise:** How are you going to automate your keep-in-touch strategy?

The Book Yourself Solid Keep-in-Touch Strategy is the key to ensuring that your marketing efforts are effective and successful. Keeping in touch with your potential clients is critical to developing trust and credibility, and keeping in touch will keep you foremost in the minds of your potential clients when they need you, your services, or the products and programs you offer.

The Power of
Information Products

*Know where to find the information and how to use it—that's
the secret to success.*
—Albert Einstein

Brand-Building Products and Easy-to-Follow Programs

Creating information products and programs based on your expertise that
are designed to serve your target market's very specific urgent needs and
compelling desires are a very effective way of demonstrating credibility and
earning trust. People love packaged learning and experiences. They're easy
to understand and therefore easy to buy. Perhaps you think that your coaching may not be as easily defined as a packaged product or program, and
necessarily has a high barrier for entry. You may underestimate what you
have to offer. As you continue to develop and enhance your Book Yourself
Solid Sales Cycle, you will want to produce products and programs that will
fully round out the many possible stages of your sales cycle, including the
early stages, where barriers to entry must be low.

I'm sure your bookshelves are lined with products and programs that
you've purchased from other coaches over the years. In fact, you're reading
one right now. How would you like to create your own?

*You are in the business of serving other people as you stand in the
service of your destiny and express yourself through your work.*

95

I just love the opportunity offered through information product crea-tion because you can follow a simple step-by-step system that leads you to the production of the kind of revenue and satisfaction that comes from bold self-expression. Let's take a quick look at the other red-hot benefits that you get from producing information products:

- Having information products—even ones that you give away for free—increases your credibility with your prospects, your peers, meeting planners, and the media because it establishes you as a cat-egory expert and sets you apart from your competitors.
- Products create opportunities for multiple streams of leveraged income. They can be given away or sold 24/7/365, with worldwide availability. You can consistently get downloads and orders for your products from people all over the world.
- Information products can help you land more clients because they speed up the sales cycle. Because your services have a high barrier to entry, your potential clients may need to jump a few high hurdles to persuade themselves they need to hire you. Having a product to offer based on your services gives potential clients the opportunity to test you out without having to take a big risk. Then if they connect with you and are well served by your product, they will upgrade from the lower-priced product to the higher-priced service.
- If you use public speaking as one of your marketing strategies, hav-ing a product at the back of the room when you speak gives you credibility, and you also have a relatively low-cost way to introduce potential clients into your business and generate ancillary revenue at the same time.
- Information products leverage your time. One of the biggest prob-lems coaches face is the paradigm of trading time for money. If all you ever do is trade your time for money, your revenues are limited by how much you charge per hour. For example, if you speak in front of 100 of your prospects and you're able to sell a couple dozen of your information products at $50 each, then you've just increased your hourly rate from $200 to more than $1,000 an hour. Again, remember, many more people are willing and able to buy an infor-mation product than they are willing and able to hire you for your higher-priced service.

Start with the End in Mind

You may be in the beginning phase of building your business and just be setting out on track to book yourself solid, but take to heart the wise advice from Dr. Stephen Covey (1989), author of *The 7 Habits of Highly Effective People*, and "Start with the end in mind." If you want to seriously build a long-lasting career as a coach, you'll want to start thinking just as seriously about creating information products.

Don't let the idea of creating products intimidate you. You can start where you are and then the sky's the limit. For example:

- Publish a free-tips booklet.
- Write an e-book.
- Produce an audio or video product.
- Create a workbook.
- Compile a reference guide.

Here are a few thoughts on your first information product:

- Keep it simple.
- Don't overwork it or feel that it needs to be perfect.
- Don't worry about being wildly original.
- Tips, guides, or resource manuals are great formats.
- Continually strive to add value to your clients' lives in any way you can.

When considering how to create an information product, start by examining the different possibilities and ask yourself, "How can I leverage my existing knowledge and experience to create a quality product that I can produce and launch in the shortest amount of time possible?"

Be sure you don't overlook any content you may already have created. If you've written an article, you have content that you can leverage into multiple formats. You can quickly and easily turn your article into an online course; use it as the foundation for an e-book, printed book, or program; or present it as an introductory presentation or webinar. A single article can be leveraged into any or all of these formats, making it possible to create an entire sales cycle from a single source of content.

Define Your Product or Program

Choose the one product idea that you're most passionate or excited about right now—and, most important, one that is in line with your current business needs. If you're starting out and need to build your database, you'll need to create a *lead-generating* product (sometimes referred to as a lead magnet) first, a product that you give away to create a connection with a potential client. You will then leverage that free lead-generating information product into other monetized information products over time. Maybe you already have a lead-generating product and you're ready to produce higher-priced information products like an audio program or a book.

As you define your product, you will need to consider not only the type of product you will create but also to whom you're selling it, the promises it makes, the benefits and solutions it offers, the look and feel you want your product to convey, and the ways in which you can leverage the content.

2.8.1 Written Exercise: For now, keep it simple. Just get your ideas out of your head and onto paper.

1. What type of product or program would you most like to create? What would you be most passionate about creating and offering to your target market?
2. To whom would you be offering this product? (Refer to target market.)
3. What benefits will your target market experience as a result of your product?
4. How do you want your product to look and feel? What image or emotion do you want it to convey?
5. How might you leverage the same content into a variety of different formats and price points for your sales cycle?

Assess the Need

It's important to be clear about your intentions for your product or program, and it's critical that your product or program meet the needs of your target market. No matter how much you might love to create something, if your target market doesn't need it, you'll be defeating your purpose.

2.8.2 Written Exercise: Answer the following questions:

- Why does your target market need your particular product now?
- What does your product need to deliver for it to meet your client's need?
- What about your product, if anything, will be different from similar products on the market?
- *Bonus:* How can you over-deliver on your promises by adding unexpected value to make your product remarkable? If you're unsure of your target market's need for a particular type of product or program, doing market research will help you ensure you're creating something your target market will find valuable. Survey friends, clients, and groups, such as online discussion groups or local organizations. And certainly search Google, using keywords that your target audience would use.

The Five Simple Steps to Developing Your Product

We discuss the five simple steps to developing your product in the following subsections:

Step 1: Choose the role you are playing.
Step 2: Choose your product framework.
Step 3: Choose a title that sells.
Step 4: Build your table of contents.
Step 5: Create your content.

Step 1: Choose the Role You Are Playing

Whatever product you choose to create, you will want to choose the role you'd like to play when delivering your content. I'll use books to illustrate my point because books are simply bigger information products and I can give you examples that you might be familiar with.

- *Expert:* Here's what I've done, and here's my theory on why it works. This is the role that I chose as the author of this book. Or maybe you're the mad professor, the reluctant hero, or the reclusive genius?

- *Interviewer:* Compile information from other experts. You can compile a product by interviewing others who are experts in their respective fields. A good example of that is Mitch Meyerson's (2005) book, *Success Secrets of the Online Marketing Superstars.* He interviewed more than 20 online marketing experts and compiled their interviews into a book.
- *Researcher:* Go out and gather information to serve the needs and desires of your target market. Compile the results to create a product that meets those needs and desires. Research can turn you into an expert at a future date. Jim Collins's (2001) book, *Good to Great,* is a perfect example. It's a research study, and it has made him an authority on creating great results in large corporations. You don't need to do a 10-year clinical study as Mr. Collins did, but the concept is the same.
- *Repurposer:* Use and modify existing content (with permission) for a different purpose. Many of the guerrilla marketing books are excellent examples of this. Jay Conrad Levinson created the "Guerrilla Marketing" brand, and then many other authors co-opted that material and offered it for a different purpose—for example, *Guerrilla Marketing for Job Hunters* by Jay Conrad Levinson and David E. Perry (2005).

2.8.3 Written Exercise: Which role most appeals to you or is most appropriate to your product or program, and why?

Step 2: Choose Your Product Framework

You'll need a framework in which to organize and present your content. A framework will make it easier not only for you to develop your content but also for your potential client to understand it and get the greatest possible value from it.

You may find that your content is ideally suited to a particular framework. If, for example, you're developing content for a product on enjoying pregnancy, the chronological framework may be the logical choice. Your content, however, may work well in more than one framework. An information product or program often uses a combination of frameworks. Here are six of the most common:

- *Problem/solution*: State a problem and then present solutions to the problem. *The Magic of Conflict: Turning Your Life of Work into a Work of Art* by Thomas F. Crum (1987) is written in this framework. He presents a number of problems that people face in their life and at work and presents solutions to those problems using the philosophical principles of the martial art of Aikido.

- *Numerical*: Create your product as a series of keys or lessons. A well-known example of this would be Stephen Covey's (1989) *The 7 Habits of Highly Effective People*.

- *Chronological*: Some products need to be presented in a particular order because that is the only way it would make sense. Step A must come before Step B, as in *Your Pregnancy Week by Week* by Glade B. Curtis and Judith Schuler (2004). (I really don't think you'd want to read that book out of order.)

- *Modular*: This very book is a perfect example. The book consists of four modules: Your Foundation, Building Trust and Credibility, Perfect Pricing and Simple Selling, and the Book Yourself Solid Six Core Self-Promotion Strategies. Within each module are additional tracks presented in a chronological framework. So you see that the book has both a main framework (modular) and a secondary framework (chronological).

- *Compare/contrast*: Showcase your creation in terms of presenting several scenarios or options, and then compare and contrast them. Jim Collins (2001), in his book *Good to Great*, compares and contrasts successful and not-so-successful companies.

- *Reference*: Reference is just as it sounds. You may be creating a product that becomes a valuable resource to members of your target market. A compilation of information is best showcased in a reference format like that in *Words That Sell* by Richard Bayan (1984). It's a reference guide of good words and phrases that help sell.

2.8.4 Written Exercise: Which framework will you choose and why?

Step 3: Choose a Title That Sells

The title of your product or program can make a big difference in whether your product sells. It's the title that initially catches consumers' attention and determines whether they look any further. In fact, when I submitted my proposal for the first edition of this book to Matt Holt, my soon-to-be editor, he wanted to talk to me right away. I was thrilled and asked him what he liked best about the proposal. His response surprised me, "Well, I haven't read it yet but I love the title so I wanted to talk to you about it." Your title must be compelling enough for the prospect to want to know more. The consumer should be able to know exactly what you're offering by reading or hearing your title. Investing time to craft a captivating title can have a significant impact on your bottom line. Here are six types of titles that you can adapt to your needs:

- *Suspense:* The Secret Life of Stay-at-Home Moms
- *Tell a story:* The Path of the Successful Entrepreneur
- *Address a pain or a fear:* The Top 10 Fears Every Leader Has and How to Overcome Them (This type of title has been around since the dawn of time but it still works.)
- *Grab the reader's attention:* Caught! The Six Deadliest Dating Mistakes (Okay, cheesy, but you get the point.)
- *Solutions to problems:* Focus: The Seven Keys to Getting More Things Done in Less Time
- *Emotional connection:* What My Son's Tragedy Taught Me About Living Life to the Fullest

---

2.8.5 Written Exercise: Choose one of the title types that fits your product or that you find especially appealing, and brainstorm a number of different title ideas. Have fun with this. Just get your creative juices flowing.

Step 4: Build Your Table of Contents

Your table of contents is another key piece in organizing your content so that it's easy for you to present and easy for your potential clients to understand and follow. Regardless of which role you present your content in, the creation of a product gives the impression that you are an expert, and this is how your target market will view you.

The table of contents should be very well organized and professional. It should be easy to scan through to gain an understanding of the concept and the main points. Creating a table of contents also enables you to break your content into manageable pieces. The thought of writing even a simple article, e-book, special report, or book may at first glance seem overwhelming, but it doesn't have to be. Well, truth be told, writing a good book can be a massive endeavor, but for the other formats, just use your table of contents, or outline, to break the process down into smaller steps that will be much easier and less intimidating to work on.

2.8.6 Written Exercise: Create your table of contents. Keep the following questions in mind:

- What are the steps in understanding your content?
- Is the flow logical and easy to understand?

Step 5: Create Your Content

Using your table of contents, create a schedule for completing the first draft of each section. If you write as little as a paragraph or two a day, you could have your content for your product or program completed in as little as a week for an online course or a month or two for a more in-depth product or program.

I suggest that you adhere to the Philosophy of the First Draft. What? You've never heard of this ancient Greek philosophical movement? Okay, maybe not. But it might help you mitigate the feeling of being overwhelmed and get you unstuck. The Philosophy of the First Draft suggests that you get it down quickly, just do a data dump, and then adhere to the next level of philosophical thinking: the Philosophy of Tweaking, which suggests that your product will be a work in progress. Do not expect an end result at this point. First follow the five-step plan for developing the structure of your product, as indicated previously. Then, use this simple three-part formula for creating your first draft, the second draft, and so on until the final draft.

Three-Part Formula for Creating Your First Draft

> *Step 1:* Based on your table of contents, choose two to five key points for each section.
>
> *Step 2:* Flesh out each of the key points per section with supportive content.
>
> *Step 3:* Repeat step 2 until you've created the final product.

Yes, it should be that straightforward. I'm even going to get down on my knees right now and beg you not to make it more complicated. I'm not actually on my knees, and I apologize if I sound patronizing when I say not to get overwhelmed. It's just that I see so many people get hung up on this step. Understandably. But, like most things, doing it is what produces more confidence and makes it less overwhelming. Keep it simple and focus on getting it done so you can get down to the business of getting booked solid.

The Simple Three-Step Product Launch Sequence

Listing your product on your website is a fabulous idea. It's a great start. However, if you don't, at present, have an overwhelming number of visitors browsing through your site, it's unlikely you'll get many orders—*even if you're giving it away for free.* However, if you want to make a splash with the new product you've created, consider using the following simple three-step product launch sequence to get your product into the hands of eager and inspired potential clients.

> *Step 1:* Prelaunch
> *Step 2:* Launch
> *Step 3:* Postlaunch

Step 1: Prelaunch

On completion of your product, you may be tempted to immediately begin promoting it. Hold off for a bit. Consider instead how you're going to warm up your audience with tidbits of content in the form of video, audio, infographics, and any other format that is easy for them to consume. During the prelaunch stage, you should focus on giving so much value that you think you've gone too far and then give more. This teaser content should be designed to get your audience thinking about the specific problems that your upcoming product offer addresses and the results it promises—without mentioning the product itself—not yet. This early stage prelaunch period can last a few days or a few weeks and can give you the opportunity to evaluate how your audience is responding to your content and adjust your product accordingly.

Perhaps a strength and conditioning coach who created a breakthrough video product on how to increase performance doing three, 30-minute kettlebell workouts a week might consider writing a series of articles, blog posts, and online press releases (I cover these in Chapter 16) that include links to two-minute video clips lifted from the product. This content, sent to an email list, posted on a blog and in article and press release directories, is designed to stimulate discussion on the topic rather than to explicitly promote the product. Instead, it encourages the audience to consider particular issues and solutions to those issues before the product is released.

Toward the end of this early stage prelaunch, make mention of an upcoming product in the same places that you seeded with valuable content. Now that momentum and interest in the topic you've been addressing has spiked, among your readers, it's time to enter the late stage prelaunch. This is when you announce the details of your upcoming product offer, which is so packed with value that, again, you and they will think you've gone too far. But you'll go even further adding more value by piling on additional features, opportunities, and bonuses like these:

- Follow-up implementation coaching calls
- Additional videos, interviews, or e-books
- Quick-start PDF guides
- Related software
- And, certainly, a no-hassle guarantee of some sort

Your potential buyers should feel like they're getting a significant return on their investment; value should overwhelm cost. You'll attempt to focus their attention on the incredible benefits of your product and the problems it solves. Hopefully, by the time you launch, your potential buyers will have very few objections to your product and believe that it is a high-powered vehicle that'll get them where they want to go.

Prelaunch Checklist

- Software to database and manage buyer's information
- Shopping cart and merchant account if you're selling the product rather than giving it away as a lead generator
- Sales page
- Completed product ready to ship or deliver digitally

Remember to test every part of the process before launching it. Guaranteed (well, almost), you'll miss something. Run sample orders to make sure that you clear up any glitches. View all of your pages and videos in all of the most popular browsers, and on every mobile device you can get your hands on. Notify your web host, merchant account provider, and shopping cart solution of your upcoming launch date if you expect a lot more traffic to your site than is usual. Sometimes, hosting companies and payment providers will freeze an account if they detect activity that is unusual or different from the norm. This happens more often than you might think and can seriously squash your product launch.

Step 2: Launch

The success of your launch is, in large part, due to the structure of your offer: how you make it, what comes with it, how long it lasts, and more. A word to the wise: be careful of what kind of tactics you use to encourage people to buy. I discuss pricing models at length in Chapter 9, so I won't discuss them here. I suggest that you carefully consider how you want to be perceived, however, when promoting your information products. Will you create a hyperkinetic, high-intensity product launch based on the principle of scarcity? Will you try to tap into the buyer's fear that they'll miss out if they don't act right away, or the perception that if they don't buy what you're offering they'll never move forward and will, basically, fail at whatever it is you're offering to help with? Or will you create a reasoned, sensible, and appropriate product launch based on integrity? Look, I'm comfortable with special time- and space-limited offers as long as they are real and based in integrity and they're not too hyped up and aggressive.

You are how you market. Consider what you stand for and how you want to be known. And, of course, how the people to whom you are trying to sell want to be treated.

Okay, so, now the big day is here! It's time to press *send* on your "we're live" email as well as announce the product launch on the social network sites to which you belong, your blog, or any other relevant platform. This is where all of your hard work pays off. Take a deep breath.

Don't stress the process. You know already the launch is unlikely to unfold as planned. Hey, it might go better than planned. The live period of the launch usually lasts from three to seven days, depending on your preference. The first day or two is a great time to introduce the urgency of acting as the time or available units are dwindling (but please see the previous note). Feel free to share new and exciting testimonials as they come in or more bonuses.

Step 3: Postlaunch

Sales generally die down after the first few days of the launch. There are ways to reignite them, however. For example, you can announce another bonus. This may encourage people sitting on the fence to go for it and hit the *buy* button. This bonus will also please all previous buyers, as they'll get extra value that they had not anticipated. Maybe you're holding a special live event to which the buyers of the product get free tickets? Or perhaps, you've added an entire product to the offer that is complementary to the topic covered in the initial product?

When you close out the launch, what do you do with the product? Are you planning on continuing to sell it from your site but at a different price point or, maybe, you're taking it off the market for six months and will then do a second launch? If you do take the product off the market, make sure you put up a special web page thanking visitors for their interest in the product and suggest that they opt in to a web form so they can be the first to be notified when the product becomes available again. This way you'll have the opportunity to earn their trust before your next product launch.

Joint Venture Partners and Affiliates

When you don't yet have a substantial group of followers or subscribers, or even if you do, for that matter, one of the keys to increasing your reach is to team up with what are usually referred to as joint venture (aka JV) partners or affiliates. I discuss this concept in Chapter 16 as it relates to driving traffic to your website, so for now, I'll just touch on a few important points of JV marketing relationships with respect to product launches.

Other coaches, who already have established relationships of trust with your target market, might be willing to partner with you and promote your product in exchange for a commission on each product sold or some other incentive. Note that I said *might*. As you'll learn when we discuss direct outreach in Chapter 12, before you make any kind of JV request of a successful professional, it's wise to have already established a relationship with them and to understand what incentivizes them. You might be surprised to learn that they are not, in fact, interested in what you think is a financial incentive. When a JV partner promotes your product for you, they expend a considerable amount of social and professional capital. There is also an opportunity cost associated with every promotion made to a group of subscribers or followers. Be prepared to demonstrate the viability of your offer with sound metrics. You need to have a sound commission structure in place as well as a detailed analysis of your opt-in and conversion rates. When you ask someone to promote a product for you, you're asking for a lot—more than you might realize at the moment. You're asking for access to what might be their most prized business asset—the trust they have built with subscribers. Read the chapter on direct outreach before you attempt any kind of JV campaign.

If you want joint venture partners to enjoy working with you, you'll want to make promoting you easy and breezy. Once you have your JV partners in place, have the following materials available for them:

- Email copy ready to use during the prelaunch and launch periods
- Affiliate accounts for your JV partners in your shopping cart system that provide custom affiliate links

Big, deep, authentic success is truly only realized when we share our gifts with others through mutually valuable, long-term partnerships. Some of your JV partners may even become your best friends and closest allies.

If you are new to the concept of launching a product on the internet, some of this can seem daunting. It can be a big process with many more moving pieces than I included in this section. Nonetheless, you can do this. Keep your launch simple at first and take it one small step at a time. Look at it this way: once you create a successful launch, you can do it again and again. Just duplicate your initial success with some small changes for the new product. Most of the hard work was done the first time around.

A Necessary Step in Your Business Development

Creating a product or program is a powerful—and possibly necessary—step in your business development. One product will turn into another and another; the possibilities are endless.

Just imagine this: you open your email first thing in the morning and you see 15 new orders: one from Switzerland, one from Australia, one from India, and a dozen from all over the United States—all for the product you recently made available on the web. It's 7:00 a.m., you're still sipping your first cup of coffee and only half awake, and you've already earned $3,479.27.

If you're just starting out, this scenario may seem more like a dream than a reality to you right now, but it's entirely possible to achieve, and it's much easier to do than you might imagine. Just follow the steps I outlined previously for creating an unlimited number of information products on virtually any topic you can think of! Before you know it, you'll be hearing the beautiful, melodic *ka-ching, ka-ching* sound of your website-turned-cash-register as the orders come rolling in.

Module
THREE

Simple Selling and Perfect Pricing

To be booked solid requires that you price your offerings at rates that are compelling to your ideal clients and that you're able to have sales conversations that are effortless and effective. It means that you must do the following:

- Perfect your pricing strategies using the right models and incentives.
- Master simple selling techniques so you can have sales conversations that feel as easy as a day at the beach.

Module Three consists of two chapters. These two chapters are the culmination of the Book Yourself Solid system because you'll learn how to make offers that are proportional to the amount of trust that you've earned and how to have a sales conversation that books new business. This is the ultimate goal—to get new clients so you can earn new business.

Remember how the Book Yourself Solid system works:

1. You'll create awareness for the products and services you offer using the Six Core Self-Promotion Strategies (you'll learn these in Module Four).

2. Once you create awareness for what you offer, potential new clients will check out your foundation for stability and security (you built this foundation in Module One).

3. If they like what they see, they'll give you the opportunity to earn their trust over time (you do this using the strategies you learned in Module Two).

4. When the circumstances are right, potential clients will either raise their hand and ask you to have a sales conversation or they'll accept one of your compelling offers and you'll book the business (this is the focus of Module Three).

All you have to do now is decide how to price your offers and learn how to be comfortable and confident during sales conversations. Let's get right to it then.

9

Perfect Pricing

Price is what you pay; value is what you get.
—Warren Buffett

What is the value, for example, of having the talent and skills to create a compelling web presence for someone or maybe a training manual for a corporation? Is it the length of time it takes for you to produce it, or the number of pages created, or, how about the number of images used? The answer is ... D, none of the above. Unfortunately, that's how many coaches price their products and service offerings—as stuff. How should services be priced? By putting a value on what they will produce.

"But it took me only a day to create my online course," you might say. How long it takes you to write something, or design something, or think up an idea, or even the amount of time you spend with a client, is irrelevant. What (should) matter to the client is the financial, emotional, physical, and spiritual (FEPS) return on investment your product or service provides—remember, I introduced you to the all-important FEPS benefits. Think about the value you provide:

- How much income will your service create?
- How long will what you create be a productive, useful resource for the client?
- How much pain will you relieve?
- How much pleasure will you create?

- How are you helping your client connect to their purpose or spirit?
- Will your work create substantial and long-lasting peace of mind?

No less important than the value you create is how you value yourself. This is another reason why the section on releasing blocks in Chapter 3 is critically important to your success. And this might just be the difference between simply making ends meet and earning healthy heaps of money. Remember your ideal client. Remember doing your best work. Remember standing in the service of others as you stand in the service of your destiny. You want to work with people who value what you bring to your partnership. But if you don't value it, they won't either.

3.9.1 Written Exercise: Think of a client who gave you rave reviews. Make a list of all the FEPS benefits the client received from working with you. Don't be stingy here. Think big. Now, put specific dollar values on all of those benefits. Again, think big. No, bigger than that. Because . . . hold on to your hat . . . you may just find that you have been undervaluing yourself and, as a result, underpricing your products and services. You are giving generously of your talents and skills and, it's likely, the value you provide is worth much, much more than what you've been charging.

Don't Buy into a Poverty Mindset

Maybe you think, "I don't want to price my services such that people can't afford them." Or maybe it was something like, "I have a new client who says they can't afford much so I'm thinking of lowering my price for them." These thoughts don't necessarily mean you have a "poverty mindset" but they most definitely play you small. Allow your expectations to be stretched. People rarely buy coaching based solely on price. In fact, people express their values through what they buy—so let them.

Most of us express our values through the things we buy. We are what we purchase. Think about it. If you didn't know me but came across my personal and business financial statements from the past three months, you'd know a heck of a lot about me, like what I value and how I spend my time.

If my financial records showed that I was at the bar every night and spent most of my money playing the slot machines in Vegas, you'd get a sense of what I value. If those records showed that I spent my disposable income on boats and fuel for the boats, purchase four books a month, and invest 25% of my income for retirement, you'd see a person with different values. I'm not even making a value judgment here. Rather, I'm simply saying that what you spend your money on is a demonstration and representation of what you value.

Most of us want the opportunity to express ourselves through the things we purchase, especially when those things are adding value to our life or work. So please give the people you serve the opportunity to express their values by buying what you have to offer.

Only you can offer you. Whatever it is you offer it is unique to you. Only you can offer a particular combination of services, skills, talent, and personality. Only you can offer the exact combination of information, style of communication, and value that makes you so uniquely you. Know that. Know and accept, and revel in your value. Come from a place of service. Raise your intention to be well compensated for what you offer. Expect to be paid well. Then ask for it. Not everyone will be willing or able to pay what you require but your ideal clients will. Put out a price that makes you feel valuable and see ideal clients joyously flocking to take advantage of the great value you offer. And, practically, you can't sustain the work you're meant to do unless you are paid well to do it. Your income is a reflection of how you value yourself as well as the number of lives you affect in the world.

3.9.2 Booked Solid Action Step: Right now raise your prices until it makes you slightly uncomfortable. You'll know you've reached the right number when you experience a slight feeling of nausea. That's your new price. Over time you'll grow into it—not the nausea, the price—and, over time, you'll continue to raise your prices, sans nausea.

Ask for what you are worth. But first, truly know and believe you have great value. Then others will know and appreciate all you have to offer. You have to know that what you offer is valuable, and you have to charge an amount that shows it is valuable. Only you can choose to think big about who you are and what you offer the world.

Pricing Models

I'm sure you've seen a number of different pricing models employed by various coaches. Some seem to benefit the coach and others are more favorable to the client. However, the picture of perfect pricing has each party thinking that they got the better end of the deal. If clients think they got more value than they paid, they'll be tickled pink and if the coaches feel that their time, talents, and efforts are valued, they'll feel like the cat who ate the canary. The key is to figure out how to create this win–win dynamic so that both parties feel fortunate. Here are a few of the often-used pricing models for selling coaching:

- *Time for money trade*: Clients pay by the hour or day for your services (for example, $100 per hour or $1,000 per day). This is a straight-forward pricing model, where clients pay for the amount of time they spend with you. This model can be used with individual clients and also for workshops with multiple participants, for example in corporate settings where you will receive a flat hourly or daily rate irrespective of the number of participants in the room with you. It's a very common model and one with which clients are generally comfortable.
- *Package pricing*: Clients buy a specific number of coaching sessions for a fixed price. The price for each session may be more cost-effective for the client than paying your per-session fee. Plus, you benefit from longer coaching time frames and increased revenue. This model can be used in private coaching, in live online workshops and in corporate training.
- *Program pricing*: A flat fee for a clear set of deliverables. If you are running online programs, selling information products, or offering a series of workshops or classes over a specific period of time, you will employ program pricing, possibly in combination with other pricing models. Coaching programs vary in price wildly from a few dollars for an online information product to many tens of thousands for live, in-person retreats.

- *Tiered pricing*: Your clients will have the choice of various pricing options, where each option comes with different benefits. Also used in the software industry and the events industry, the "gold" package might be the entry-level option, while the "platinum" and "diamond" options include extra benefits, bells, and whistles.

- *Recurring fee for an open-ended amount of time*: Commonly referred to as a retainer, for which a monthly payment is offered for a certain amount of work. Many coaches use this model so that they are "on call" for their clients as they need them, for an occasional call or email without necessarily having a fixed schedule. Other coaches use this model in their group continuity programs or masterminds, where the client is in a group with others and can pick and choose their level of engagement with the benefits on offer. It's also popular for consultants in advisory capacities who may be expected to attend board meetings and be available for advice and guidance on day-to-day issues. Sometimes a time period is associated with the retainer but the arrangement is typically not associated with a period of time and can be canceled at will or with some reasonable amount of notice.

- *Retainer plus back-end*: Less commonly used by coaches than other service providers (for example, marketing agencies or systems improvement specialists), but sometimes used by business coaches. The client pays a fixed monthly retainer and the coach receives a pre-negotiated percentage of either savings or increased revenue or profit. Can be difficult to monitor and there are many variables at play that can affect the client's outcome. Be sure to draw up water-tight contracts with an attorney if choosing this route.

- *Flexible pricing*: This can apply to all of the pricing models. This is very common in the corporate market where the final cost is based on negotiations rather than a sticker price. Coaches often offer flexible pricing, also known as sliding scale pricing, based on the client's ability to pay or the coach's desire to work with the client. Just be careful that you don't get into the habit of sliding down the scale too easily just to make the sale. You'll end up working a lot but for not enough money. No point in that, is there?

- *Free coaching*: Giving clients an opportunity to try your services before they buy. This can be useful as a marketing strategy; however, I'd encourage you to find other ways to demonstrate your value through your sales cycle without trading your time for no money. I will talk more about this shortly. If a client is talking to you about working with you, that should be a sales conversation rather than a private demonstration. Don't confuse free coaching with pro bono coaching, where you make a decision to donate your time or products to those who may need it but are not in a position to pay.

- *Outcome-based pricing:* You charge based on whether or not your client achieves the result they are looking for. Clients pay more if they achieve their desired results and less if they do not. This is a risky proposition for the coach because you're ultimately not the one "doing the work," but it can be attractive for your prospect. You may have seen this type of pricing wrapped up in a guarantee, where the coach promises to "work with you until you get the result you want."

- *Penetration pricing:* Offer low prices to get into a market. Once you've created a name for yourself, begin to raise your prices. Most coaches end up increasing their rates as their time and experience grows. If you choose this model, just make sure you don't stay here too long. Remember: raise your prices until you're slightly uncomfortable.

- *Low barrier to entry pricing:* Usually used when selling coaching products rather than services, although you can certainly apply it to group experiences like one-day workshops or online classes or products. You make your offer at a very low price point to get clients in the door who will then, hopefully, buy additional products or other services at a higher price point. This is also known as *loss leader pricing* because you may be willing to take a loss upfront for a financial gain down the road.

- *Bundle pricing:* Offering a combination of products or products and services together in a single package to increase the size of the sale can offer savings to both the buyer and to the seller. Very common in online products and program launches, with "bonuses" being used to increase the value of the offer. The buyer gets more value for less money and the seller gets more profit for less marketing effort. However, if you bundle your products, "Don't wrap all the Christmas presents in one box," says economist Richard Thaler. The benefits of the product or service should be enumerated rather than lumped together. So, if you buy "this" we'll also throw in "that." And, if you buy "that" we'll also throw in "this." Or, if you buy "this," you can also have "this" at a reduced price. You want to be sure the client values and appreciates each and every product, program, and service they're getting from you.

- *Promotional pricing*: A discount or other incentive applied to one of your offers, products, or programs for a limited period of time, or a bundle that is not usually available. This is very common with coaches who have a library of courses that are launched and relaunched throughout the year, and prospects are happy to snag a deal during the promotional period. See more on this following.

- *Economy pricing*: Offer the lowest prices in the market as a way of differentiating yourself. This is unlike loss leader pricing in that all your prices are always low when you use economy pricing—it becomes part of your brand. It's very difficult to recommend this to most coaches because you really need a large number of clients in an online community, for example, to be able to pay your bills. Also, offers with low prices can often be perceived as low value.

- *Prestige pricing*: You may choose to price your services at a price point higher than is typical for your industry in order to create a sense of prestige for your offers. You may serve fewer clients but end up making more money. You're in the expertise industry, and it is certainly the case that the most respected experts will be expected to charge premium rates.

When considering which of the various preceding pricing models you are going to employ, first consider your objective. You may be thinking, "Uh, Michael, are you dense? I want to make as much money as I can—that's my objective!" Well, yes, but you're reading this book to think more strategically about your business and how you grow it, so humor me for a moment. Consider the following four different pricing objectives:

1. *To maximize long-term profits:* This should be your default approach. You're building something to last a lifetime, something that will support your dreams, not to mention your family, so you always want to focus on long-term pricing. Any of the pricing models can be applied to achieve this objective.

2. *To maximize short-term profits:* Generally chosen when you need to make a bunch of money fast. You might consider bundle pricing to sell more of what you already offer. Or, maybe, aggressive promotional pricing will help. Lots of options here.

3. *To gain market share:* That's just a fancy way of saying you're starting up the business or introducing a new product or service and need to create awareness about who you are and what you have to offer the world. Flexible pricing may be the way to go. It will help you get in the game and build up a large group of ideal clients who are out in the world talking about your best work. Which, of course, will bring you new, ideal clients.

4. *To survive:* Hey, look. Sometimes things get rough. You might face, say, a complete global economic recession. Sometimes survival *is* enough. This is when you employ whatever strategy you think is going to get you through to the next quarter. Do what you have to do to make it.

When to Lower Prices, Discount, and Offer Specials

The answer is not always clear but the question remains the same: when should I use promotional pricing and lower prices or offer discounts and specials? Sometimes you want to offer price discounts or special packages to motivate potential clients to act. Other times, you'll feel the need (or desire) to lower prices because of factors beyond your control, like economic conditions. Or maybe, you're in complete control and have found a cheaper, more economical way to offer your services that enables you to lower your prices while increasing your profit margins. Either way, leveraging a variety of discounting tactics and other incentive devices to get clients faster and increase sales can be, to put it mildly, a godsend.

As a general rule, I don't think coaches should ever offer discounts on their one-to-one offers. Sure, use bundle pricing and package pricing and flexible pricing to lower the per-session fee, but don't send an email to your entire database saying, "all my one-to-one coaching is now 50% off!" as that is likely to confer the wrong message—even if it's accurate—about your ability to sell your services. Save the discounts and incentives for your products and packages and online programs.

And use them with care. There's a fine line between over-the-top infomercial-like promotional pricing and authentic, clean, believable, appreciated-by-the-client, and respectful use of discounting tactics and special offers. However, don't be afraid to be fully self-expressed in your sales promotions. There's nothing wrong—in fact, there's something very right—about giving your ideal clients an opportunity to take advantage of your services. Remember what I said before: people buy to express their values. You're giving them an opportunity to express their values through the work you do together.

Here are some discount strategies you might like to employ:

- *Quantity discounts:* See previous point about bundle and package pricing. You may be able to encourage clients to buy more of your services if they can get better prices the more they purchase. This model is very common for coaches. For example, a coach may sell sessions in 5, 10, 15, and 20 packs. The price per session will decrease for each subsequently larger pack, making the 20-pack the best deal. You may even decide to offer a value-added bonus to the buyer of the 20-pack: a free, day-long VIP workshop for the client and 10 of their closest friends, for example. Yes, you're right, what a great value-add to the client as well as a remarkable marketing opportunity for you—10 brand new potential clients brought right to your doorstep.

- *Pay-in-full discounts:* Reward clients who pay for your programs or services in full with a lower rate. They will be more committed, pay less than if they pay by installments, and you will receive the full value of the contract upfront.

- *Seasonal discounts:* Encourage clients to buy at certain times of the year in anticipation of seasonal needs. Or offer off-season discounts. A fitness coach can increase sales in the winter by offering a "summer body" program at a special price.

- *Markdowns and time sensitive discounts and offers:* Mark down your prices for a particular amount of time or until a certain number of sales is made. For example, "50% off for the next five days" or "the first 10 people to sign up get a free upgrade to the VIP track."

- *Free coaching:* Give away free sessions as a sales tactic to get clients. Does it work? Sometimes. Should you do it? Depends on whom you ask. Some swear by it. Others have sworn off it. And yet, still others curse every time they do it because it's so frustrating. Generally, I don't recommend it. Think about it. How does it look to a potential client that you're offering free services to anybody who happens to stumble across your website—in demand, successful, and valuable—or sitting around with lots of time on your hands just trying to give your stuff away for free in the hope that someone will hire you? Much more likely the latter. Credibility is built in large part on perception. And, anyway, what happened to your Red Velvet Rope Policy? Sure, get on the phone with someone to see whether they get past your red velvet rope and give them an opportunity to fall in love with you at the same time. Learn about their needs, talk about how you can help, and book the business. In Chapter 10, you'll learn how to have effective sales conversations.

Now, I'm not completely against giving away free sessions, in fact, here's how I used free sessions to produce 65% of my new business during my first year in business. I included an offer for a 20-minute "laser coaching" session into my sales cycle, but only after someone had demonstrated that they were serious about learning from me. If someone downloaded my seven-part email mini-course (see why information products are important to the lead generation and conversion process?) I would send them the first two lessons during week one. Each lesson included two paragraphs of education followed by a detailed, written exercise. Then, instead of starting off week two with lesson three, I would send a "congratulations and reward" email, offering praise and appreciation for the work put in to the first two lessons (all of this was automated). As a reward, I offered a complimentary 20-minute telephone coaching session to address any questions they had about the material in the first two lessons. A number of procedures needed to be followed, however, to book the session, which I spelled out in the "congratulations and reward" email:

- The session had to be scheduled using my public calendar. I made only a few spots available on Friday afternoons so that a waiting list developed quickly. This way I didn't look like I was sitting around twiddling my thumbs, hoping someone would show up.
- If they missed the session or didn't reschedule with 24 hours' notice, they missed the opportunity and could not reschedule (again, all of this was automated).
- If they were more than a few minutes late to the phone session, I wouldn't pick up. Bad timekeeping and a lack of respect for others are both Red Velvet Rope Policy violations in my book.

- And, finally, one week before the scheduled session, they had to send me an email with their responses to the exercises from the first two lessons. This helped because if they had not already done them, it got them to do the exercises. Getting clients to consume your work is as important as getting them to hire you.
- By reviewing their written exercises, I knew what they needed before they dialed my number. It showed me what they were struggling with and how to help them. So, in just 20 minutes, I could solve a few of their problems and create an impressive result.

You might think that all these rules would put potential clients off. You're trying to get clients, not force them to jump through flaming hoops. But, you know what? Over 65% of the people who signed up for the free 20-minute session became clients.

If I were starting out today, I might use this strategy again, or I might leverage online learning platforms and communities to offer the same process to potential clients through a short online challenge or week-long program. Plus, with the advent of online video and webinars, which weren't available when I was starting out, there are more ways to convert clients to working with you than necessarily requiring them to get on the phone with you. However, for your most important one-to-one clients who will be working with you privately, I'd still recommend a screening call.

Figure out a way to use this strategy in your sales cycle and you'll get the opportunity to do something valuable, and free of charge, for your potential clients. You'll build your reputation, demonstrate credibility, and book more business. Then, once you're booked solid, you'll have so many referrals coming in that you won't need to do this anymore.

When to Raise Prices

Whenever you can, but there's no need to race to the top of the pricing ladder to be successful. Here are a few examples of why and how to do it:

- *Just for the heck of it:* Sometimes, raising prices may simply, and beautifully, lead to a much deserved increase in profit.

- *Economic conditions:* You will need to raise prices with inflation (rising costs unequaled by productivity gains). Inflation usually gets carried over to the consumer, which is why it's such an economic problem.
- *You're in demand and overbooked:* If demand for your services has increased, you'll be doing the Book Yourself Solid happy dance and it may be a good time to raise prices.
- *Training and skill development:* If you've recently upgraded your certifications or completed a significant training that is highly relevant to your clients' needs, it may be a great time to raise prices.
- *Upgrading your packaging:* If you upgrade your website with a complete redesign and in doing so seriously upgrade the look and feel of your brand, you can raise your prices. If you see clients in person and upgrade your offices, again, increasing the perceived value of your brand, you can up your prices. Credibility is, in no small part, based on perception.

Sometimes, when coaches get overbooked, they complain about it. Oh, how easily we forget what it was like when we were struggling our way up the ladder. Worse still, I've witnessed many a coach resist raising prices, which would have enabled each of them to work with fewer clients, for fear of losing business.

I used to see an acupuncturist from time to time in an attempt to reduce pain in my knee. He was likely the most experienced acupuncturist in my small town and had an overbooked practice because of it. One time I was on the table and while he was treating me, he commented that he was overworked and couldn't keep up with the demand.

He indicated that he didn't want to change the model of his business, in that he still wanted to see patients himself. He didn't want to manage other acupuncturists, nor did he want to raise his prices. So, even though he had a fist full of needles at the ready, I said, "Why don't you just double your prices?" His answer? "But, Michael, if I double my rates, I'll lose half my clients." I'll pause here to let that sink in.

First of all, he wouldn't have lost half his clients but even if he did, he'd still make the same money *and* have twice as much free time. More likely, he'd lose just a few clients but make much more money overall because of the price increase. Ironically, I stopped seeing him because it was too hard to get appointments that fit my schedule. So, if you're booked solid at rates that are too low, it might actually lose you clients.

If you do raise prices, it's a good idea to let clients know why. There's nothing wrong with saying that you're fortunate to be in high demand and are raising your prices so that you can give more attention to your clients. Or, that certain expenses related to serving your clients have increased and you're raising your prices accordingly. People like the truth. I'd prefer to be open and honest with my clients, running the risk of disappointing a few of them, than be manipulative or obtuse, running the risk of damaging my reputation. Just be sure to let them know what the new rates will be and when they go into effect. Give them reasonable notice so they can adjust to the changes. And, most important, remind them of the continuing benefits they'll get from working with you.

Although all coaches raise their pricing over time, you should also leverage your time and increase your revenue with online products and group coaching programs. A group coaching program, well managed, means that your clients can pay less and you can earn substantially more than your one-to-one hourly rate. This is a luxury that isn't afforded to many other industries. Most professionals need to hire new staff to increase their capacity. Plumbers, bookkeepers, cleaning firms, even software companies need to hire fast and often as they grow. The digital landscape means that you can serve many hundreds or even thousands of people without compromising on the hours of sleep you're getting.

10

Super Simple Selling

Art is making something out of nothing, and selling it.
—Frank Zappa

As a coach you may not want to think of yourself as a salesperson. You're in the business of helping others, and the sales process may feel contradictory to your core purpose. If you're uncomfortable with the sales process, it's likely that you view it as unethical, manipulative, or dishonest. Looking at it that way, who wouldn't be uncomfortable?

Many coaches also feel uncomfortable charging for services that either come easily to them or that they love doing. There is often a sense that if it comes easily and is enjoyable, there's something wrong with charging others for doing it.

Add the fact that coaches sell themselves as much as they sell a service, and the whole idea becomes even more uncomfortable. It may feel like you're bragging and being shamelessly immodest.

Becoming comfortable with the sales process requires that you let go of any limiting beliefs you may have about being worthy of the money you're earning. In fact, developing the right comfort level might also require a shift in your perspective on the sales process itself.

Letting Go of Limiting Beliefs

Most people who are successful get paid to do what they do well. You don't usually become successful doing something that you find difficult. You become successful when you exploit your natural talents. Imagine Tom Hanks saying he shouldn't get paid to do movies because he's really good at it and loves it. Or Stephen King saying he should write books for free because he enjoys it.

Tom Hanks, Stephen King, and anyone else you can think of who is, or was, wildly successful at what they do, work to the bone at becoming even better at what they are naturally gifted at doing. They create extraordinary experiences for the people they serve, whether it's an audience, a fan, or a client. That's why they—and you—deserve to be paid top dollar.

If you've been feeling like you can't, or shouldn't, be paid to do what you love, you must let that limiting belief go if you're to be booked solid.

If you don't believe you are worth what you are charging, it is unlikely that a lot of people are going to hire you based on those fees. You need to resonate fully with the prices you are setting so that others will resonate with them as well. To do so, you may need to work on shifting your beliefs so that you feel more comfortable with charging higher fees, rather than lowering your fees to eliminate the discomfort. Understand the far-reaching financial, emotional, physical, and spiritual (FEPS) benefits that you deliver and stand firmly in that value.

There is an old joke about a guy who gets into a cab in New York City and asks the driver how to get to Carnegie Hall, and the driver responds, "Practice, practice, practice." You're going to increase your pricing with practice. It's just like practicing a martial art, or a sport, or singing. Singing is a great example because your voice becomes more resonant the more you practice. At first it's uncomfortable, but over time, it becomes easier and more natural. The same thing will happen when you quote your fees. The more comfortable you feel when setting your price, the more other people will feel that comfort and the energetic resonance that comes with that comfort, and they'll happily pay you what you're worth.

Shifting Your Perspective

The Book Yourself Solid paradigm of sales is all about building relationships with your potential clients on the basis of trust. It is, quite simply, about having a sincere conversation that enables you to let your potential clients know what you can do to help them. You aren't manipulating or coercing people into buying something they have no real need or desire to buy. You're making them aware of something you offer that they already need, want, or desire.

Thinking in terms of solutions and benefits is the *aha* to the selling process. It's the key to shifting your perspective.

When you think in terms of solutions and problems solved, clients are compelled to work with you. You are a consultant, a lifelong advisor. When you have fundamental solutions and a desire to help others, it becomes your moral imperative to show and tell as many people as possible. You are changing lives.

Successful Selling Needs the Right Amount of Trust at Just the Right Time

It's no accident that I introduce sales here in Chapter 10; after I've taught you how to set your foundation and build trust and credibility. One of the reasons that so many sales conversations are *unsuccessful* is because they're had at the wrong time—usually too soon—before you've earned the proportionate amount of trust needed for the offer being made. Plus, your clients buy when it's right for them, when something occurs in their life or business that compels them to hire you. If these two factors, trust and timing, come together at just the right moment, you'll have a *successful* sales conversation and book the business. But this only works if you've built a solid foundation, demonstrating that you have done the following:

- Have a Red Velvet Rope Policy so you work only with ideal clients.
- Understand why people buy what you're selling so you know exactly to whom you are selling and what they want to invest in.

- Have developed a personal brand identity so you decide how you're known in the world.
- Are able to talk about what you do without sounding confusing or bland, or like everybody else, and without ever using an elevator speech.

If you've set this foundation, a potential client will give you the opportunity to earn their trust. But you'll only earn trust if you do the following:

- Use the standard credibility builders and have a high degree of likeability.
- Have designed a sales cycle that starts with no-barrier-to-entry offers including your always-have-something-to-invite-people-to offer.
- Regularly and respectfully keep in touch with the people you're meant to serve.
- Have simple lead-generating information products that enhance your credibility and speed up your sales cycle.

Then, and really only then, are you ready to have sales conversations that work.

The Secret to the Book Yourself Solid System

This simple four-step process is the secret to the Book Yourself Solid system:

1. You execute a few of the six core self-promotion strategies, which create awareness for what you have to offer.
2. When a potential client becomes aware of you, they'll take a look at your foundation. If it looks secure, if they feel comfortable stepping onto it, they'll give you the opportunity to earn their trust—but only the opportunity.
3. That's when your plan to build trust and credibility comes into play. As a potential client moves through your sales cycle, they will come to like you, trust you, and find you credible.

4. When their circumstances dictate that they need the kind of help you provide, they'll raise their hand and ask you to have a sales conversation. You have a sales conversation the Book Yourself Solid way and book the business.

The process is simple. The process is sound. It can turn your business life around. And, most important, the process is a complete, repetitive, and self-perpetuating system. While potential clients are going through this process, you're continuing to create awareness for what you have to offer using a few of the six core self-promotion strategies. This gets more new potential clients checking out your foundation for stability and security. They'll like what they see, stand on it, and give you the opportunity to earn their trust. You earn their trust (over time) and when the circumstances are right for *them,* they'll either raise their hand and ask you to have a sales conversation or they'll accept one of your compelling offers and you'll book the business. The process repeats itself over and over and over again. It's systematic. Once you've set up your own Book Yourself Solid marketing and sales system, it works like a charm. Just rinse and repeat.

The Super Simple Selling System

Now, let's talk about how to have the sales conversation. I've created the Four-Part Sales Formula for super simple selling—it practically works on its own. Why? Because, once trust is ensured and a need is met, using this four-part formula during your sales conversations is a natural process for booking business. But, please, just like the Book Yourself Solid Dialogue, this is meant to be an open and free-flowing conversation, not a sales script.

Book Yourself Solid Four-Part Sales Formula

When a potential client expresses interest in working with you, open with a simple question:

Part 1: What are you working on? Or *what is your goal?* Or *what are you trying to achieve?* Listen. Be curious. Take your time. Once you feel certain you know what he wants to accomplish and by when, simply ask some of the following questions.

Part 2: How will you know when you have achieved it? What results will you see? What feedback will you hear? What will it look like? What feelings will you have? Again, take your time. Listen deeply. Get your potential client to connect at every level with all of the FEPS benefits of the outcome they are seeking. Anchor your potential client in that place. Once you feel like the potential client has clearly articulated these benefits, make sure they are fully in the hiring frame of mind, and then ask . . .

Part 3: Would you like someone to help you with that (achieve your goal, and so forth)? If they say no, wish them the best of luck and keep in touch with them. If they say yes, then offer . . .

Part 4: Would you like that person to be me? Because, you know, you are my ideal client. (To which they'll say, "What do you mean?" because no one has ever said that to them before.) *Well, you are someone with whom I do my best work.* (They'll ask "Why?" and you'll tell them . . .) *Because you are . . .* (Here is where you list the qualities that make them who they are and enable you to do your best work.) As you're listing these qualities, you'll see their face brighten as they sit up straight and say, "Wow. That is so me! Thank you for noticing." You'll say, "So, shall we look at our calendars to plan a time to get started?" And the answer will be . . . drumroll, please . . . "Absolutely, yes!"

Don't use the preceding phrases verbatim. Instead, just use the Book Yourself Solid Four-Part Sales Formula as a framework for a super-duper simple (successful) sales conversation.

3.10.1 Written Exercise: Practice without pressure. Try this process with a good friend or colleague and see what happens. Ask them to call you at random a few times over the course of a week and say, "Hi, I've been getting your newsletter for a while, and I think you may be able to help me. Can we talk about your services?" And, instead of doing that thing that everyone does—talk about themselves and their business for 20 minutes—ask them what they're working on or what they're trying to achieve or what problem they're trying to overcome, and you'll be into part 1 of the Book Yourself Solid Four-Part Sales Formula. Super simple.

About the Gap

Notice that between part 2 and part 3 of the Four-Part Sales Formula, there is a gap between where the potential client is and where they want to be. You will be sorely tempted to step into that gap to demonstrate your talent and your skill. You might be tempted to "coach the gap," to solve the problem. After all, you want to help; you want to serve. But when you step into the gap, you actually do a disservice to your potential client because creating lasting change takes time. If your potential client goes away from the sales conversation believing that the problem has been "fixed," they likely won't see the lasting value of what you can deliver and, consequently, won't hire you. Stay inside the Four-Part Sales Formula.

If They're Uncertain

What if potential clients are not ready to start working with you? No problem. They go back into your sales cycle process. You continue to keep in touch. Book Yourself Solid is not about qualifying and disqualifying leads. Book Yourself Solid takes the long view. It's about creating long-term relationships. The good news is that someday the benefits you provide will be a priority. Something in your potential client's life will change that compels them to hire you. However, if you haven't kept in touch and followed up, they'll look to someone else to help them reach their goals. But, because you're going to become a master at keeping in touch and following up, you'll be waiting in the wings, ready, willing, and able to help them accomplish their goals. (Go back to Chapter 7 and review the keep-in-touch strategy if you need to.)

These are the lovely, easy steps to simple selling and booking yourself solid. Start small, end big, and remember: successful selling is really nothing more than showing your potential clients how you can help them live a happier, more successful life.

Cut the Crap Out of Selling

Traditional and trite sales tactics that include, but are not limited to, closing techniques, assuming the sale, overcoming objections, and so forth were originally developed in the late 1800s by John H. Patterson of the National Cash Register Company (who, ironically enough, was found guilty of violating antitrust laws). These contrived sales strategies, created by a convict, are still perpetuated by sales trainers. And for good reason. They give us something to do when we're lost. They provide a standard by which to measure. And the worst part is that they work . . . a little . . . sometimes. But clients detest them.

People don't buy because you want them to. If you really want to be successful when selling, listen to your potential clients. If they don't like the old, generic, overused, and clichéd tactics, why are you still holding on to them? (Maybe you're not, but you know, or work with, someone who is.)

Do what you must. Ditch the canned 1-2-3, sometimes pushy, usually insensitive, and almost always repetitive sales strategies glamorized in the past.

I've offered you the Book Yourself Solid Four-Part Sales Formula to use as a framework for your sales conversations. You can and should certainly adapt it to your asynchronous sales offers in videos, webinars, and online sales pages. But remember that there is no perfectly packaged process, magic bullet, or foolproof method to crumble every gatekeeper in your path and book every piece of business. It doesn't exist. We must be willing to learn, adapt, and listen to our potential clients.

When you do this, you'll never have to use a canned close again. But you will connect brilliantly with the values your customers want to express. Remember:

- Trash the level-setting statements and the conversation helpers and just listen while customers tell you what they really want.
- Ditch the pitch of the day and only make relevant sales offers that are proportionate to the amount of trust you've earned.
- Use the Red Velvet Rope Policy and don't look at everyone as a dollar sign. Maximize your time and energy, and build credibility when you work with people you are meant to serve.

I'm certain you care about what you do: the people you serve, the services you sell, and the reputation you've earned. You wouldn't be reading this book if you didn't. Do not let your guard down for one second. Think bigger about who you are and how you will serve your clients.

When you keep your focus and maintain your integrity, you'll never, ever, be put in the same category as those stereotypical, shady, smooth-talking, handlebar-mustache-twirling, sleazeball "salespeople" ready to screw over the next poor sap just to take home the commission. Your service is important to the world. You are important to the world. Cut the crap out of selling and set yourself apart.

The Book Yourself Solid Six Core Self-Promotion Strategies

You've diligently worked through Modules One, Two, and Three. You have a foundation for your coaching business. You have a strategy for building trust and credibility. You know how to price and sell your services. Watch out, because you're not only on your way to liking marketing and selling, but you are now dangerously close to loving both.

> By the time you complete Module Four, maybe you'll be in a full-on, mad, passionate love affair not only with the idea of marketing and selling. We can only hope.

Just like any new love affair, you want to give yourself time to absorb the newness of it all. Don't let the multitude of strategies, techniques, and exercises in Module Four overwhelm you. Pick the strategies that are most aligned with your strengths and run with them—you don't need to execute all of them. In fact, only three of the strategies are mandatory, whereas three of them are optional. Can you guess which are mandatory and which are optional?

The Book Yourself Solid Six Core Self-Promotion Strategies
1. The Book Yourself Solid Networking Strategy
2. The Book Yourself Solid Direct Outreach Strategy
3. The Book Yourself Solid Referral Strategy
4. The Book Yourself Solid Speaking Strategy
5. The Book Yourself Solid Writing Strategy
6. The Book Yourself Solid Web Strategy

Give yourself an A-plus if you guessed that the mandatory strategies are networking, direct outreach, and referrals. You don't survive without using those basic strategies for creating awareness for what you offer.

You might have guessed that speaking and writing strategies are optional, but are you surprised to hear that the web strategy is also optional? Yes, having a professional website that effectively starts conversations with potential clients is necessary 99.9% of the time for coaches, but beyond that, you need not learn or use all of the additional web marketing strategies. If you're not web or tech savvy and have absolutely no desire to become so, then you shouldn't worry about all the various bells and whistles the web offers. If you can outsource this, great. If you have the resources to hire people to run these efforts for you, then go for it. But, if you try to dive into the web with no real interest or aptitude, you're sure to become overwhelmed, and fast. We know this might sound blasphemous to an expert in search engine optimization or a Facebook ad strategist, but there are many coaches who build their business offline and send what is called direct traffic to their site rather than drive traffic from other online sources. More on this in Chapter 16, but our point is that you can get booked solid with solid networking, direct outreach, and referral strategies alone.

Start with the strategies that speak to you first. The only possible mistake you can make is to try all of these strategies at once. You run the risk of watering down your efforts, becoming frustrated with the results, or worse, quitting before you see any results. I suggest that you use the three mandatory strategies—networking, direct outreach, and referrals—and pick one of the optional strategies—web, speaking, or writing—to start.

The mandatory strategies will ensure that you're creating awareness for the products and services you offer, and the one optional strategy will supercharge your promotional efforts. Then, over time, as you get more and more proficient with the mandatory strategies, feel free to add in more of the optional strategies. In the process, do your best to enjoy, embrace, and profit from the Book Yourself Solid Six Core Self-Promotion Strategies.

Knowing how to do something and actually doing it are two very different things. For years, I've seen many a talented coach struggle to get clients because, even though they understood what they were supposed to do, they just didn't do it. Watching others struggle so much hurts my heart, and solving this problem, for the people I serve, became an obsession. Thankfully, for me, and fortunately, for you, I believe I've solved the problem.

Remember, the Book Yourself Solid system is supported by both practical and spiritual principles. From a spiritual perspective, I believe that if you have something to say, if you have a message to deliver, and if there are people you want to serve, then there are people in this world whom you are meant to serve. Not kinda, sorta, because they're in your target market . . . but *meant to*—that's the way the universe is set up if you're in the business of helping others.

From a practical perspective, there may be two simple reasons why you don't have as many clients as you'd like: either you don't know what to do to attract and secure more clients or you know what to do but you're not actually doing it.

The Book Yourself Solid system is designed to help you solve both of these problems. Module Four will show you what to do to attract and secure more clients. But these Six Core Self-Promotion Strategies must be executed every day. Yes, *every working day*. You don't need us to tell you that your future rests on your ability to execute these strategies with daily discipline. However, you might need us to help you do the following:

- Identify exactly what you need to do each day to book more business.
- Definitely get it done, daily.

This module will show you exactly what to do daily. Most important, the concepts and action steps laid out in the following pages will help you create relentless demand for the services you offer so that you can energetically build a cadre of high-value, high-paying, inspiring clients.

CHAPTER

11

The Book Yourself
Solid Networking
Strategy

Some cause happiness wherever they go; others, whenever they go.
—Oscar Wilde

Networking, Ugh!

It's possible that—like the thought of marketing and sales—the thought of networking may make you cringe. When most coaches hear the word *networking*, they think of the old-school business mentality of promotional networking at meet-and-greet events where everyone is there to schmooze and manipulate one another in an attempt to gain some advantage for themselves or their business.

Who wouldn't cringe at the thought of spending an hour or two exchanging banalities and sales pitches with a phony smile plastered on your face to hide your discomfort? If it feels uncomfortable, self-serving, or deceptive, chances are all those business cards you collected will end up in a drawer of your desk never to be seen again because you'll so dread following up that you'll procrastinate until they're forgotten.

Take heart, because it doesn't have to be that way. The Book Yourself Solid Networking Strategy operates from an entirely different perspective—networking is all about connecting and sharing with others. All that's necessary is to shift your perspective from one of scarcity and fear to one of abundance and love. With the Book Yourself Solid Networking Strategy, the focus is on sincerely and freely giving and sharing, and by doing so, building and deepening mutually beneficial relationships with others. Networking is all about making lasting connections.

Making the Shift to the Book Yourself Solid Way

The first step is to change your perspective of what networking really is. Do you believe that networking has something to do with the old-school business mentality of scarcity and fear that asks these questions:

- How can I push my agenda?
- How can I get or keep the attention on myself?
- What can I say to really impress or manipulate?
- How can I use each contact to get what I want or need?
- How can I crush the competition?
- How can I dominate the marketplace?

The Book Yourself Solid Networking Strategy (one of abundance and, dare I say it, love) asks instead these questions:

- What can I give and offer to others?
- How can I help others to be successful?
- How can I start and continue friendly conversations?
- How can I put others at ease?
- How can I best express my sincerity and generosity?
- How can I listen attentively so as to recognize the needs and desires of others?
- How can I provide true value to others?
- How can I fully express myself so I can make genuine connections with others?

When we use the word *networking,* let's think of *connecting,* instead. Does that help make the concept of networking more palatable? We don't get contacts, we don't find contacts, we don't have contacts; we make *connections* with real people.

> *A connection with another human being means that you're in sync with, and relevant to, each other. Let that be our definition of networking.*

When people ask me what is the most important factor in networking success, I always have a two-word answer: other people. Your networking success is determined by other people—how they respond to you.

If you keep asking yourself the preceding value-added questions and follow the Book Yourself Solid Networking Strategy that I'm about to present to you, you'll create a large and powerful network built on compassion, trust, and integrity, a network that is priceless and will reap rewards for years to come.

The Book Yourself Solid 50/50 Networking Rule

The Book Yourself Solid Networking Strategy employs the 50/50 networking rule, which requires that we share our networking focus evenly between potential clients and other industry figures, like suppliers, publishers, conference organizers, and other influential professionals. Most people think of networking as something you do primarily to try to reel in clients. That's not so.

Although the Book Yourself Solid Networking Strategy adds value to the lives of people who could become your clients, you'll also want to spend 50% of your networking time connecting with other industry figures. Networking with them provides you with an opportunity to connect and share resources, knowledge, and information. Bear in mind that working solo does not mean working alone. This chapter is focused on increasing the value of your network of other professionals who can open doors of all kinds for you. You can create so much more value when other talented people are involved.

Have You Got Any Soul?

The absolute best education I have ever received on the concept of networking was from Tim Sanders (2002) in his book, *Love Is the Killer App: How to Win Business and Influence Friends.*

Tim Sanders's message is that being a *love cat* is the key to business success, and it's at the heart of the Book Yourself Solid Networking Strategy. He quotes philosopher and writer Milton Mayeroff's definition of love from his book *On Caring*: "Love is the selfless promotion of the growth of the other." Tim then defines his idea of business love as "the act of intelligently and sensibly sharing your intangibles with your biz partners."

What are these intangibles? They are your knowledge, your network, and your compassion. They are the three essential keys to networking success.

Networking requires that you consciously integrate each of these intangibles until they become a natural part of your daily life, everywhere you go, and in everything you do. Yes, I said *daily life*. Networking isn't something you do only at networking events. It's an ongoing process that will bring terrific benefits.

Share *Who* You Know, *What* You Know, and *How* You Feel

Here's how you practically go about sharing your intangibles with your partners, potential clients, suppliers, and friends:

- *Share who you know:* This is everyone you know. It's as simple as that. Whether family, friend, or business associate, everyone in your network is potentially a good connection with someone else, and you never know whom you might meet next who will be the other half of a great connection.
- *Share what you know:* This means everything you've learned—whether through life experience, observation, conversation, or study—and everything you continue to learn.
- *Share how you feel (in ways that make other people feel better about themselves):* This is all of your compassion, the quality that makes us most human. It's our ability to empathize with others. Sharing

your compassion in every aspect of your life will bring the greatest rewards, not only for your bottom line but also in knowing that you're operating from your heart and your integrity in all your interactions.

Note: Give each of these three intangibles freely and with no expectation of return. After all, that's how love is meant to operate, too. Although it may seem calculated to plan a strategy on them, the fact remains that when you're smart, friendly, and helpful, people will like you, will enjoy being around you, and will remember you when they or someone they know needs your services.

Share Who You Know

To whom do you want to give your business or recommend to other members of your network? It's the people who have served you in some way; the people who are friendly, nice, smart, and helpful; the people who will go the extra mile; give that little bit more than anyone expects; and who genuinely strive to provide the best service they can with integrity. It's the people who are upbeat, always have a ready smile, and from whom you walk away feeling supported and energized.

If you are that person in each and every interaction you have with others, whether business or personal, your network is going to grow exponentially, and those people are going to remember you and want to do business with you. They're going to link you with others in their network with whom you can make beneficial connections, and they're going to refer you to everyone they know who could possibly use your service or products.

There is one thing that is essential to consider with respect to sharing your network. You must do what you say you're going to do—always. And if you don't, apologize and make it right. If you make commitments and don't fulfill them, you'll damage your reputation and close doors that were once open to you. If you don't make commitments to connect, no one will do it for you. These habits of commitment making and fulfilling are essential to developing yourself into a masterful connector who truly and meaningfully adds value to the lives of others.

Each business day, introduce two people within your network who do not yet know each other but you think might benefit from knowing each other. This is not a referral for a specific work opportunity but rather a way to connect two people who may find some benefit in knowing each other. Maybe they are both in the same field or share some business connection. Maybe they are both into martial arts or golf. Or, maybe they just live in the same town. Either way, all you're doing is creating an opportunity for connection. If they're the kind of people who value meeting others, then something special might happen. Hey, you never know, you might be introducing two people who are going to save the planet from climate calamity or fall in love and get married.

4.11.1 Written Exercise: List three people in your network who consistently support you by sending referrals, giving you advice, or doing anything else that's helpful. Then identify someone in your network for each of these three people whom you could connect them with. Who do you know who will add value to their work or life? Is it a potential client, a potential business partner, or a potential vendor?

4.11.2 Booked Solid Action Step: Try it now. Go through your address book and find two people who share something in common, something that each one of them will find relevant about the other and introduce them to each other.

The people you listed in the preceding written exercise and the people you connected in the Booked Solid Action Step are going to appreciate the opportunity to connect or the recommendation that you make, and when someone they know needs your service or product, they'll be more likely to remember you and to reciprocate.

Remember, too, that the six degrees of separation theory says that you are only six people away from the person or information you need. (In your field, your degrees of separation from anyone you need or want to connect with are even fewer.) Everyone you meet has the potential to connect you (through their network and their contacts' networks) to someone or some piece of information that you need. So step out of your comfort zone and make a sincere effort to connect with people you might not usually interact with. The more diverse your network of connections is, the more powerful and effective your network becomes. It opens doors that might otherwise remain closed.

4.11.3 Written Exercise: Think of the types of people or professions that are *not* represented in your current network. List five that would expand and benefit your network, as well as ideas for where you might find them.

Every once in a while I get some pushback about sharing my network that goes something like this: "But, Michael, I don't know that many people, so this won't work for me." You might be surprised to discover that you can create 45 connections from a network of only 10 people. Bump it up to 20 people and you've got 190 connections. It may seem like funny math, but it's not. It's factorial math.

Here's how it works for just 10 people:

Introduce Person 1 to Persons 2 to 10.

That's nine connections.

Person 2 has met Person 1, but needs to meet Persons 3 to 10.

That's eight connections.

Person 3 has now met Persons 1 and 2 and needs to meet Persons 4 to 10.

That's seven connections.

Person 4 has now met Persons 1 to 3 and needs to meet Persons 5 to 10.

That's six connections.

Person 5 has now met Persons 1 to 4 and needs to meet Persons 6 to 10.

That's five connections.

Person 6 has now met Persons 1 to 5 and needs to meet Persons 7 to 10.

That's four connections.

Person 7 has now met Persons 1 to 6 and needs to meet Persons 8 to 10.

That's three connections.

Person 8 has now met Persons 1 to 7 and needs to meet Persons 9 to 10.

That's two connections.

Person 9 has now met Persons 1 to 8 and needs to meet Person 10.
That's one connection.
That's a total of 45 connections created out of only 10 people.

If you start with 20 people, you end up with 190 connections because
19 + 18 + 17 + 16 + 15 + 14 + 13 + 12 + 11 + 10 + 9 + 8 + 7 + 6 + 5
+ 4 + 3 + 2 + 1 = 190.

Your world is much bigger than you might think. And you don't really
need to know much about math; you just need to know that connecting
people is a good thing to do.

Share What You Know

The answers to most questions are offered in books. Even better, we get to
choose what we learn and from whom. Then armed with this information,
we're in a great place to share it with others, including the books themselves.

You may be thinking, "But if I'm always referring to other people's
work, won't they just forget about me and get everything they need from
the book or resource I referred them to?" Good question. First of all, if they
love the book or information that you referred them to, it's highly likely
they'll associate much of that value with you. They will feel connected to
you because you helped them achieve a goal or change their life, or simply
learn something new, the value of which is not to be underestimated. The
more knowledgeable you are, and are perceived to be, the more trust and
credibility you'll build in your network. Reading books is, by far, the best
and most efficient way to increase your knowledge. Sharing those books is
an excellent way to demonstrate that knowledge and help other people at
the same time.

Reading a book on a topic that is related to the services you provide
offers an easy way to start a conversation with potential clients or contacts.
In fact, they may start the conversation with you instead with one simple
question, "What are you reading?" I realized this gem of a networking technique by accident. I was born and raised in New York City, where almost
every New Yorker rides the subway. You bump into friends, sit next to politicians, and see celebrities. Plus, it's simply the best way to get around. It's
also one of the best places to make new friends. Think about it; you're constantly bumped, pushed, and shoved by people you don't know. So instead

of fighting all the time, most New Yorkers decide the path of least resistance is simply to strike up a conversation. If you have a book in your hand, what do you think this conversation is going to be about? You guessed it: the book. And what better way to get into your Book Yourself Solid Dialogue than to explain why you're reading the particular book you're holding in your hand.

Of course, this doesn't just apply to New York subway cars. Everywhere you go, you're running into, meeting, and connecting with other people. What if you always had a book in your hand that enabled you to share what you know about your particular area of expertise, for the betterment of the person you're talking with? I know that not every person you meet or run into is a member of your target market, or at first thought, can send you clients, but it doesn't matter. You're just finding opportunities to add value to those you meet by sharing what you know—as long as it's relevant to them.

4.11.4 Booked Solid Action Step: Try it with this book. Carry it wherever you go and explain to people why you're reading it. You'll have the opportunity to talk about the Book Yourself Solid philosophy of giving so much value that you think you've gone too far and then giving more, and how it's in sync with your values and what you do as a service provider. You'll then be able to get into your Book Yourself Solid Dialogue with ease.

Ask yourself what knowledge, once acquired, would add the greatest value and make you more attractive to potential clients and business partners, and then go after learning it. Your investment in books—buying them and reading them—will pay dividends you can't even imagine.

Here are a few examples of books that will help you grow your business:

- *Profit First* by Mike Michalowicz (Portfolio, 2017)
- *Duct Tape Marketing* by John Jantsch (Thomas Nelson, 2010)
- *Your Body of Work* by Pam Slim (Portfolio, 2013)
- *Never Split the Difference* by Chris Voss (Harper Business, 2016)
- *UnMarketing* by Scott Stratten (Wiley, 2016)
- *Lean In* by Sheryl Sandberg (Knopf, 2013)

- *Hug Your Haters* by Jay Baer (Portfolio, 2016)
- *Fascinate* by Sally Hogshead (Harper Business, 2016)

4.11.5 Written Exercise: List five books you've read that you know are must-reads for your target market. Think about and jot down the names of any specific people who come to mind for each book.

4.11.6 Written Exercise: List five books that have been recommended to you as must-reads or that you know contain information that would add value to your target market. Then go out and make the investment in at least one of them this week.

4.11.7 Written Exercise: Books aren't our only source of knowledge. As I mentioned previously, our life experience, observations, and conversations are all sources of knowledge as well. Think about the many areas in which you're knowledgeable and list a minimum of five. Have fun with this and just let it flow. If you know a lot about skydiving or ikebana (the Japanese art of flower arranging), include it! You never know what subject might help make a connection.

Let's take it up a notch. Once a week, send a book to someone with whom you'd like to develop a meaningful business relationship. Include a nice card with a note about why you're sending them the book—what it's meant to you and why you think it'll be valuable to them. Follow up three weeks later by phone to see how they're enjoying the book. This strategy is especially beneficial for those who are not particularly comfortable with small talk because now you've got something to talk about.

Now, let's take up one more notch. Sharing magazine, journal, and newspaper articles can work even better than books because the recipient of the information can consume it so quickly. Each day, send personally or professionally relevant articles to three people in your network. I know what you're thinking, *Michael, c'mon, how much time is that going to take? What do you think, I'm just sitting around with nothing to do?* No, of course not. I know how busy you are. But, if you want more clients, you need a stronger network. If you're not willing to build it, do you really deserve more clients? Just sayin'. . .

For example, if you are developing a professional relationship with Bob, who owns a small engineering business and focuses on high technology, and Monday morning the *New York Times* publishes an article about the state of the high-tech engineering industry, you'll be able to send the article to Bob before he even turns on his computer. Your email will include a link to the article and a little note that says, "Good Morning, Bob, I saw this article and immediately thought of you. Wonder if you've seen it? Pretty interesting when the author says that . . ."

You might just make Bob's day by sharing some very relevant and timely information that he might otherwise have missed. Moreover, Bob is going to feel so fortunate you're out in the world thinking about him and his needs.

Review three publications that are relevant to your industry each day and then decide to whom you are going to send various articles.

4.11.8 Booked Solid Action Step: Try it now. Go to your favorite online publication, browse through today's articles and when you find one that is relevant to someone in your network, send it to them with a note as suggested earlier.

Share How You Feel

In a business like yours that is based on service, people will generally not hire you unless they feel you have compassion for what they're going through. Expressing that compassion is the first step to a successful working relationship. How do you do that? Listen attentively. Be fully present when making connections, smile as often as possible, make eye contact, and ask engaging, open-ended questions that express your curiosity and interest.

Take the time to add value to the person you're connecting with by offering information or resources that speak to their needs. If you don't have what they need, think about who in your network would meet their needs and how to go about acting as the link for them. Remember, this is done with no expectation of any immediate return.

4.11.9 Written Exercise: Note a recent situation, business or personal, when someone else expressed compassion for you. Think about how you felt following the interaction. How do you feel about that person because of the compassion they showed for you?

Can sharing your compassion be a marketing tactic? Absolutely. Do you do it manipulatively or to try to gain some favor? No, that is not the Book Yourself Solid way. You can be deliberate and developmental in the way that you share your compassion—that's not manipulative—it's thoughtful.

Send a card or an email to someone in your network at least once a week just to share your compassion. If you know they're going through a difficult time, send a note expressing sympathy. If they have just been honored with an award, shower them with praise. If they recently experienced a family triumph, like the marriage of a child, congratulate them. These simple, yet powerful, gestures make people thankful to know you. It keeps you on top of their mind. And, most important, you're making other people feel better about who they are and what they do.

These Booked Solid Action Steps are your new daily and weekly networking activities and you don't even need to leave the house to get them done:

- You'll share your network by introducing two people each day who may benefit from meeting each together. You'll come across as a real connecter, someone who thinks about the needs of others, and that's an amazingly attractive quality.
- You'll share what you know by sending one book a week, and at least two articles a day, to important networking partners. It'll make you look like a smarty-pants, give you something to talk to them about, and in the process build your relationship.

- You'll share your compassion with one person in your network each day, making them feel better about themselves and in the process thankful that they know you. Want to share compassion with more than one person a day, by all means, be my guest.

Let's do some more math, basic math, this time. If you adopt these habits and introduce two people each day, share articles or a book with two people each day, and share compassion with at least one person each day, that means you'll be connecting with at least five people each day (2 + 2 + 1 = 5). If you do that Monday through Friday, you'll be connecting with at least 25 people a week (5 × 5 = 25). There are generally four weeks in each month so if you connect with 25 people each week, that means you'll connect with 100 people a month (25 × 4 = 100). Do this all year long and you'll connect with 1,200 people each year. That's a numbers game worth playing. That alone can get you booked solid.

These simple, yet meaningful, networking strategies will get, and keep, you booked solid for many years to come. You just have to do it—each and every business day. I believe the Book Yourself Solid Networking Strategy is a critical key to your success.

The Book Yourself Solid Network of 90

Make a list of 90 people, a mixture of potential clients or industry professionals with whom you already have a relationship. The relationship doesn't have to be very strong, as it will become stronger over time as you work your networking muscle. If you don't know 90 people today, don't worry. Start with whoever you have. You will add to it over time.

This is your Book Yourself Solid Network of 90. This list sits on your desk. It lives on your computer and travels with you when you're on the road. Why 90 and why must you keep it with you at all times? Because your success is, in large part, determined by the quality of your relationships, keeping this list by your side will ensure that you're thinking of them and, if you make a habit of sharing your intangibles with them, your relationships will become stronger than you ever thought possible. And 90, because contacting three people from your list every day is manageable, and means that you will be in touch with these people roughly once a month.

> **4.11.10 Written Exercise:** Identify a minimum of 10 and a maximum of 90 people you'd like to remain in regular contact with. This list should be made up in equal parts of peers and prospects.

Here's what you do with your list:

- Each day, reach out to the three people at the top of your list.
- Share your knowledge, your network or your compassion with these people. You can write a quick email, send a text message, a postcard, or a handwritten note.
- After you reach out to these people, put them to the bottom of the list, and tackle another three people tomorrow. That means you'll be in contact with them every month at a minimum.
- Be flexible. If you don't see an opportunity to make a relevant introduction to the third person on your list, send them a note to say that you're thinking of them.
- Be pragmatic. You might run into somebody on your list every week at the gym. That's great. If you've had a meaningful exchange, put them to the bottom of the list. If a colleague has a birthday and they were at the top of your list last week, of course you should still wish them a happy birthday, before finding them in your list and putting them to the bottom again. It's a framework, not an exact science.
- Think big. If you have 120 or 180 people you'd like to stay in touch with on a regular basis and it's not overwhelming, go for it! Ninety is a manageable number of connections for most people, but if you're a super-connector, feel free to supercharge this strategy by adding more names.

This networking activity occurs every business day: you'll reach out to a minimum of three people, each and every day, and you'll follow up with people who reply to you, each and every day. This is critical. Dedicated, disciplined, and determined action is key to your networking success.

4.11.11 Booked Solid Action Step: Reach out to the first person on your network of 90 and then add them to your follow-up system.

Networking Opportunities

The possibilities for meeting people are endless. Any time you're sharing your connections, knowledge, and compassion, you're networking. Any time you're learning more about what others do and know, you're networking. Anytime you link or connect two people you know, you're networking.

Informal Networking Opportunities

These are the ones that we might not think of as networking but that we can't afford to overlook. We have dozens of these every day:

- Casual chat in line at the grocery store
- In exercise class at a gym or in a coffee shop
- Speaking with your neighbor while walking your dog

Let's take the neighbor you see while walking your dog as an example. Every day you walk the same path with your dog. Each time, you smile and chat with your neighbor as your dogs sniff each other. After a while, you begin to greet one another by name, and you know enough about him to ask after his family. He mentions he was looking forward to a special evening out with his wife the following night for their anniversary but then sighs and says, "But our babysitter canceled at the last minute. I wish [one of the phrases to always be listening for] that I knew of a good backup to call." You recall that your friend Sally seems to know every sitter in town. You pull out your phone, look up her number, and give her a call. "Sally, meet Bob. He's looking for a great sitter for tomorrow night, and you know everyone, so of course I thought you might be able to help," you say as you hand your cell phone to Bob.

Now this exchange has absolutely nothing to do with business. Or does it? On the surface, it might not seem to. However, who do you think Bob is going to call when he, or someone he knows, needs your services? Bob is thrilled with you because you've saved his special night out. And Sally is pleased too because you've given her high praise and allowed her to show off her knowledge of who's who in the world of local babysitters. Both of them feel better following their interaction with you, and that makes you memorable. And, most important, you've increased your connection factor with each of them. Your connection factor is how much trust you've built with each person in your network. The more value you add to a person's life, the more they are going to trust you.

4.11.12 Written Exercise: Think for a moment: have you recently missed any opportunities for making a deeper connection with someone? List one connection that would have been made if you had just shared your knowledge, your network, or your compassion.

Formal Networking Opportunities

These are the more formal, business meet-and-greet opportunities that can be fun and enjoyable and offer great rewards:

- Chamber of commerce meetings
- Networking or leads groups—Vistage, BNI, or EO, for example
- Trade association meetings (important)
- Yacht clubs (you might need a boat for this one)

4.11.13 Written Exercise: Do some research and come up with three additional business networking opportunities like the ones I've listed that you can attend with the intention of adding value to others as well as enhancing your network.

Networking Events—What to Do

- *Arrive on time:* This is not the time to stage a grand entrance by being fashionably late or to tell any stories about why you're late. Nobody cares. If you're late and it's noticed, apologize and leave it at that.
- *Relax and be yourself:* Contrary to conventional wisdom, you don't have to fit in. It may sound trite, but be yourself, unless when you're being yourself you end the evening with your tie wrapped around your head doing a nosedive into the shrimp salad. Seriously, people want to meet the person who is out in front, who is writing the rules and taking the lead, not the one who is following the pack. So don't be afraid to be fully self-expressed. If you are, you'll be more memorable.
- *Smile and be friendly:* Both men and women may worry that smiling too big will be construed as some sort of a come-on or that they're desperate for attention. This fear of being misunderstood will hold you back. Let it go. Better to err on the side of a big, friendly smile than to be considered unfriendly or standoffish.
- *Focus on giving:* If your focus is on giving of yourself, you're going to get returns in spades. If you focus on what you can get, you will be much less successful.
- *Prepare for the event:* Learn the names of the organizers and some of the key players. Identify what and how you can share with others at the function: whom you know (without being a name dropper), what you know (without being a know-it-all), and what you can share from your heart (without making assumptions) with the people who will be at this particular event. You never know what might change someone's life.
- *Introduce yourself to the person hosting the event:* This person may be a very valuable addition to your network. Never forget to say, "Thank you."
- *Introduce yourself to the bigwig:* If there's someone you want to meet at a big seminar or event, someone famous in your industry, do you go up to them and say, "Here's what I do and here's my business card"? No. You start by offering praise. You say, "I just want to tell you your work had a great effect on me" or "Your work inspired me

to do this or that." Then the next time you are at the same event, you could say, "I would just love to hold your coffee cup." Meaning, "I would love to assist you in some way that would add value to your life or work." Or don't wait and do it by email after you've met at the event (but read Chapter 12 before you do). They may say, "I don't think so," but what have you got to lose? Then again, they may respond by saying, "Yeah, you seem like a really genuine and considerate person. I've got some stuff you can do." Don't forget that successful and busy people always have more on their plate than they can reasonably handle. They're always looking for talented people to help make their life easier. If you can help reduce someone's stress or work level, you've made a friend for life.

- *Offer something when first meeting someone, whenever possible:* Offer praise (as in the previous example), compassion, or a connection. When you can say, "I know someone you've got to meet" or "There's a great book I think may offer the solution to your problem," they are going to see you very differently from the person who shoved a business card in their face and said, "Let's stay in touch." If you can leave them feeling even better, uplifted, and energized after his interaction with you, they're going to remember you.

- *Start conversations by asking questions:* This is a great approach, especially if you're nervous. It takes the spotlight off you and enables the other person to shine. It enables you to learn something new at the same time.

- *Identify two or three things you'd like to learn from the people at the function:* People are drawn to others who are curious and interested.

- *Make eye contact:* It expresses respect and interest in the person you're speaking with. And stay focused on the person you're speaking with. If you're speaking with Jan, but your eyes are constantly scanning the room for someone more important or relevant to you, don't you think it might make Jan feel unappreciated?

- *Wear comfortable clothing but dress well:* If you're constantly fidgeting or worrying about how you look in clothes that aren't comfortable or don't fit properly, you'll be self-conscious and others will sense it.

- *Take the initiative:* Go up to people and make friends. People love to be asked about themselves, their hobbies, or their family. This is the time to get to know a few personal tidbits that will give you the opportunity to find a common interest that makes connecting easier and more natural.

- *Offer a firm handshake:* Hold your drink in your left hand. This eliminates the need to wipe your damp hand on your clothes before shaking hands. And, guys, don't think you need to shake hands differently with a woman from the way you do with a man. A firm handshake (not a death grip) is always appropriate.

- *Be inclusive:* Ask others to join your conversations; this is very important. Don't monopolize people, especially those who are in high demand, like the speaker from the event. It makes the speaker uncomfortable. Remember, they're there to meet lots of people, too. It also annoys others who want to meet the person you're trying to keep to yourself. Tip: if you want to be helpful, ask the speaker if there is anybody you can introduce them to, or simply be sure to keep including people in your conversations with them. This way, you'll be seen as a very generous and open person by the others at the event, and the speaker will remember you as someone who helped them easily network and navigate the event.

- *Ask for a business card and then keep in touch:* It's your responsibility to ask for a card if you want one, and it's your responsibility to follow up. Quality, not quantity, counts when making genuine personal connections. If you race through an event passing out and collecting business cards from anyone and everyone as though there were a prize for the most cards gained at the end of the event, you'll do yourself a huge disservice. And remember, just because someone gives you their business card does *not* mean you have permission to add them to your mailing list. You do not. You can certainly send a personal email as a follow-up, and you should, but you should not and cannot start sending email blasts. You don't have permission to do that.

- *Always have a pen with you:* When you receive a business card, write a little note about any commitment to follow up, what you talked about, any personal bits or unusual things that will help you to remember the person and to personalize future contact, and be sure to include the date and name of the function where you met.

- *Take photos:* Ask permission to get a selfie or ask somebody to take photos of you and the people you meet. Rather than posting it immediately on social media, offer to send it to the person you're speaking with and they may choose to put it up online. Plus, you'll probably need to exchange contact details to share the pictures with them.

- *A note for introverts:* Remember that networking is not speed dating. You don't need to work the whole room. Focus on creating one or two deep connections. Honor your own need for space.

Networking Events—What Not to Do

- *Don't try to be cool:* And don't overcompensate for your nervousness by bragging about your success; this is a major turnoff.
- *Don't let "What do you do?" be the first question you ask:* Let it come up naturally in conversation.
- *Don't sit with people you know for the majority of the event:* Although it may be more comfortable to sit with the people you know, it becomes too easy to stay with them, and if you do, you'll defeat the purpose of being there. Step out of your comfort zone and get to know new people.
- *Don't wear cologne, perfumes, or essential oils:* Many people are sensitive to these kinds of smells, and they can be overpowering. Men seem to overdo this. If I shake your hand and your cologne transfers to my hand, you've gone way overboard. It's like marketing your territory —invasively so.
- *Don't juggle multiple items:* Travel light to eliminate the necessity of juggling your coat, purse, briefcase, drink, or buffet plate. Keep that right hand free for handshakes and for jotting down quick notes on business cards.
- *Don't complain about networking or the event you're attending:* In fact, don't complain about anything. The cycle of complaining is easy to get drawn into, especially at events where almost everyone is a bit uncomfortable. Although complaining is an icebreaker, it's not an attractive one. Change the subject—for example, "Have you tried the shrimp?"—or take the opportunity to recommend a great book.
- *Don't take yourself too seriously:* Remember to relax and have fun.

Online Networking Through Social Media

You're probably using social media for both personal and professional purposes, or it may be an entirely new frontier just waiting for you to stake your claim.

In an October 2009 *Wall Street Journal* article titled, "Why E-Mail No Longer Rules," the writer, Jessica Vascellaro, predicted that in the next 5 or 10 years, email will become a thing of the past. "E-mail has had a good run as king over communications, but its reign is over. In its place a new generation of services is starting to take hold. Services like X and Facebook and countless others vying for a piece of the new world. Just as email did more than a decade ago, this shift promises to profoundly rewrite the way we communicate in ways we can only begin to imagine."

The author was wrong.

Yes, social media has changed the way people communicate online but it has not replaced email communication and won't anytime soon. On the one hand, the growth of social media is good for you and your ability to exploit it for networking and marketing purposes—it's mobile, it's easy, it's quick, and it's free. On the other hand, the fact that it's easy, quick, and free is also a problem. It means more junk—more irrelevant noise clogging up the bandwidth. So use your social media wisely and well. If you do, it will speak volumes about who you are, what you stand for, and how you do business.

Social Media—for Marketing or Networking?

Social media can be used for marketing purposes through pay-per-click ad campaigns, live broadcasts, promotions, and the like. However, when beginning to build a social media platform on Facebook, LinkedIn, or whatever the flavor of the month may be, I suggest using it primarily as a tool for connecting, relationship building, and creating value by sharing your intangibles as we discussed before. When I introduce you to the Book Yourself Solid Web Strategy in Chapter 16, I'll share various ways to use social media for both marketing and building relationships. It's too much to add to this chapter. Just remember the bottom line: *Think relationships first, business second.*

You Are Always Networking

Your profits will come from connections with people who can send you business—whether that's by way of a satisfied client who refers others to you; or another professional who has the ability to book you for speaking engagements, write about you, or partner with you; or the neighbor who appreciates your big, friendly smile and the recommendation you made for a great babysitter when he desperately needed one.

With the Book Yourself Solid Networking Strategy, the prospect of creating a phenomenal network of connections doesn't have to be overwhelming or intimidating. We all connect constantly, with everyone, every day. Now we just need to do it consciously, with greater awareness, until doing so becomes a natural and comfortable part of our daily lives.

Then follow up. Keep in touch. It is imperative that you get every one of your connections into your database and act on each relevant connection.

So You've Got Spinach in Your Teeth

I've given you a lot of techniques in this chapter about what to do, what not to do, and how to interact with others when you're networking, but there's a big difference between techniques and principles, and it's the principles that are most important to remember and begin implementing. If you can incorporate the principles, you'll naturally do well.

For example, everyone says when you meet people at a networking event you're supposed to look that person in the eye, give them a firm handshake, smile, and nod your head, but if you do that and don't take the giver's stance, it won't matter how slick you are. However, if you always take the giver's stance and share who you know, what you know, and how you feel, even if you have spinach in your teeth and your palm is sweaty, you'll be fine, because people are going to respond to who you are as a human being. In fact, they'll share their compassion with you by gently letting you know about the large piece of spinach entrenched between your two front teeth.

So what do you think? Are you ready to network your way to more clients, more profit, and deeper connections with people? Sharing your knowledge, your network, and your compassion will bring you one step closer to being booked solid.

12

The Book Yourself Solid Direct Outreach Strategy

You miss 100% of the shots you don't take.
—Wayne Gretzky

As a professional coach, you'll need to proactively reach out to potential clients to make offers and to marketing partners and other decision-makers to create opportunities. In fact, the most important direct outreach you do might well be to other coaches, businesses, and professional associations to network, cross-promote, and build referral relationships.

Let's clearly define what direct outreach is *not* before detailing exactly what it is and how to do it authentically, easily, and successfully. It is *not* spam, which has typically been considered unsolicited mail or email sent without permission to mailing lists that have been purchased or scraped. However, I think the way people now see spam has grown in scope and definition. Today, there are many more ways you can be labeled a spammer—even when you think you're standing in the service of potential clients or business associates.

As you know, spam is not the Book Yourself Solid way. It never has been and never will be. Before the advent of the internet, direct outreach was a very common marketing strategy. I suppose it's no less common today, but unfortunately, it is often perceived as spam. You must be very careful and

161

discerning with respect to how you use the Book Yourself Solid Direct Outreach Strategy.

You can now be labeled a spammer by sending an unsolicited email directly to a potential client that contains any kind of sales message or promotional or business offer. The same goes for cold-calling. Many people just consider that another kind of spam, because it's unsolicited. Even direct outreach to an individual on social media can get you pegged as irrelevant or worse, a spammer. Even posting public comments online can get you called out for spamming if they smack of self-promotion.

Clients now find you. That doesn't relieve you of your marketing responsibilities. You need to create awareness for what you offer so that when potential clients go looking for the kind of services you offer they find you. If you don't like the fact that clients want to find you, rather than the other way around, then blame Google. It has changed the way customers and businesses interact. When people go searching online they're willing to wade through junk in search of what they want because they feel in control of the process. When they find what they want, and if it's you, they'll give you permission to market to them.

Just because it's easy to broadcast our messages through email and social media platforms doesn't give us permission to force people to pay attention. We have to earn their attention—more than ever. My colleague Seth Godin, the father of permission marketing, puts it this way, "Go ahead and make what you want, as long as you stand behind it and don't bother me. If you want to sell magnetic bracelets or put risqué pictures on your website, it's your responsibility, your choice. Want to find a website featuring donkeys, naked jugglers, and various illicit acts? It's junk, sure, but it's out there. You just have to go find it. Junk turns into spam when you show up at my doorstep, when your noise intercepts my quiet."

This is why, even though it's easier than ever to make noise and get noticed, direct outreach has become trickier than ever. When you reach out, unsolicited, to a potential client or business associate about a business opportunity, their default assumption is that you're a spammer interrupting their peace and quiet. Is it fair? That doesn't matter. Until there's a cure for selfishness, one that eliminates spammers and their spam, it's the reality that you and I have to deal with. Don't make noise that interrupts others' quiet.

You will find yourself using the Book Yourself Solid Direct Outreach Strategy time and time again when you want to reach out to these types of people:

- An ideal client or a referral partner within your target market
- The decision-maker at an organization or association to cross-promote, secure speaking engagements, submit articles for publication, and more
- The press
- Myriad other business development opportunities.

Direct Outreach Gone Wrong

Sometimes the easiest way to understand a concept is to see real examples of what works and what doesn't. I don't want to scare you off from doing direct outreach. Just the opposite—I want to encourage you to do more of it, but in a way that will make sure you come across as a thoughtful, considerate, empathetic, relevant, and high-integrity professional with value to add. To make sure you're always perceived this way, I'm going to show you a series of direct outreach messages sent to me that went terribly wrong. I've changed the names of all of the people involved to protect the innocent but the following are actual messages from real people. In fact, I'm pretty sure they were sent by decent, hard-working professionals. Unfortunately, they haven't yet learned how to do direct outreach and, as a result, their messages landed like a ton of bricks.

Let's start with this brick, which landed in my LinkedIn inbox.

LinkedIn Recommendations

Maria Venter is requesting an endorsement for work.

Dear Michael,

I'm sending this to ask you for a brief recommendation of my work that I can include in my LinkedIn profile. If you have any questions, let me know.

Thanks in advance for helping me out.

– Maria Venter

Endorse Maria Venter. It only takes a minute. Your endorsement can help Maria Venter:

- Hire and get hired
- Win customers and partnerships
- Build a stronger professional reputation

This email was sent to you by Maria Venter (email@website.com) through LinkedIn because Maria Venter entered your email address. If you have any questions, please contact customer_service@linkedin.com.

This request from Maria is problematic for a number of reasons:

- Let's start with the fact that I don't know her.
- If I don't know Maria, why would I recommend she get hired, win customers and partnerships, and build a stronger professional reputation?
- My LinkedIn profile states that I don't check email at LinkedIn. Rather, I request that people email me at a public email address, which I list.

What should have Maria done instead?

- She could have started by giving me a recommendation first if she thought I deserved one. It's always better to offer something before asking for something.
- If it was important to her that we connect, she could have attempted to meet me at an event, if it was convenient for her.
- She could have commented on my blog posts or one of my social media profiles. This would have been noticed and appreciated.
- She could have sent me an email to my public email address expressing some appreciation for my work or find some other way of making a personal connection through any number of other activities that don't ask for anything in return and don't make any assumptions.

My suggestions have nothing to do with professional status. I would approach anyone this way. Of course, if the person you're reaching out to is already familiar with your work or your name, the connecting process usually speeds up. And, if you're thinking that it's just novice business owners whose direct outreach goes wrong, think again.

This next email is from a publicity and promotions manager at a marketing firm that represents supposed best-selling authors and large publishing houses. They asked me to participate in a promotion for an author they represented. Now, I don't know the sender or the author and have no connection to the publisher of the book. Again, I've changed the names of all parties involved.

Dear Mr. Port,

    I have not heard back from you on my email below. This is a great opportunity to get your products out in front of a huge audience looking for this kind of material (our previous book campaign was seen by over 5 million people)! Not only will you be offering your subscribers an incredible package, but you will also be directing more traffic to your website and building your own mailing list. Remember, there is no cost involved.

    Click on the link below to view a previous campaign we put together for John Smith's *New York Times* best-selling book, XXXXXX: http://www .longurltoasalespage.com.

    Please let me know right away if you would like to participate or if you have any questions.

Thank you, Andrea

Assistant Publicity and Promotions Manager

Progressive Marketing Firm, Inc.

What's so bad about a PR or marketing firm reaching out to an author to see if he'll help promote another author? Nothing. Nothing at all. In fact, one of the primary ways authors get noticed is through promotion from other authors. So, what's wrong with this one?

- I don't know any of the parties involved, and they're sending me what is clearly a form email. It's not personalized in any way.
- Andrea makes all sorts of assumptions about why I would want to promote this author. She has no idea what really makes me tick and didn't take the time to find out.
- In the last line, Andrea tells me to let her know "right away" if I want to participate. She clearly demonstrated a lack of respect or appreciation for my time, schedule, life, and so forth. It's not wrong to try to encourage someone to act quickly when promoting a product or

service, but this is not such a promotion (her biggest mistake is that she thinks it is). Fundamentally, it's a request to a colleague to help out another colleague and at this point, after all the other offenses in this email, telling me what to do and when to do it is off-putting.

- This is actually the fourth email Andrea sent to me about this "opportunity." If I didn't respond the first three times, might that be saying something? And, to add insult to injury, every time Andrea sent me an email I wrote back asking her to stop emailing me. Obviously, she ignored my requests. It just confirms my suspicion that I was added to a "list" of authors to whom they're trying to get to participate in their book promotions. That makes it real, honest-to-goodness, 100% spam.

What should Andrea have done instead? Well, because I didn't request any information on her promotions or the authors she represents, she could have sent me a short note to this effect:

My name is Andrea Tiffonelli. I'm the Assistant Publicity and Promotions Manager for Progressive Marketing Firm, Inc. We represent authors and help them promote their books.

I'm writing to you today to let you know that I'm a fan of your work and really loved your most recent book, *Steal the Show*. Before I read it, I dreaded public speaking. Now I actually look forward to it.

Again, just saying "hi" and thanks for your work. If there is anything I can do to be of service to you, please just say the word.

Sincerely, Andrea Tiffonelli

Assistant Publicity and Promotions Manager

Progressive Marketing Firm, Inc.

What works so well about this alternative version of the email?

- She's not asking anything of me on her first contact.
- She quickly tells me who she is and what she does right off the bat.
- She offers praise and demonstrates that she is actually familiar with my work.

- She closes by offering her support with no expectation of anything in return.

This is how you start a relationship. Over time, a few more, relevant and personal interactions like this would earn her the proportionate amount of trust and credibility needed to see if I'd be interested in getting involved in one of her author promotions. Does it take time to learn about someone and get to know one's work? Yes. But it makes your direct outreach well received and that's the goal.

Here's another one. It's long. Very long. Which is just one of its many problems. There is, however, one simple fix that could have saved this effort. Can you tell what it is?

This is Jerry Faber and I'm working with Tom Rose, The ███ Coach, looking for a few very special joint venture partners for his upcoming Quick-Start 3-Day ███ Workshop.

███ are Hot and getting Hotter! And anybody who wants to have a successful online business needs ███ as part of their funnel. So we want to offer you the opportunity to host a preview call with Tom for his highly acclaimed ███ Workshop.

Tom has been teaching this workshop for the past five years and has helped hundreds of frustrated writers become successful authors. (You can see his long list of testimonials at www.firstwebsite.com.)

I'm contacting you because Tom and I believe that you and Tom are speaking to the same target market, and that this offer will be very lucrative for you while providing great value for your list.

This opportunity pays from $200 to $1,000 commission on every sale (depending on which level your subscribers register for).

For the complete details on this JV opportunity go to: www.secondwebsite.com.

Basically, here's the way this JV works.

Once you agree to do a JV call with Tom (The call is on "The Seven Biggest Mistakes People Make When ███ And How To Avoid Them" and it has converted from 11% to 22%), we'll set up the pages for the call and send you a link to all of the materials you will need to promote it, including a promo email series, blog posts, and tweets to mail to your list.

Then, over the coming weeks, we'll "drip" great content on them (unless it's the week of the Workshop. We do a final Q and A call that week).

If they buy, on or after your call with Tom through your affiliate link, you will get the following commissions.

Platinum Plus Package pays $1,000. Platinum Package pays $500. Gold Package pays $200.

You can see the sales page at: www.thirdwebsite.com.

If you're interested in doing a JV call with Tom, please let me know. You can email me directly at: jerry@gmail.com.

If you have any questions, feel free to email me at jerry@gmail.com.

Or, if you're ready to get started, email me at jerry@gmail.com and I'll send you everything you need to get started as soon as we can get the web pages set up.

Thank you for your time. We truly appreciate it—and look forward to having the opportunity to joint venture with you. And we'd like to give you a gift for taking the time to read this email:

www.fourthwebsite.com is a PDF with 28 ways to use X. We hope it helps you prosper even more!

Best Wishes,

Jerry Faber for Tom Rose

The [xxxx] Coach

P.S. If you want to know more about Tom, you can see his bio at: www .fifthwebsite.com.

You can see his videos at: www.sixthwebsite.com.

Holy cow. Where do I start?

- It's insanely long.
- Tom and Jerry are making all sorts of assumptions about why I would be interested in this joint venture.
- It's filled with hyperbole like "... are Hot and getting Hotter! And anybody who wants to have a successful online business needs ..."
- Jerry mentions the marketing funnel, which demonstrates that he's not particularly familiar with my work because I write quite a bit about how I don't like the philosophy behind the marketing funnel for selling services.

- He thinks he needs to tell me how a JV like this works.
- He gives me his email address three times within three sentences.
- He wants me to look at six different websites.
- He offers me a "gift" of an e-book on how to use X for taking the time to read his email. Does he think I'm unfamiliar with X and how to use it?
- And what might be the biggest offense of all, he tells me that I'll be blasting my email newsletter subscribers, tweeting to my followers, and promoting Tom's product on my blog. If Tom and Jerry think that I would indiscriminately promote someone I don't know to my subscribers, readers, and followers, for a few dollars in commissions, then it's obvious they don't know how I operate and they don't have a lot of respect for their subscribers.

So, what should Jerry have done? Did you figure out the simple fix to this total disaster of a direct outreach attempt? If you're thinking that he should have simply sent me a short note asking if I even do these kinds of joint ventures, you're absolutely right. If he had, I would have told him that I don't and no love would have been lost. Instead, Tom and Jerry wasted my time (and theirs) asking me to read this unrequested email about their JV opportunity. Here's what a better direct outreach attempt could have looked like.

Dear Michael,

My name is Jerry Faber and I work with Tom Rose, who teaches courses on—creation. I enjoy your work and really like your style. I don't want to take up much of your time, so if I may ask one quick question . . .

I'm wondering if you ever promote products from other experts in exchange for commissions on sales. If so, would you consider learning more about Tom and a joint venture campaign we're putting together? If not, I completely understand and I thank you for your time, nonetheless. Both Tom and I appreciate your work and hope to have the opportunity to meet you at some point in the future.

If there is anything we can do for you, please don't hesitate to ask.

Sincerely,

Best Wishes,

Jerry Faber

for Tom Rose

www.onewebsitehere.com

Even if Tom and Jerry used the letter I suggested, they're still not guaranteed a response. But they would at least have come across as professional and respectful, two of the most important components of credibility.

Here's one more short one. Can you figure out what's wrong with this note? Besides the fact that I received it through my personal Facebook profile—which clearly states, just like my LinkedIn Profile, *"Please don't contact me here. Instead, please send to* questions@heroicpublicspeaking.com."

> Michael, please accept my friend request. Tell me about what you do. I see you have written books. What are they called? What are they about? I'm also working on a book and a project you might be interested in. I would like to discuss potential business opportunities with you.

Here, this woman asked to "friend" me. Of course, my Facebook profile explains what I do and lists all six of my books. So perhaps it's just my ego talking, but one would hope that she would make a little effort to at least scan the page—do a little homework on me. She's asking me to take my time and do her work for her. Time is precious. Don't ask people to part with it. They need to offer to do so. To fast-forward the process and ask for business without building some foundation is more than just ineffective; it's a turnoff.

You Will Connect More When You've Got the Skinny

It doesn't matter if you are prospecting, door knocking, outreaching, introducing, or just plain canvassing. If you do any or all of these without knowing the person or business you are contacting, you may as well be calling the president of the United States. At best, you'll find yourself winded, your time wasted, or your wares unwanted. Or, at worst, humiliated. No one wants to feel like a cheesy, shady, pushy, or unprepared salesperson.

So, you say at the end of the day you want to create a never-ending pool of heartwarming and bank account–filling clients? You want to capture more sales? You want to get booked solid? Make more money? Create a nest egg? Then show up front, center, and in the know with all the people you want to know. There's no minimizing your overall effectiveness and confidence when you're packin' preparation. So find out:

1. *What motivates the person?* What really gets the person's juices flowing? What makes their eyes sparkle? It might be business, family, or hobbies. Look at the photos, books, and other things sitting on or near their desk or on their website or social media pages. What are they reading, referring to others, or genuinely interested in?

2. *What has the person accomplished?* Do an online search. Go to their site and do a Google Image search if you don't know what their smiling face looks like yet. Who is singing their praises? Have they won awards, received acknowledgments, public recognition, or publication announcements?

3. *What common interests might you have?* How have your paths crossed? Express your compassion, enthusiasm, and understanding for these shared interests. Keep your focus coming back to the person. Use these common interests as a starting place to learn more about how they feel and think about the world.

4. *Who are the person's peers?* Do you have any mutual friends, or do your social circles overlap? Do you have common social media connections? And are you involved in these circles? Be informed and stay connected.

5. *Who is their competition?* Know the opportunities and challenges they face in their business. What challenges will you help them overcome? And what opportunities will you, ultimately, help them fulfill?

6. *What unique benefits do you offer?* What do others love about the way you do business? Be easy. Know your strengths. Show up as the kind of person people love being with and want to do business with.

7. *What excites you about knowing or working with this person?* We all want to feel appreciated, acknowledged, and respected. Share how the person's work and opinions have influenced or affected you. Stay positive, be yourself, and be complimentary.

8. *What do you believe is possible for the person?* No matter how confident or successful we appear, all of us have limiting beliefs. Can you see areas of business or life in which the person has been holding back? Describe in detail (but keep it to yourself, for now) the true potential you see for the person based on what they want and need. As you get to know each other, you *may* decide to share what you see.

9. *What is your current status or role in the person's life?* Don't overrate or exaggerate who you are or why the person should work or connect with you. Be realistic about what you bring to the table and how you see the relationship unfolding. The best relationships grow slowly and with a foundation of trust.

10. *How can you become an indispensable asset to the person?* Do you truly know how and why the person should know or work with you? Do you believe that their life will be happier, easier, fuller, richer, or just plain better with the benefit of you and your services?

Sales offers aren't always sensible. Connecting isn't always cool. Even if your proposition seems picture perfect, life, decisions, and relationships are always wrapped up in underlying influences. Some of these foundational influences we can see quickly at first glance, and others take a bit more time.

But, when you show up knowledgeable and prepared, you address the human needs of the people you want to serve, and you are closer to meeting both the other person's needs and your own. You might have a shot at getting what you ask for. Plus, aren't conversations just easier and more fun when you know and share these commonalities. Doors stop slamming. People start playing and they start paying, too.

When initiating your direct outreach strategy, please make sure that your efforts are targeted, individualized, valuable, and legitimate so they are not perceived as spam and are instead appreciated and acted on.

Using the Book Yourself Solid Direct Outreach Strategy is all about making personal connections. Whichever of the following direct outreach tools you employ, you should be reaching out to others from the heart in a way that is genuine and authentic for you.

When I was an actor (that was my first career in the mid-90s) I had a modicum of success. I appeared in *Sex and the City, Third Watch, Law & Order, All My Children, The Pelican Brief, Down to Earth,* and many other shows. I also did hundreds of television commercials and voice-overs, but hung up my hat for what I thought was the meaning and stability of a career in the corporate world. Boy, was I wrong about the "meaning and stability" thing. Anyway, in my acting days, I recall blowing auditions because I was trying to knock it out of the park. Instead of focusing on getting the callback, I was focusing on getting the part. What I should have done was focus on getting the callback. Then, once I had the callback, work on getting the second callback. Then, once I had the second callback, work to get the producer's meeting. Once I had the producer's meeting, work to get the screen test, and so on. Do the same thing with your direct outreach. Take it one step at a time and you'll do fine, and it will feel more authentic to you.

Only One Link in the Chain of Destiny Can Be Handled at a Time

There are lots of different tools that you can use to reach out to other people. You can write emails, letters, or postcards. You can reach out to people on social media. You can use the phone. And you can do what I call the whatever-it-takes direct outreach, as long as it doesn't get you arrested; like parachuting into the backyard of the CEO of Google because you think you have a great service to offer his company. It will get you noticed but also get you arrested.

These tools can be instruments with which you can make beautiful music or they can be weapons of mass destruction. It just depends on how you use them. My mantra is Winston Churchill's quote: "It is a mistake to look too far ahead. Only one link of the chain of destiny can be handled at a time." Keep that on the top of your mind as you progress through the direct outreach process, and you'll be able to avoid desperate direct outreach measures. You'll build trust over time instead and end up swimming in success.

When reaching out to others, you'll go through multiple stages of relationship development. At each stage of the process you'll, hopefully, build more trust and earn more credibility with your new friend, much like the Book Yourself Solid Sales Cycle process that you learned in Chapter 6. And, just like the sales cycle, no relationship will develop in the exact same way. There isn't a secret formula that will guarantee everyone will love you and do exactly as you wish but there is a way to know whom to contact when, how to make contact, and whether to do it again—and the method requires a well-developed social intelligence.

Socially Successful Conduct

When I'm asked, "What other marketing books should I read?" in addition to some of the books listed in the previous chapter, I also recommend *Social Intelligence: The New Science of Human Relationships,* by Daniel

Goleman (2017), a popular science writer. Why a book that draws on social neuroscience research to help learn how to market and sell coaching services? Because, social intelligence can be defined as a person's competence to comprehend their environment and react appropriately for socially successful conduct. And socially successful conduct is what ensures successful direct outreach.

Understanding the concepts people use to make sense of their social relations can help you understand things, like *What situation am I in and how do I talk to this kind of person?* You can also learn rules that help you draw references, like *What did he mean by that?* as well as plan your actions so you can decide, *What am I going to do about that?*

You may or may not like this concept, depending on your interpretation of self, but your ability to succeed in many entrepreneurial endeavors is, in large part, based on your self-awareness and social savvy. Being able to understand yourself and what's going on with others and then skillfully responding to them is a question of social intelligence, not how many different clever pitches you've memorized or methods you've got on hand to impress someone.

According to Goleman, humans are wired to connect, neurologically speaking. Holy rapid-fire synapses, Batman. That means you are wired to market and sell. But really, all brain function aside, you've already got the mental crampons to do the steep climbing and naturally scale to the top of your class.

Marvel at this. The news gets even better. Goleman doesn't believe that these competencies (the ability to connect) are necessarily innate, but rather can be learned capabilities, if worked on and developed to achieve outstanding performance. There's nothing phantom about your direct outreach success. To perform at your highest level and enhance how you connect to real people in the real world, increase your social intelligence. With diligence, reflection, and the commitment to improve, set aside time to study yourself:

- *Self-awareness:* The ability to read your own emotions and recognize their impact on others while using gut feelings to guide decisions
- *Self-management:* Involves controlling your emotions, impulses, and the ability to adapt to changing circumstances
- *Social awareness:* Your ability to sense, understand, and react to others' emotions while comprehending social networks
- *Relationship management:* The ability to inspire, influence, and develop others while managing conflict

While you are at it:

- Toss the trite sales pitch and never formulate another "smart" thought. Develop the keen ability to listen and hear what others truly want and need.
- Tear up the how-to-get-anything-you-want-in-three-easy-steps manual and increase your empathy by entering into the realm of others' feelings.
- Step away from the PowerPoint presentation and study your self-presentation so you can foster credibility, trust, and connection confidence.

Social intelligence is defined as a person's competence to comprehend their environment and react appropriately for socially successful conduct. This brand of intelligence is therefore *the* most important component of your direct outreach strategies.

Understanding the concepts people use to make sense of their social relations can help you improve your social awareness, presence, authenticity, clarity, and empathy. Bottom line: you'll be more attuned to the needs and desires of others, which will make you more relevant and influential.

The Book Yourself Solid List of 20

Make a list of 20 people within your industry with whom you'd like to develop professional relationships. These are people whom you do not yet know—influencers within your target market who can help you get booked solid. This is your Book Yourself Solid List of 20. The list never leaves your side.

It sits on your desk. It lives on your computer and travels with you when you're on the road. Why 20 and why must you keep it with you at all times? Because your success is, in large part, determined by the people within your industry who are willing to refer others to you or to put you in front of your ideal clients or endorse you, you need to keep these people at the top of your mind. Keeping this list by your side will ensure that you're thinking of them and, if you do, you'll begin to notice opportunities to connect with them and get to know them. And 20, because it's a large enough number to keep your focus expansive but narrow enough that you won't feel overwhelmed.

4.12.1 Written Exercise: Identify a minimum of 3 and a maximum of 20 people you'd like to reach out to directly and personally. (For now, this list should focus on people who you want to add to your network, not potential clients.) At this moment, you might not think you can fill out your list of 20, but now that you know what you need to do, you'll start to take notice of the people you should add to this list. You'll see in a minute how your list can grow far beyond just 20 people.

Here's what you do with your list:

- Each day, reach out to the person at the top of the list.
- After you've reached out to this person, if you connect with them in a meaningful way, take them off your List of 20 and start sharing your network, your knowledge, and your compassion through your Network of 90. Then add a new person to the bottom of the list so you always keep the list at 20.
- If they don't respond to you, move this person to the bottom of the list, and they will take the 20th position. The person who was in the 20th position will move up to the 19th spot, and each person on the list will move up one more position. If the person who moved to the bottom of the list because you didn't hear back from them the first time doesn't respond a month later when they move back into the first position and you reach out to them again, then take them off the list. To keep contacting someone when you're getting no response isn't good form, as we've already discussed.

This direct outreach activity occurs every working day: you'll reach out to one new person, each and every day, and you'll follow up with people you've already reached out to, each and every day. This is critical. Dedicated, disciplined, and determined action is key to your direct outreach success. Remember, the Book Yourself Solid List of 20 is your wish list. They are your list of 20 people who could have a significant impact on your business through their referrals, introductions, and advice. Do this daily and you'll be booked solid in no time flat.

4.12.2 Booked Solid Action Step: Reach out to the first person on your list of 20 and then add them to your follow-up system. Then add a new person to your list of 20.

Making Your Case

When you get to the point in a relationship when it's time to make your case for something you want, usually after the initial courtship, the next step is to expand on your reason for contacting that person and make your case. To do this, there are three things that others take into account, whether consciously or unconsciously, when they consider a proposal you make:

- Is it going to be successful?
- Is it worth doing?
- Is this person able to do what they say they can?

If you get a resounding yes! for each question, you're in. If your reader raises an eyebrow at even one of the questions, you've probably gone as far as you're going to go with this person. For your direct outreach to be effective, all the questions must be answered in the affirmative. Also, to make sure all your bases are covered before you make any calls or send out any letters or email, ask yourself the following questions:

- Do I connect with the reader about one of their accomplishments?
- Do I indicate that I will follow up?
- Do I know how I'm going to follow up?
- Am I being direct without pushing?
- Am I being real in the message?
- Am I clear about the next steps?

Whatever-It-Takes Direct Outreach

You can do a lot to grab attention, but attention is only valuable if it shows you off in a light that's flattering. If you're a creative soul with a strong and developed sense of play, you'll have a lot of fun conceiving of and executing no-rules, attention-grabbing direct outreach campaigns. Because, yeah, there may be a time when someone you really want to connect with is just not paying attention.

Twenty years ago, when I was a vice president at an entertainment company, I had a boss who swore, literally, every which way till Sunday that I had to get a particular executive at a big cosmetics firm to agree to sponsor one of our events. The only problem was that the executive wouldn't take my calls. I tried to explain to my boss that I didn't think they were the right fit for us, but he disagreed and directed me to make it happen.

After a few more weeks of trying to get a meeting with the executive, I was about to give up when his assistant, the toughest gatekeeper I'd ever encountered, let slip that the executive was at lunch when I called. Just making pleasant conversation, I asked, "Oh, yeah? What'd he go for today?" "Chinese. It's his favorite . . ." she replied, without thinking much about it. "Okay, thanks. Have a nice day!" I said, and hung up.

The next day I had a $250 order of Chinese food delivered to him at that exact same time. Inside the order was the proposal for the project. Twenty minutes after the food arrived, I called him. This time I was put right through. I said, "Will you take a look at my proposal now?" "No," he answered. "Why not?" I asked. "Because I don't like any of the dishes you sent over." "What do you like?" I asked. "Moo shoo chicken with Mandarin pancakes," he said. I said, "If I send these over tomorrow, will you read my proposal and take a meeting with me?" He said, "No, but I will read your proposal. If I like it, then I'll take a meeting with you." I said, "Great. When would you like me to follow up?" He told me and we said goodbye. He did like the proposal and subsequently took a meeting with me, but we never actually made a deal. It turned out that our companies really weren't a good fit. But we became friendly, and he introduced me to one of my first clients after I left the corporate world and started my own business. You just never know.

One of my clients was trying to connect with a meeting planner at a large multinational corporation and couldn't get the planner to give him the time of day. After all his other direct outreach attempts failed, he sent her a coconut with a note that said, "You're a tough nut to crack. How about it?" She was still laughing when she called him to schedule an appointment.

Think creatively about what kind of fun, outrageous, no-rules, attention-grabbing direct outreach strategies would work for you. Really let loose and let the ideas flow freely.

4.12.3 Written Exercise: Jot down one wild, wacky, and unique way to make a personal connection, especially with anyone you've been unsuccessful connecting with in the more traditional ways.

Direct Outreach Plan

There are many ways to connect with potential clients and customers, but none of the concepts I laid out are effective without a plan. After you identify a person or organization you'd like to reach out to, what do you do? Do you create a plan and then execute the plan? No? Well, that's okay because now you will and you'll be delighted with the success your new plan will bring. Each day, when working with your Book Yourself Solid List of 20, here's how to keep it simple:

- Identify the individual you're going to reach out to.
- Choose the steps you'll take to connect with them.
- Create a schedule for your initiatives.
- Execute the plan.
- Evaluate the plan.

Patience and Persistence Pay Off

Remember that there is no *trick* to direct outreach. The magic formula to direct outreach, if there is one, is a consistent and open course of action throughout the life of your business. Direct outreach, like networking and keeping in touch, is something that must become a part of your regular routine. It takes time, but if you're patient and persistent, you *will* book yourself solid.

CHAPTER

13

The Book Yourself
Solid Referral Strategy

For it is in giving that we receive.
—Saint Francis of Assisi

Imagine enjoying deeper relationships with every client you work with while attracting three or four times as many wonderful new clients as you have right now. The key lies in generating client referrals. By starting an organized referral program, you can immediately connect with an increasing number of potential new clients.

Think for a minute about how you seek out high-level services or products. Perhaps you need a new physician or accountant; or maybe you want to put a new addition on your home. It's not likely that you make your choice of service provider based solely on a Facebook ad or a Google search. The likelihood is that you will look for a referral from someone you know, someone who has had an experience with the particular service you seek. The same is true when people are looking for coaches. This is why having an organized referral program is so important for your success.

Because your clients enjoy and respect working with you, they will be eager to recommend you to their friends and family. In fact, the vast majority of your new clients already come to you as a result of word-of-mouth referrals, either directly or indirectly.

You can increase your referral quotient exponentially. How many referrals do you get without a referral system right now? Now triple or quadruple that number. That is the potential increase in clients you could be working with as early as next month. Referral-generated clients are often more loyal, consistent, and better suited to you than any other category of potential clients you could find.

Quick Referral Analysis

Let's look at how you've already received referrals. By identifying a situation in the past when a client or colleague, or someone else altogether, referred a client to you, you will recognize patterns that will help you consistently produce the results you desire.

4.13.1 Written Exercise: Start by remembering the last time a quality referral came to you:

- From whom did the referral come?
- What was the referral for, specifically?
- Did the referral need your services immediately?
- How were you contacted—by the person making the referral or the potential client?
- Had you educated the referrer about your services before they made the referral?
- How did you accept the referral and follow up?
- Is that new referral still a client today?

You may have already noticed some of your strengths in generating referrals, or perhaps parts of the process need a little of your attention. Either way, we're creating an easy and profitable process.

Finding Referral Opportunities

Referral opportunities are all around you, and most are slipping through your fingers right now because you either aren't noticing them or you aren't acting on them. Pay close attention and mentally seek out every possible situation in which you could see yourself asking for referrals.

> **4.13.2 Written Exercise:** Create a referral tracking log based on the seven questions in the preceding written exercise and begin to track daily referral opportunities. Your referral-tracking log should focus on the details of your referral interactions. Doing so will help you see what works and what doesn't work in the referral process. If you study these interactions, you can learn from them and adjust your behavior accordingly while significantly increasing your referral quotient. You're going to be pleasantly surprised at the plethora of untapped referral opportunities that are appearing before you every day.

Beginning the Referral Process

Are you ready to begin working with eager new clients who have heard about your expertise and seek the benefits you offer? Never forget how profitable and prosperous your coaching business can be. How committed are you? Are you convinced that this is something you absolutely must do?

Step 1: Identify Your Clients' Benefits

Keep their benefits in mind when you speak to your clients about referrals. These are the reasons they work with you and why they would want others to do the same. Refer to the work you did in Chapter 2.

> **4.13.3 Written Exercise:** Create a list of the benefits your clients will experience by working with you. Keep going until you've exhausted all the possible benefits.

Step 2: Identify Why Others Would Refer Clients to You

What are the emotional, social, and professional benefits that go along with being someone who refers people in need to those who can help?

Examples: They feel great helping their friends improve their business or life in a specific way. They feel special having made a positive influence in their friends' lives. They feel important and knowledgeable about something. They feel connected and accepted when they introduce friends and business associates to a high-quality professional. They feel confident that they are a valuable resource in their friends' lives and that they have sent them to someone who is qualified, committed, and well-liked.

4.13.4 Written Exercise: Bring to mind your two best clients and list the reasons they would want to refer their friends and family to you. Again, think in terms of benefits. How did they feel after having referred their friends and family?

Step 3: Identify the Types of Referrals You Seek

Examples: Family members, friends, neighbors, acquaintances, work associates, small business owners, executives, and so on.

Don't forget your Red Velvet Rope Policy of working only with ideal clients with whom you do your best work.

4.13.5 Written Exercise: Write down the types of people you want your clients, associates, friends, and family to refer to you. Your friends and family may have no idea whom to refer to you.

Step 4: Identify the Places Where Your Referrers Meet Ideal Referrals

Your goal here is to help your clients and other acquaintances understand who in their lives will benefit most from your offers and where they cross paths with these people. You are helping them get a clear picture of the people in their lives who must meet you and work with you. With these two things in mind—whom your referrals should be referring and where they will meet them—you have all you need to start on the referral path.

Examples: At the office, taking the kids to school, neighborhood events, sporting events, lunch appointments, after-work socializing, charity functions, the gym, political events.

4.13.6 Written Exercise: Write down the places where your referrers would meet or connect with good referrals for you.

Step 5: Clarify and Communicate How Your Referrers Make a Referral

Let's focus on how to help your referrers have a simple conversation with a potential referral that will effectively connect them to you and your offerings. You can't leave this to chance. Being able to articulate what you do in a way that makes you stand out from the crowd and truly connects you to the people you're meant to serve is not only necessary but also essential for booking yourself solid.

What do you want them to say? How do you want them to talk about what you do? What specific words and phrases do you want them to use? Do you want them to say that you are "the best"? Do you want them to mention that you recently received an award for outstanding community service? Get very specific. Think of yourself as a one-person PR firm. You decide how you want people to talk about you.

4.13.7 Written Exercise: Write down how you'd like your referrers to refer their contacts to you.

Step 6: Ask for Referrals

If you want to increase your referral quotient by 50%, the best strategy is to ask for referrals. This is the simplest part of the Book Yourself Solid

Referral Strategy, as well as the most important. The preceding and following exercises will help you ask effectively. Please make sure to complete these exercises thoughtfully before you run off and just ask for referrals willy-nilly. What you can start with today is seeking out opportunities for referral conversations. Here are a few excellent situations that naturally lead to a referral conversation:

- Your ideal client thanks you for a great session or work well done.
- Your ideal client asks you for more services.
- Your ideal client asks for clarification on a process or concept.
- Your ideal client describes a past problem that you helped fix or goal you helped her achieve.

And here are some obvious situations:

- Your ideal client mentions a friend or business associate who's been facing the same challenges your client faced.
- Your ideal client mentions they are going to an industry conference for a few days (and you serve businesses or individuals within that industry).

Or you can create the opportunity for a referral conversation by doing the following:

- Thanking clients for their energy and enthusiasm during your session or project.
- Clarifying their goals or making a suggestion to work on their own.
- Asking clients how they are feeling about the work you're doing together or about past challenges.
- Complimenting clients on their progress—always.

Once you get clients talking, ask them about the value they get from your work together. Use this as an open door to have them talk about how your services could benefit other people or organizations they have relationships with.

Step 7: Facilitate the Referral Connection

Offer to meet, consult with, or advise anyone who is important to your clients. Let them know that you want to help educate their friends about the benefits of your services.

Ask them to make the introduction today. There are times when you can take the burden of calling or sending the email off of your referrer. Not because your referrer doesn't want to make the referral happen but because life sometimes gets in the way. People are busy and they can get distracted by other tasks on their to-do list. If *you* actually make the connection and do the follow-up, it's sure to happen.

The same is true any time you personally meet potential clients. They say they're going to call you, and even if they have the best of intentions, things come up that get in the way, and you don't get a call. So I suggest that when you meet someone you really connect with and who has expressed interest in your services, you call them; don't wait for them to call you.

Step 8: Follow Up with Referrals and Referrers

Contact new referrals and introduce them to what you have to offer—in a meaningful, connected, and helpful way. This is where your always-have-something-to-invite-people-to offer comes into play. It gives you a really easy way to start a conversation with the potential client and extend a no-risk, no-barrier invitation that is compelling and attractive. All you have to do is make a generous invitation and you've started the Book Yourself Solid Sales Cycle.

When beginning a relationship with potential clients, consider the following:

- Hold private meetings or demonstrations to eliminate any fear or embarrassment they may have about trying something new.
- Learn about any past experience with coaching services that they may have experienced and, most important, what they hope to achieve.
- Tell them what to expect, how you work, and the benefits they will experience.

- Include administrative details, too, such as what to have available if anything. Help clients feel as comfortable and prepared as possible.
- Provide third-party articles and facts that support your analysis in describing benefits they will achieve.
- Invite clients to work with you, and remember the Book Yourself Solid Super Simple Selling system. Offer a specific date and time that suits their schedule.

Practice Your Referral Presentation

Don't leave this up to chance. Be fully prepared and rehearse your presentation ahead of time. Know what you're going to say, and in addition, do the following:

- Speak with lots of expression, get excited, and show the passion you have for the benefits your services can offer.
- Smile.
- Be confident.
- Open your heart.
- When your potential client starts speaking, hush up and listen.

4.13.8 Booked Solid Action Step: Make the commitment to ask for referrals every day for five days straight.

Are you as excited as I am about the dozens of potential clients you're going to meet? Just think about all those potential clients who've been searching and waiting to be introduced to an expert like you. I hope and expect that you will serve your potential clients and community by immediately starting to ask for client referrals. Once you start speaking with your potential clients on a deep and personal level, they will see you as far more than just your title. They will see you with more value, dimension, and a higher level of respect.

This meaningful connection is the key to achieving a greater level of prosperity and personal satisfaction. It's the Book Yourself Solid way.

Who Wants What You Want?

Although some of your clients, friends, family, and colleagues may refer others to you without your having to ask, many won't. As I mentioned previously, it isn't that they don't want to; they're just busy with their own lives and it hasn't occurred to them. Although it may feel awkward at first to ask for referrals, give it a try. You'll be surprised at how willing they are to do so once you've brought it to mind. Certainly, if they've worked with you, they'll want their friends, family, and business associates to experience the same great benefits they have. And they'll enjoy being able to help you as well. When someone has a positive effect on one's life, even in small ways, it feels good to give something back, and referrals are a great way to do it.

Other Professionals—the Other Source of Referrals

Other professionals who offer services and products that are complementary to your own, and work with your target market, are ideal sources of referrals. That's why we spent so much time on the 50% of your networking strategy that focuses on other industry figures. When you operate from a perspective of abundance and cooperation, rather than from scarcity and competition, it becomes easy to reach out to others to develop relationships that can be mutually beneficial.

The more you refer to others, the more they'll be inspired to refer to you.

Many coaches have a formal referral group with five or six other professionals who serve the same target market but offer complementary services and products. Each member of the group works to send referrals to each other member of the group. If you join a high-integrity referral group, you'll greatly extend your referral reach. You'll also build your reputation by having others talk about you and your services.

Affiliate Fees and Rewards Programs

Reward those who refer others to you. A reward could be anything from a formal affiliate program, through which you pay cash for referrals, to coupons for discounts on your services, products, or programs or highly personalized gifts.

I'm not a big fan of setting up cash-based referral program unless you're selling online products, programs, or events and others in your industry want to make a concerted effort to generate revenue by promoting what you're offering. In that case, it makes sense.

However, it's not normal practice for experienced, high-level coaches to pay for referrals for private coaching services. But, finding a way to show your appreciation and reward for the referrer is essential, nonetheless.

I do it through gifts. Not gift baskets or gift cards. They're too trite. Instead, I find a way to personalize gifts based on the recipient's hobbies, interests, and passions. For example, I'm writing this while flying a plane to Toronto to work with the CEO of the largest electronics company in North America (well, I'm sitting in the cabin, a professional is in the cockpit). I received this opportunity because a colleague of mine told him to hire me. This CEO trusts my colleague. All the CEO needed was my name and phone number, and he was ready to hire me. I didn't have to sell myself.

My colleague would find it tacky if I sent him a referral fee. So, instead, I hired an artist to paint a huge picture of his dog, Rupert, using the color scheme of his newly redesigned office. He'll hang that on the wall of his office, and it will serve as a constant reminder of my appreciation for him.

Say you charge $1,000 per month for your services and you currently have 10 regular clients. You're currently earning $10,000 a month. Now let's say that you receive 10 referrals at $1,000 per month. That's another 10 clients for another $10,000 a month. If you give a referral fee of 10%, you'll be paying each referrer $100 per referral for a total of $1,000 in referral fees. Would you spend $1,000 to make $10,000 for a profit of $9,000 and a new monthly income of $19,000, almost double what you were making? Of course, you would.

However, are people really going to make a concerted effort to send you referrals because you're offering them $100 per month? I haven't found that to be the case. It's rare that someone will make a referral simply because you're offering a small referral commission or reward. They'll do it because they believe in you and what you stand for. The fee or reward is just a nice bonus that makes them feel appreciated.

Strike While the Iron Is Hot

Nurture the relationships you develop with those who refer others to you, and *always* follow up right away on any referrals you get. You'll then create not merely satisfied clients but raving fans by delivering your best work. Before you know it, you'll be booked solid.

14

The Book Yourself
Solid Speaking Strategy

It usually takes me more than three weeks to prepare a good
impromptu speech.
—Mark Twain

The Book Yourself Solid Speaking Strategy is extremely effective way to get in front of potential ideal clients to demonstrate your knowledge, talents, and strengths. But it's not for everyone. It's not mandatory. There is no reason you should use this strategy unless you'd like to speak to groups of people, large or small. You're not a more impressive person because you want to speak in front of others. In fact, many do it just for the approval of the audience or to sell something to them instead of being in service of them and reaping the rewards of that service. There is nothing deficient about you if you don't want to use this strategy for marketing yourself.

The wonderful thing about sharing your knowledge is that it's rewarding for both you and your audience. They will leave your presentation or event with a kick in their step, feel a little smarter, and think a heck of a lot bigger about who they are and what they have to offer to the world. You've also given them an action plan that will help them implement what they learned from you. You will benefit because you'll know you've helped others, which is the reason you do what you do. And you'll increase awareness of your services and products at the same time.

To get in front of your target market, you can promote yourself or have others promote you. When you promote yourself, you're inviting your target market to something that is going to help them solve their problems and move them toward their compelling desires. When you are promoted by others, your surrogates put you in front of your target market. You may want to travel both routes.

I won't address the details of being a professional speaker, someone who makes a living speaking to organizations, but rather how you can use public speaking to create awareness for what you have to offer and get booked solid. If you're interested in becoming a professional speaker, pick up a copy of my *Wall Street Journal* best-selling book, *Steal the Show*. But it's not just for professional speakers. It's for all people who want to shine when they're in the spotlight. If you're going to do a lot of public speaking, it will become your bible. Also, if you'd like more help with your public speaking, visit HeroicPublicSpeaking.com for free video resources and information on our training programs and events for individuals and corporations.

Self-Promotion

Of course, all of the Book Yourself Solid Six Core Self-Promotion Strategies require that you promote yourself in one way or another. Even using the Book Yourself Solid Speaking Strategy to get other people to put you in front of your target market requires that you promote yourself to the person who is going to give you that platform.

First, let's look at pure self-promotion, such as inviting your target market to events that you produce—not necessarily big workshops or conferences, but simple, community-building, meaningful, enlightening events at which you can shine, show off your products and services, and build your reputation and credibility in your marketplace. These types of speaking and demonstrating events might fall into the category of an always-have-something-to-invite-people-to offer or they may be one-off events.

Webinars and Online Meetings

Start a monthly or weekly call for clients to learn the benefits of working with you. Prepare a new, timely, and relevant topic every time. Pick up a magazine in your industry and use one of the articles to inspire your topic, invite guests to discuss their area of expertise, and ask your clients to tell you what they'd most like to hear about. The rest of the call will naturally flow into a Q&A session. Here are a few ideas to get you started and to spark your inspiration and creativity for your own unique ideas:

- Any coach can offer a monthly or weekly Q&A on their field of expertise. No planning is necessary—just show up and shine.
- Financial coaches can offer quarterly conference calls on updates on tax law along with planning strategies for decreasing tax liability, for example.
- Business coaches can offer weekly conference calls on the best strategies for hiring people and managing teams.
- Marketing coaches can offer web conferences where they share strategies and techniques that are working today for online lead generation.
- Life coaches can offer regular meetings on their area of expertise: reducing anxiety, increasing focus, and setting boundaries.

If you're doing a webinar or online meeting it won't cost you a dime after you've paid for your meeting software. Record each session and put it up online, on social media or on your website. Highlight small sections and share them as snippets online. Those who couldn't make the actual session will still have the opportunity to listen to it and benefit from it. Archiving and sharing the calls is also a wonderful way of immediately establishing trust and credibility with new web visitors and attracting new prospects to check you out.

Demonstrations and Educational Events

These opportunities are similar to online meetings except that they're conducted in person. Demonstrations and educational events are an excellent way to reach potential ideal clients if your services are physical or location-based or if the people you serve are all located in the same town or city. This approach is also a great alternative if you feel that an online call doesn't speak to your strengths. This format is another opportunity to get creative and express yourself. For example, you could create some excitement with an open house or outdoor demo at a park or at any other venue. Don't just invite your potential clients but also your current clients, friends, or colleagues who know the value of your services and are willing to talk about their experiences with you.

- Fitness coaches and personal trainers can offer a weekly physical challenge for clients and potential clients. Ask clients to bring a new friend every week. Each week a new type of workout would be planned with a social event afterward.
- Professional organizers and clutter coaches can offer a monthly makeover in which they go to a potential or new client's office or home, along with a small group of 10 or 15 people (it's not bad to have a waiting list for these types of offerings), and the professional organizer reorganizes the space and teaches the guests the basics of how to be more productive and effective through an organized office.
- An image consultant or personal style coach can do something similar with the monthly makeover concept. They could even offer a contest or raffle each month, and the winner would get the makeover.
- Any coach can host a no-cost or low-cost morning retreat. Be playful and adventurous. It doesn't have to be expensive, just creative. Allow clients to get to know you and meet other people with similar interests and goals. Make it as simple as serving tea, whole fresh fruit, and scones—and share your wealth of knowledge.
- Start a niche club. Consider cool stuff clients would enjoy. Think about activities that you love. Start a creative brainstorming club, weekly play group, or fun family outing. I know a dentist who organizes bike rides—of the Harley Davidson variety. He gives out bandanas for everyone to wear. And, yes, they are black with a big white tooth on them. It's not a coincidence that most of the folks who participate in these regular rides are also his clients.
- Start a book club. Almost everybody who is interested in personal or business development is an avid reader of self-improvement literature. Get together once a month to discuss the ideas and implementation of books you recommend that align with your own beliefs and interests.

Introduce these offerings at the end of your Book Yourself Solid Dialogue. Add, "I'd like to invite you to _____" or "Why don't you join me and my clients for a fun, playful _____." Try out different venues and topics until you discover the one that works for you. Remember, the difference between the typical client-snagging mentality and the Book Yourself Solid way is that the typical client-snagging mentality plays it safe so as not to look foolish. The Book Yourself Solid way asks, "How can I be unconventional and risky so as to create interest and excitement for my services?"

You will never be at a loss for different things to try or experiences to create for your clients and potential clients. You want to invite as many people as possible to these events for three important reasons:

- You want to leverage your time so you're connecting with as many potential clients as possible in the shortest amount of time.
- You want to leverage the power of communities. When you bring people together, they create far more energy and excitement than you can on your own. Your guests will also see other people interested in what you have to offer, and that's the best way to build credibility.
- You'll be viewed as a generous connector. If you're known in your marketplace as someone who brings people together, it will help you build your reputation and increase your likeability.

4.14.1 Written Exercise: Create three ways that you can instantly add value to your potential and current clients by way of an invitation.

Getting Promoted by Others

Now let's address the second approach: getting promoted by others to speak or demonstrate. If you're speaking for exposure, which I believe is very effective for many people, you probably won't be paid upfront for most of the speaking you do, except possibly an honorarium and travel costs. You're doing it for the opportunity to address potential clients and to interest them in your offerings. There's an assumed trade involved. You receive marketing opportunities, and the association or organization that brings you in to speak or demonstrate gets great content that serves their constituents. The key is to balance the two. If you are invited to speak and you spend 90% of your time talking about what you have to offer, you won't be well received and you certainly won't be invited back. However, if you don't make any offers at all, you'll be sure to miss great opportunities for booking yourself solid. Before I became a professional speaker, this was my primary marketing strategy.

Booking Your Way Up

If you would like to be promoted by others, you need to develop trusting relationships with decision-makers at associations and organizations that serve your target market. In the business world, these people are often called *meeting planners*. At your local associations, these people may be called *communication* or *education directors* or something altogether different. Bottom line: they are the people who can get you in front of your target audience.

There are thousands of associations and organizations that serve your target market. For example, colleges and universities all across the country sponsor executive extension courses, community learning programs, and all kinds of management and small-business seminars and workshops. And to create comprehensive programs, the colleges and universities will often invite guest experts, like you, to make a presentation on their area of expertise. Trade associations and networking groups all need speakers to address their memberships, and this phenomenon continues to expand in the public sector as well as become a big part of the local communities they serve. The most potentially rewarding venues will offer you audiences that include potential buyers for your products and services. Some of the venues or organizations may even have name recognition that is prestigious, like a university club or well-known business networking group.

There is a general hierarchy of associations and organizations that can sponsor you and your services. I start the list with the lower-level organizations and associations and work up to the highest-level organizations and associations. The lower-level organizations are usually smaller and less prestigious, but don't let the hierarchy fool you. You can fill your coaching practice by speaking in front of members of the lowest-level associations and organizations, but you don't necessarily have to start with the lowest and work your way up. It may help to have previous speaking experience with some of the lower-level associations and organizations for you to get booked with the higher-level associations and organizations.

Level One

Your entry point to speaking and demonstrating is with local not-for-profit community groups or organizations like the community center, churches, YMCA and YMHA, service clubs, or political action groups and chambers of commerce. Some of these groups serve a particular target market, but most are made up of individuals who share similar interests. They're good places to find potential clients and great places to work on your material and practice speaking and demonstrating in front of other people.

> **4.14.2 Written Exercise:** Identify several level-one groups or organizations that you can contact.

Level Two

Seek out local for-profit business groups, learning programs, and schools, including schools of continuing education and networking groups like Business Network International, Vistage, universities, and others.

These organizations are higher up the value scale for you because they serve more targeted groups of people who are really there to learn what you have to offer. Furthermore, they tend to be slightly more prestigious than the local not-for-profit community groups.

> **4.14.3 Written Exercise:** Identify several level-two groups or organizations that you can contact.

Level Three

At level three, you'll be speaking at local and regional trade associations. There are more local and regional trade associations than you can count or ever speak to in a lifetime. Do a quick search on Google to find associations for everything from home-based businesses, electricians, and computer programmers, to lawyers, and family winemakers. Local and regional trade associations and organizations are excellent opportunities for you to connect with your target market because you know the exact makeup of your audience.

Another avenue to consider, depending on your target market and the kind of services you provide, is businesses, both large and small. Even if you don't work with businesses directly, every business is made up of individuals, and they will either be in your target market or know somebody who is in your target market. I put the smaller businesses on level three and the larger corporations on level four. Many companies offer educational workshops, programs, and conferences just for their employees. Sometimes, they'll bring in a speaker for a lunchtime session. Other times, the setup is more formal, and you'll speak to large groups of people at a conference center. Just be clear on why you're targeting a particular business. Know what you have to offer them that will serve their needs and what opportunities the business or the individuals who make up the business offer you.

4.14.4 Written Exercise: Identify several level-three local or regional trade associations or businesses that you can contact.

Level Four

From here you're just going to keep moving up the trade association ladder, from local and regional trade associations to national trade associations and then to international trade associations. There's even a Federation of International Trade Association.

4.14.5 Written Exercise: Identify several level-four national or international trade associations that you can contact.

How to Find Your Audiences

Most of the information you'll need about associations and organizations that serve your target market is on the internet. An obvious statement, I know. They're easy to find but it can sometimes be difficult to identify from a website whom to contact, but it's the best and cheapest way to start. If you're serious about using the Book Yourself Solid Speaking Strategy as your go-to marketing strategy, you can also pick up a copy of the *NTPA: National Trade and Professional Associations of the United States*. It contains the name of every trade association, its president, budget, convention sites, conference themes, membership, and other pertinent information. You might also consider referencing the *Directory of Association Meeting Planners and Conference/Convention Directors* and the *Encyclopedia of Associations* at your local library.

4.14.6 Written Exercise: Identify the decision-makers for the organizations you chose in the previous written exercises. Put them on your list of 20 and then go through your network to see who you know who might be able to connect you with these decision-makers or someone else who might know these decision-makers.

4.14.7 Booked Solid Action Step: After reading this chapter, contact these decision-makers using your newfound direct outreach strategies and begin getting booked to speak.

Get Booked to Speak

Meeting planners and their respective counterparts get lots of offers from people like you to speak to their constituents. That's why it's critical that you follow the Book Yourself Solid system. If you have a strong foundation and a trust and credibility strategy in place for your business so you understand why people buy what you're selling, know how to talk about what you do, have identified how you want to be known in your market, know how to have a sales conversation, are a likeable expert within your field, and have created brand-building information products, not only will you get all the clients you want but you'll also earn the respect of the decision-makers at the associations and organizations for whom you'd like to speak.

Do your homework. If you're going to contact a meeting planner or education director, make sure you know as much as you possibly can about their organization. You'd be surprised at how many people overlook this step and cold-call these meeting planners without having done their homework. The meeting planner knows it within minutes of the conversation.

Talk to organization members first, if possible. Learn about their urgent needs and compelling desires. They know best what they need, so learn it from them and then reach out to the decision-makers. You'll get booked a lot faster that way. Even better, if possible, have a member or board member refer you. How much do we love it when other people talk about us so we don't have to? So much.

Send an email first and follow up with a call. And as always, be friendly, be relevant (meaning that you offer your services only if you can really serve the group), have empathy (step into the shoes of the meeting planner), and be real (no big sales pitch).

What You Need to Present to Get Booked

Each meeting planner, depending on the organization and type of event they're planning, will ask you to submit different materials in order to be considered. If you're trying to get booked at the local community center, a simple phone conversation may do the trick. If you're trying to get booked to speak at the largest conference in your industry, more is expected. In this case, you'll be asked for a video, session description, learning objectives, speaking experience, letters of recommendation, general biography, introduction biography (which is what is used to introduce you right before you present), and more. By the way, we can help create speaker demo videos for you. Simply contact us at questions@heroicpublicspeaking.com. Even if five organizations ask for the same materials, it's likely each one will ask for them in their own special way. Here's a word to the wise: make sure you follow instructions. People, especially meeting planners, like that.

Your Invitation to Speak

When invited to speak or present a program, a preliminary meeting or phone call usually sets the stage for further interaction with the person responsible for the program. During the initial contact, you and the meeting planner can usually nail down the topic to be covered and the length of time expected for the presentation. From the time you receive your invitation to the time you write thank-you notes, knowing the key players and how to connect with them is vital.

Know Your Audience

Start by considering your audience. Do as much research as you can on the people who will be attending your presentation so that your learning objectives can be directed right at their needs and desires. Work to understand the culture of the group you're speaking to so you can understand how to best communicate with them. Your audience will influence your choice of vocabulary (technical jargon) and may even influence how you dress. Knowing your audience well will also help you decide how much background material you need to deliver for you to effectively communicate your message.

Ask if you might have an opportunity to interview some of the leadership personnel (and even more exciting, some of those who will be attending the seminar or conference) to determine who they are along with their personal goals and agendas. Will they allow you to involve them in the presentation?

Setting up for success in advance will remove much of the stress of preparation and it'll give you more confidence when delivering the actual presentation. Once again, a reminder that a strong foundation leads to super performance.

Knowing Your Audience—Questionnaire

Experience has proven that at this point it is appropriate to present a questionnaire that gives you background information specifically tailored to this particular audience. Developing various forms to help you present effectively and evaluate your performance gives you the professional edge when talking with the person in charge of the program.

The kind of forms you can create might include the following:

- Pre-questionnaire—to know your audience in advance
- Audience evaluation forms
- Follow-up forms

Be Prepared

Of course you will find out where your presentation is to be held and what audiovisual equipment will be available to you, if any. You don't need to use slides or any other visual aid if you prefer not to. Ninety-nine percent of the time, slides are not only a waste of time and space, but they are also distracting, dysfunctional, and can seriously damage a speech. Put down the clicker. It usually just shoots bullet points and kills an otherwise good presentation.

Clarify how long you'll be speaking and what your audience will be doing before and after your presentation so you can incorporate that information into your planning. It's even a good idea to end a few minutes early. You'll find that, even when you bring down the house, your audience will appreciate a little extra free time.

Don't forget to remind the facilitator of your requirements closer to the presentation date. Remember, they are juggling a lot of information. Your presentation may be a small part of a larger conference.

Know Your Speaking Venue

Ask to visit the speaking site. As a guest speaker, an appointment with the conference chair, facilitator, or meeting planner is important, as you probably will have only one chance to determine several factors:

- Room setup, speaking area, time of access to facility and meeting room
- Location of restrooms
- Setup and breakdown time allowed for your presentation—staff help?
- Your technical and physical needs—who provides what?
- Back-of-room sales—permitted or not?

Steal the Show

Now that you're going to be booked to speak, you need to put together a presentation that steals the show. Keep your presentation as simple as possible. To be an effective speaker, you need to either teach your audience something that they don't know or haven't yet fully realized, but will really value learning, or give them an experience that changes the way they see the world. Ideally, you want to do both.

When putting your program together, start by considering your venue, the primary learning objectives, and the amount of time you have with your audience. I know how much you have to offer, and I know you want to give so much value that you knock people right out of their chairs. Believe it or not, you'll do that by delivering a reasonable amount of content rather than an overwhelming amount of content. It's likely that your audience is going to be rushing from somewhere else and then rushing to somewhere else after you've finished. So simplicity and clarity is a winning approach. Again, it's important to never run overtime. Even if you get a standing ovation and they scream, "Encore! Encore!" you must still end on time. Only amateurs run over their allotted time.

Develop Your Introduction

Your introductory bio needs to do one of two things, or both. Demonstrate that you've done what they want to do or know what they want to know.

If it does, the audience is much more likely to listen to you right from the get-go. The fact that you live in New Jersey, have a spouse, 2.2 kids, and a dog, isn't important to them. If you have 11 children and have climbed Mt. Kilimanjaro, well, that's interesting and should be included. Remember that your written bio and spoken introduction bio are different. The spoken introduction bio should read naturally and be brief and to the point.

Who will introduce you? Send your introduction in advance but take at least two copies with you, as it will probably have been lost amid all the conference preparation papers. Go over the introduction with the facilitator in advance and explain that you do not want ad libs. Be sure the person introducing you knows how to pronounce your name correctly and that any other information is clearly understood. If your name isn't easy to pronounce, writing your name phonetically in your introduction and asking the presenter to say it out loud a couple of times is a sensible precaution to take. Take this seriously even if you think you have a name that is easy to pronounce. I've been introduced more than once as Michael Porter, the esteemed author and Harvard Business School professor. The person introducing you may be a sponsor or some other VIP, and until you become better known, may not know you from Adam and, frankly, may not care. My name, by the way, is Michael *Port* (just one syllable).

Know Your Material

The best way to give the impression that you know what you're talking about is to really know what you're talking about. You must understand your subject very well and be able to answer related questions. However, it is impossible for anyone to know everything. If you're asked a question for which you don't know the answer, there is no shame in answering, "I don't know, but I'll find out and get back to you." Or you might ask if someone in the room knows the answer. Very often, you'll find that someone does.

In preparing your presentation, take the time to survey friends, clients, and others in your network who represent the kind of people to whom you'll be speaking. Learn as much as you can about what others are saying about your topic and make sure that your presentation passes the "so what?" test. Deliver it to a test audience and make sure they don't say "so what?" at the end of the presentation.

Wrap Up and Follow Up

Be sure those participants have your contact information and that you have contact information for participants where possible. Your follow-up strategy will also include thank-you notes and personalized gifts to those who helped make your presentation a success: the person or organization that invited you to speak, the facilitator who introduced you, anyone else who helped with room preparation, and so on.

You may want to remind the organization of the availability of follow-up materials as part of your keeping-in-touch plan. Make notes of what you learned so that you can apply it to future presentations and particularly to the current organization, should you be asked back again.

Fifty Public Speaking Performance Tips You Can't Afford to Ignore

Use these tips when you're preparing for a presentation. However, if you haven't yet read my book, *Steal the Show*, but you're about to read these tips, please know that *these are just tips,* snapshots of a more comprehensive process for developing speeches and performing with professionalism and passion.

My suggestion is to, no matter what kind of presentation you're preparing for, take a few moments to review the following items as a checklist to ensure that you're ready to steal the show.

1. *You Don't Have to Tell Them What You're Going to Tell Them*
   You've probably heard it before: "Tell them what you're going to tell them. Tell them. Tell them what you've told them." That's not bad advice. But it's not always the case. It doesn't have to be that way. After all, every other speaker is doing it. If you're going to make your audience sit up and pay attention, wouldn't it be worth doing something that every other speaker isn't doing? Try a pattern-interrupt instead. Open with a surprise, a shock, or an interaction. Open with something that makes a connection, or something that entertains, or something that leaves you exposed. Be different. Be memorable. It's

often the journey that's exciting. If you already know where you're going, you might not pay as much attention along the way.

2. *Cut, Cut, Cut*

   I often see (and you often see) extraneous detail added into stories and speeches that disrupt the flow. Cut to the meat. Cut to the chase. Include specifics at critical parts of the story. You don't need to pad out your speech to make an impact. Instead, you need to focus—with intention—on what's important. Your audience needs a lot less information to get to the *aha* moment than you might think.

3. *An Entire Story Is Designed to Serve the End*

   Whatever precedes the punch line must serve the payoff. See Tip 2. Does the audience need to know what color socks you're wearing or how long it took you to get to the venue? The only things that matter are things that serve the story.

4. *Establish Right Away That You Know What the World Looks Like for Them—and What It Could Look Like*

   Vividly paint the picture. Meaningful speeches are transformational experiences for your audience. Start out by showing "This is what you've got today, and this is how it could be." This builds immediate rapport and hooks the audience's interest. You know them. You understand them. You've got their back . . . and you've got a better way.

5. *Reward Them for Contributing in Some Way*

   Don't encourage interaction just to ignore it. Your audience isn't made up of chimpanzees: they don't need treats. They're intelligent beings, who do, however, need some acknowledgment.

   Imagine being asked to participate in something—whether it's holding a door open for a friend or running a project—and not even getting a nod of thanks in return. You start to feel bad right away.

6. *Use Open Hands with Your Palms Up Instead of Your Finger for Pointing*

   Sometimes the finger looks like a gun. It also feels accusatory even if you don't mean it to be. Instead, extend your hands with your palms up as if offering up alms. It's more gracious, more inclusive, and more giving.

7. *People Say Yes When We've Affected Them Intellectually, Emotionally, or Physically*

   Can you include those three elements in your presentation? Can you give your audience intellectual gristle to chew on? Can you make them gasp or cry or laugh with an emotional connection? Can you get them physically engaged (you can tell by the way they're sitting) with your ideas and message? If not, learn how and start today.

8. *Outline Your Content and Then Unpack It*

If you're teaching a curriculum like, say, Book Yourself Solid, which is distinct from a message-based speech like my Think Big Revolution keynote (you can see a 16-minute trailer of it on YouTube.com), outline first, then go back and unpack it. This isn't the same as "tell them what you're going to tell them." It's a learning plan for what's coming next. It serves as both a high-level overview before you get granular and a teaser for the exciting content still to come.

9. *Use Props*

What can you show or demonstrate or depict with objects rather than words? Can you stimulate your audience visually as well as aurally? Props aid recall: if you want to be remembered, you can be visually arresting (without dying your hair) by using props to drive your points home. Most speakers don't do this. That's just one of the reasons why you should.

10. *Use Contrast and Extremes to Create Excitement and Keep Attention*

Contrast can be emotional, physical, and structural. This basic technique is integral to every great play and film, and every great piece of music. Consider your performance like a roller coaster ride. Can you take me to the edge of a cliff before artfully lowering me, with love and care, to a safe place? Can you make the highs higher and the lows lower?

11. *Keep Moving Forward*

Never let your energy drop. You're on stage to take your audience to their final destination. Keep your foot on the gas pedal. You'll have uphill moments when your speed slows but the power and intensity increase. You can be both calm and energetic simultaneously. The great actor does this brilliantly. You, as a speaker, need to do this as well. The best way to be effortlessly spontaneous is to rehearse to the point of mastery. How often do you have to stop to think about "spontaneously" adjusting your shoelaces? Never. When you know your material, you can deliver it like it's the first time every time you perform it.

12. *Stand and Land*

    Let your punch lines, point lines, and purpose lines land. That means you don't move while you're delivering them. You remain physically rooted to the spot so that your body reinforces the gravity of your words.

13. *You Can Move and Talk at the Same Time*

    People do it all the time in real life. The idea that you can't walk and talk at the same time is ridiculous. But don't sway, and don't move when you're landing your most important points (read Tip 12 again).

14. *Don't Say, "I'm Glad to Be Here"*

    Show them that you're glad to be there instead. Your audience should see it in your actions and hear it in your words. Besides, what's the alternative? That you're pissed off that you're there?

15. *Don't Tell Them You're Going to Tell a Story, Just Tell the Story*

    If you tell them you're going to tell them a story, it's likely that they'll prepare themselves to judge the story. When people find themselves in a story, however, they are usually more engaged. People are driven by their curiosity for answers. Stories stimulate that curiosity. If you can create a sense of wonder for the listener, you can take them on a journey of exploration and insight.

16. *Be Conscientious About Connecting the Dots or You'll Lose Your Audience*

    If you're presenting a series of interconnected concepts or stories or characters, make it as simple as possible to understand. Remember: even though you know your story inside out, your audience is hearing it for the first time.

17. *Give Them Time*

    If you like to encourage note-taking during your performance, make sure you give people enough time to write down what you want them to write down. Spell things out if necessary. You'll lose your audience very quickly if they've got their heads stuck in their notebooks or laptops and you're already on to your next point.

18. *Never Apologize for the Amount of Time You Don't Have*

    The minute you apologize for what they're not getting, your audience will start to feel that they're missing out on something. They should feel that the amount of time you have is the perfect amount of time. You can blow their minds in just a few minutes. Look at all those great TED Talks for inspiration.

19. *Let Them Go Early*

    Audiences always like to be let out a few minutes early—even if they love your performance. There are no prizes for endurance in performance. Let them leave a few minutes ahead of schedule; they'll thank you for it.

20. *Enlist the Self-Proclaimed Experts in the Room*

    There's often somebody in the audience who knows more than you—or thinks they do. Get them on your side. Talk them up. Kill them with lavish praise. It'll help knock the chips off their shoulders and get them to support you and your message.

21. *Embellishment Is Positively Okay*

    You'll paint a more vivid picture with brighter colors. It's a performance, a show. Be honest, but embellish for the sake of your performance. You can combine multiple stories into one story if it produces a better result. Go for what is most dramatic and effective to get your message across. This is different from lying. Lying is something you do to make yourself look better.

22. *Remember That They Don't Know What You Know*

    It's the first time they've heard your info. Don't assume prior knowledge. It can only help your message if you're comprehensive and to the point.

23. *Don't Use Acronyms*

    Or, if you do, explain them the first time around. Take the time to make them clear.

24. *Show Them What the World Will Look Like if They Don't Change*

    Make it clear that if they don't follow your advice, or come with you on your journey, their world will probably remain the same as—if not get considerably worse than—it is today. Just do this respectfully and without hyperbole.

25. *Study Standup Comedy*

    Watch standup comedians for their approach. Watch their setup, delivery, and payoff. See how they own the stage. Standup comedians can even turn a water bottle into a tool for creating magic moments.

26. *Be Careful Using Idioms*

Across cultures—even cultures that share a language—there are big idiomatic differences that can turn your message opaque for an audience that doesn't "get it." If you're an American talking to a British audience about bangs, bleachers, boondoggles, or fanny packs, you've likely lost them already.

27. *Don't Make Jokes About Difficult Topics*

Stay away from jokes that are awkward, insensitive, or otherwise confrontational. If you want to make yourself the butt of your jokes, that kind of self-deprecating humor can work very well. This doesn't mean you can't lighten up the mood when talking about difficult subjects, but that's different from poking fun or making jokes at other people's expense.

28. *If You Tell Them You Care About Something, You Also Need to Tell Them Why*

It's not good enough to say, "I'm a strong proponent of women's rights." It may seem obvious but you've got to hook them in with your reasons. Your why is what makes your beliefs more powerful and your case stronger.

29. *Boom, Boom, BANG*

The rule of three is one of the most important performance techniques you can use to grab attention and make people laugh. It's powerful, it's potent, and it packs a punch. (See what I did there?)

30. *Understand Stage Blocking*

You need to remain physically open so everyone in the room can see you at all times. That means you don't hide or turn to face anybody other than your audience . . . unless it's for dramatic effect.

31. *Deliver Big Moments Center Stage (Usually)*

Centering yourself physically on the stage is the same as bolding and centering a headline in a newspaper. It says: "This is important—pay attention." When you designate center stage as the pivotal place for your performance, you can more effectively use the rest of the stage to support your main message. There are always exceptions to this concept, so be sure your blocking works before the big day.

32. *That Said, Don't Head Straight for Center Stage*
When getting onstage for the first time, avoid making a beeline directly to the center before starting your speech. Doing so looks stiff and clunky.

33. *Learn How to Rehearse*
Rehearsal is the key to a successful performance. It's also the most effective method for reducing anxiety and calming pre-performance anxiety. If you know what you're going to do because you're well-rehearsed, you'll feel more prepared and, thus, less anxious. It's not just repetition, but training. If you have to stop a rehearsal, start back up at the exact same emotional, physical, and energetic state. Otherwise, you'll lose the through-line and arc of the speech.

34. *When You Land a Joke, Bask in the Glory*
If public speaking is notoriously difficult, making people laugh when you're performing is devilishly tough. So, when you nail a joke, be sure to bask in the moment.

35. *Voice and Speech Training Are Not Something You Master in an Hour*
It takes some time. I studied voice and speech daily for three years at NYU's Graduate Acting Program, and I'm still learning. Voice and speech training can make you sound more substantial so people will pay attention to you. It can also help you manage your nerves.

36. *Don't Push*
Pushing is a theater term for overacting. When you push, you can't show emotion. When you push, the work feels false and self-absorbed. It's insincere. Insincerity is the enemy of truth. Truth is integral to performance.

37. *Just Because You're Feeling It, Doesn't Mean They Are*
Major emotion for you as the speaker doesn't always translate to major emotion for your audience. It's only in rehearsal and practice that you find out what works and what doesn't. You might be moved to tears while your audience is bored to tears. Big difference. Your job is getting the audience to think differently, feel differently, and/or act differently. How you feel doesn't matter. Achieving your objectives for the people in the audience does.

38. *Get Everything in Before the Audience Claps*
Then, get off the stage quickly. Don't let them see you doing house-keeping or making routine announcements. It breaks the theatrical experience.

39. *You Can Also Stay Onstage at the End if You Invite Them to Join You There*
That way, you're hosting the party. You don't want them grabbing you in the restroom: nothing dissipates magic like a damp hand-shake in the gent's restroom.

40. *Anyone Can Make a Sexy Sizzle Reel*
Meeting planners want to know you can hold the stage for an extended period of time. Make sure you can show them video of 5 to 15 minutes of continuous performance in which you deliver a strong message and truly engage the audience. Any good editor can piece together a bunch of good lines from different speeches but it doesn't tell the audience that you can hold and own the stage.

41. *Get Right to It*
Most speakers waste time on too much exposition and preparation and the audience starts thinking, "Let's go already." Instead, hit the accelerator hard and launch straight on. Let them know what they're in for by what they experience from you in the first 30 seconds.

42. *Stop Using the Storyteller Voice*
It's false. Tell a story to 10,000 people the same way you'd tell the story to your best friend. Don't use some dramatic made-up voice. Study your favorite speakers. They make you feel like it's just you and them in the room.

43. *Simplify*
You have no time for self-indulgence. You must be clinical and sur-gical with your material and your message. Don't use overly obfus-cating verbiage when you can say things simply. See what I did there? We get attached to bits that really don't further the story or resonate with the audience, perhaps because they're funny or easy for us or have a special meaning to us. But it's not about us. It's never about us. It's always about them.

44. *You Don't Need to Slow Down*
Most speech teachers tell you to slow down. Sometimes that makes sense. But if you're worried about speaking too quickly, you're

focused on the wrong thing. Instead of slowing down, focus on pausing. Speakers who speak too slowly have a soporific effect. Sometimes, I speak quickly. But I pause at the right places. That creates rhythm. Sometimes, I slow down when it serves the speech to slow down. Audiences can easily absorb the important points if you give them pause time.

45. *If You Have to Explain a Joke, It's Just Not Funny*
No joke gets funnier with explanation. Choose a better joke or let go of it altogether.

46. *Never Turn Your Back to the Audience*
Unless it's intentional to make a point or convey an emotion, of course. When you need to move upstage (that's toward the back of the stage, away from the audience), walk backward if possible. Try not to turn your back on them.

47. *Never Yell at Your Audience*
This shouldn't need saying, but sometimes we get so fired up about what we believe in that we start shouting at the audience. Be aware of how you're coming across. Also, if you need to get everybody's attention after a coffee break, for example, simply raise your hand and stand silently. People will get it and follow. If you yell at an audience to come back to their seats, you'll lower your status and potentially create some animosity with the audience members.

48. *If You Think You're Going to Rise to the Occasion, Don't Bet on It*
Under pressure, you don't rise to the occasion; you fall back on your training. If you think you're going to somehow be inspired to come up with the right material during the speech without significant preparation, don't bet on it.

49. *Have Fun*
Some speakers will often book a speech and then worry that they didn't prepare for it and wind up frustrated at how poorly they're giving it. That's not a particularly powerful place to be when performing. The more fun you have, the more fun the audience will have. If you enjoy giving the speech, they will be much more relaxed receiving it from you. You can make mistakes, lose your place, and even trip all over yourself, and still steal the show.

50. *Read* Steal the Show

Read *Steal the Show: From Speeches to Job Interviews, to Deal-Closing Pitches, How to Guarantee a Standing Ovation for All the Performances in Your Life.* It's a *Wall Street Journal, USA Today,* and *Publisher's Weekly* bestseller. And, the president of Starbucks, Howard Behar, said, "*Steal the Show* is the most unique and practical book on public speaking ever written." So, there's that.

Many Rules Are Made to Be Broken

But to break the rules of performance, you need to know what the rules are. You need to know why they exist and exactly why you're breaking them. When you break the rules with a real purpose, you can achieve a better and more effective result.

Be prepared if you want to make life-saving, world-changing speeches. That's what *Steal the Show* can do for you: make you a much, much better public speaker and performer in all aspects of life.

A performance can be about wowing an audience, but it can also be about simply connecting with one person. Most important, you don't have to be an entertainer to be a performer. And you don't have to think of yourself as a performer today to use what I teach here and in *Steal the Show* tomorrow.

To Speak or Not to Speak, That Is the Question

It's important to be aware of what your talents are and to not use the speaking strategy if public speaking isn't one of your strengths, which isn't to say you can't get better at public speaking and performing—you can. You integrate what you learn by melding your first presentation into your second, and so on. However, I wouldn't suggest using the speaking strategy as one of your primary self-promotion strategies if you really aren't comfortable speaking in public or just don't want to.

Having said that, I'd like to make a key distinction: even if you're feeling stage fright at the thought of public speaking, that doesn't mean you don't have the ability to be a good public speaker. I'm nervous before almost every single speech I make. I'd be worried if I weren't, because it's natural to feel nervous in such a situation. If you're drawn to speaking and would like to give it a try, then by all means, go for it.

> *If you feel called to share a message, it's because there are people in the world who are waiting to hear it.*

Your job is to work hard to find the people who are waiting to hear your message and not let the naysayers—the people who don't like what you're doing—deter you from finding those you're meant to serve. This principle can drive you and keeps you going when the going gets tough. It prompts me to say again to you, if you feel called to speak, to share your message, there are people out there waiting to hear it.

The Book Yourself Solid Speaking Strategy is a great way to establish yourself as a category authority, get your message out to the world in a bigger way, and enable you to reach more of those you're meant to serve.

CHAPTER

15

The Book Yourself
Solid Writing Strategy

Words are, of course, the most powerful drug used by mankind.
—Rudyard Kipling

Article writing is an effective way to create awareness for your services and build your reputation. Using the five-part Book Yourself Solid Writing Strategy you'll learn how to write effective articles and post them online, one of the most effective ways to generate traffic to your website.

You'll also learn how to analyze some of the different offline writing markets and the steps to get editors to publish your articles. Writing articles and publishing them online and offline will help you establish your reputation as an expert while generating interest in your products, programs, and services. By publishing online and offline, you will imprint your position as a category authority as widely as possible.

If you consider yourself a writer, you're going to say, "Yes, this Book Yourself Solid Self-Promotion Strategy is for me and I'm going to jump on this right now." If you don't picture yourself as a writer, you might be inclined to skip over this chapter, but please don't. Even nonwriters can learn to write effective articles.

My fourth-grade teacher said I had the worst spelling she had ever seen in her 25-year career in teaching. Many years later, when I told one of my childhood friends that I had sold a book to a big-time publisher, he questioned how I could do that without his help. He still had an impression of me as the kid who didn't even like to write five paragraphs for a high school essay. But I wound up writing a lot more than five paragraphs— and a few good ones, too.

The point is that I don't want you to miss out on this important self-promotion strategy simply because you think you can't write. If you can speak, you should be able to write well enough to use the Book Yourself Solid Writing Strategy. You're not writing the Great American Novel here. You're writing to educate the people you serve and promote the services you sell. Even if writing isn't one of your natural talents, it's a skill that can be learned well enough for you to master the Book Yourself Solid Writing Strategy and can be improved on through practice.

How to Get Out of Writing

Does the thought of having to write an article still make you cringe? Okay, I get that. There are two other ways to gain the benefits that article writing provides without going anywhere near a keyboard:

- Hire a ghostwriter.
- Collaborate with another subject matter expert who likes writing.
- Use article writing software and other artificial intelligence (AI) tools to help you.

Ghostwriters are professional writers who will custom write an article for you on the subject of your choice for a fee. Your name and business information appear in the byline. Sure, it costs a little, but it's still a comparatively inexpensive marketing tool. And once you've got it, you can use it in many different ways:

- Send it to related websites and newsletters that accept submissions.
- Publish it in your own electronic newsletter.
- Upload it to your own blog and announce it to your mailing list.
- Submit it to print publications that cater to your area of expertise.

You can get a lot of mileage out of one article, especially if it's of professional quality.

Collaborating with another subject matter expert who likes writing is another way to get the word out about your services. If you know someone who can write well, consider pitching a joint venture to this person. You provide the expertise, and they provide the writing skills to prepare an article based on your supplied information. Then both of your names and website addresses appear together in the author's box at the end.

This sort of collaboration is a great way to solve the I–dislike–writing problem while effectively promoting two businesses at once.

And finally I'd be remiss not to mention AI. With a quick prompt or reference point, "you" can put your name to an essay or article that has been written for you in a matter of minutes. This is already a powerful tool. A word of warning, however. At the time of this writing, AI can pump out lots of "commodity" articles with titles like, *Unlock Your Success: Why an Executive Coach Is Your Missing Puzzle Piece* but can't offer you much in the way of vision or voice. In addition, there are plenty of permission, copyright, and plagiarism concerns when it comes to AI. We'll see. Maybe, by the time you read this, it'll be different. I can only imagine what you'll be able to do with these tools.

Whether or not you decide to embrace tools like this is up to you. I will just remind you that with great power, as they say, comes great responsibility.

The Five-Part Book Yourself Solid Writing Strategy

The publishing part of the article writing strategy really isn't that scary. What most people find daunting is the actual writing of the article. So, let's start with how to do that.

Part 1: Deciding on the Subject
Part 2: Choosing an Ideal Topic
Part 3: Creating an Attention-Grabbing Title
Part 4: Writing Your Article
Part 5: Getting Your Article Published

Part 1: Deciding on the Subject

What is your subject? A subject is a broad category of knowledge: dancing, boating, fashion, business, society, and recreation are all subjects. It's possible you already know a great deal about the subject of your article, or maybe you're curious about a new subject and want to expand your knowledge of it. To help identify a direction for your writing, ask yourself these questions:

- What am I passionate about?
- What interests me on a personal level?
- What is the scope of my expertise?
- What life lessons have I learned?
- What is my target audience interested in learning?

Answering these questions will help you find good subjects. Of course, you should always remember the golden rule of writing: write about what you know. If you feel stuck, it might be because you've strayed from a subject that relates to your area of professional expertise because this is probably what you have the most knowledge about. Or, it might be because you're trying to demonstrate that you're smart by attempting to write like an academic.

Don't forget to explore your personal interests as well. Consider subjects based on hobbies, family, community involvement, or charity work. Your life experiences can provide you with endless ideas for article writing.

4.15.1 Written Exercise: List three subjects you would feel comfortable writing about on the basis of your passions, your personal interests, your areas of expertise, the life lessons you've learned, and what your target market is interested in learning. Once you've chosen one subject area to write about, you're ready to narrow it down to an ideal topic.

Part 2: Choosing an Ideal Topic

A topic is a specific, narrow focus within your subject area. Subjects such as marketing, sales, and exercise are too broad to write about, especially because article pieces are usually between 500 and 3,000 words. Have you ever noticed that most articles and books (other than reference materials) are focused on a narrow topic? The reason is simple—it makes the writing (and reading) more manageable.

Let's say you're a dancing coach. You might choose a topic like how modern dance evolved from folk dance, how dancing contributes to heart health, comfortable clothes to wear while dancing, or the growing interest in a certain style of dance.

The following examples demonstrate how to narrow a broad subject area to reach a focused topic.

From Broad Subjects to Focused Topics

Dancing→ Dancing for Women→ Fitness Dancing for Grannies

Dancing→ Dancing for Men→ Smooth Moves for the Dancing Don Juan

Dancing→ Dancing for Couples→ Ballroom Dancing for Latin

Boating → Water Sports → Water Skiing Safety Tips

Boating→ Angler Fishing→ Hot Bait for the Angler Catching Weakfish

Boating→ Safety→ Preventing Hypothermia

Fashion→ Style→ Walking in Style and Comfortable

Fashion→ Seasonal Trends→ Top 10 Looks for Fall Fashion→

Teens→ Prom Night: Get the Red Carpet Look for Less

4.15.2 Written Exercise: List three focused topics you would feel comfortable writing about based on the subjects you chose in Written Exercise 4.15.1.

Determine your objective for writing: Now that you've chosen a focused topic for your article, you need to establish a clear purpose or objective. Are you writing to inform, persuade, explore new territory, or to express your personal opinion? Knowing your objective will help you zero in on the content of your article. Ask yourself these questions:

- What do I want to teach the reader?
- What life experience do I want to share?

- Do I want to venture into new territory?
- How do I want to be known?

Let's examine these questions in more detail. One of the most popular types of article is the how-to article, in which you teach your readers something. This is a great place to start, especially for new writers, because you can simply tap in to an area of expertise you already have, cutting out the need for hours of research. Likewise, sharing an experience that taught you a life lesson is another straightforward way of telling a story that can really affect people.

Or you can do the research on a brand-new topic, educating yourself and your readers at the same time. This keeps the writing process fresh and interesting for you.

Articles that provide links within the content to good resources (perhaps pages of your own website) are a great way to help your readers while establishing yourself as a reliable source of information.

Deciding now what sort of expert you want to be known as will help you determine the objective of your articles. Let's say you're a life coach for men navigating midlife crises. Writing a series of articles on keeping your marriage healthy and rewarding after 40 is a great way to tap in to your existing knowledge base while establishing a reputation for yourself as somebody who truly understands the fears and concerns of their target market. That kind of credibility can drive new business to your door without spending a cent on advertising.

Understand your target audience: So far you have narrowed your subject to a focused topic and established your purpose for writing the article. Now it is time to consider your reader.

As we discussed in Chapter 2, your target market is a group of clients or prospects with a common interest or need that you can meet. The same is true for the target audience of your article: a group of people united in their common need for the information you have to share.

To zero in on who they are, ask yourself these questions:

- What do I know about my audience: income, age, gender?
- How educated is my audience: specialized, literate, minimal education?
- How much do they already know about my topic?
- What do they need to know that I can teach?
- Are there any misconceptions about my topic that I can clear up for them?

- What is my relationship with my target audience?
- How else can I help my readers?

Digging deep to ponder and answer these questions about your readers will help you develop a mental picture of their lives and their needs. Let's say you decided to run in a marathon, but you've never run in one before. You know there must be thousands of other people out there just like you who would like to run, get fit in the process, and just feel the satisfaction of knowing they can do it. Your target audience in this case would be people who are highly motivated, health conscious, open to challenges, curious, and willing to try something new. Defining them was easy because they are just like you. Of course, writing about this would only be worthwhile as a self-promotion activity if these were the people you wanted to serve.

If you know that people in your target market need simple information on the topic you want to write about, and you can describe them as we just did, that knowledge will help you to define:

- What you will tell them
- How you will tell them: your tone, vocabulary, and style of writing

Hot buttons: Another way to understand more about your readers is to study the emotional hot buttons that make all of us tick. We share common hot buttons about health, wealth, and relationships. The readers in your target market will have more specific hot buttons related to their own personal situations. Midlife mothers don't usually worry about getting dropped from the sports team, but college athletes do. Knowing what these buttons are can help you choose topics and write articles to tap in to your audience's basic interests in life. Now that you have a topic for your article, it's time to start writing.

Part 3: Creating an Attention-Grabbing Title

I discussed in Chapter 8 how the title of your information product can make a big difference in whether it sells. The same concept is true when creating attention-grabbing article titles. In fact, some writers say it's the most important part because without an arresting title, no one will bother to read the rest of your article. Here are some additional tips to help spark your creativity when writing attention-grabbing titles:

1. Select a few choice words that sum up the main point of the article. Example: *How to Renovate Your Kitchen Without Spending a Fortune*

2. Tell the reader what they will learn. Use specifics: "95% of all" or "two out of three." Example: *New Report Shows 54% of School-Age Children Are Couch Potatoes*

3. Hint at the solution your article provides. Example: *Cook Low-Carb Meals That Don't Leave You Craving*

4. Use questions in the title to involve the reader. Example: *Are You Sleep Deprived and Don't Even Know It?*

5. Curiosity is a powerful tool, so consider a teaser title. Example: *What Your Face Shape and Your Choice of Dog Have in Common*

6. Promise results. Explain how your article will solve a problem for the reader. Example: *Get Over Your Fear of Flying in Five Minutes*

7. Promise to teach them something using phrases like "How to" or "Five Steps to Improve." Example: *How to Belly Dance in Three Easy Steps*

4.15.3 Written Exercise: Create three titles based on your topic choices. Remember, titles need to summarize in a few words what your article is about and be intriguing enough to make people who are interested in that topic—and even those who aren't—want to read more. If you can fit it in your top keyword phrase, so much the better.

Part 4: Writing Your Article

The introduction: The introduction contains the nugget of your story, a short capsule that summarizes what's coming in the body of the article. It builds on the topic already presented in the title and explains why that information matters to the reader, which is why it's so important to know who your target audience is.

Some writers tend to back into their story by dropping their lead nugget down to the third or fourth paragraph, but this is a dangerous tactic.

In nearly all cases, the first paragraph of your article should reflect the title, elaborate on it, and hint at all the juicy information to come.

Your introduction is also the place where you set the tone for the entire article, so be sure to speak directly to your readers using the words they use frequently. A casual style will endear you to your readers much more than an academic or technical style of writing. Above all, a strong introduction presents ideas that entice the reader to keep reading.

A compelling introductory paragraph answers everyone's most pertinent question: what's in it for me? Know how your information will benefit your readers and express that in your opening statement to them. If you can't imagine what benefit they will gain from your article, it may be wise to go back and refine your topic.

4.15.4 Written Exercise: Write your lead-in paragraph by presenting the most important information first. Remember to address the topic presented in your title and explain to your readers what they will gain from your article. Here's where you get to appeal personally to the readers by telling them how you can help them learn something new, solve a problem, or simply entertain them for a short while.

The body: The body of your article is where you fulfill the promise made in your title and lead-in paragraph by expanding on your theme. Here are a few tips to make the writing of this, the longest part of your article, easier:

- *Try to stick to one idea in each sentence and two or three sentences in each paragraph:* Concise bits of information are much easier for your readers to handle and are much less intimidating than long blocks of writing.
- *Use subheadings:* These are like mini-titles that explain what's coming next and help break up the writing into manageable sections. Subheadings also help you organize the presentation of your information, somewhat like an outline. Put them in bold text or all capitals to make them stand out.
- *Use lists:* Giving your readers information formatted with bulleted lists, numbered lists, or any other visual device also makes the writing

easier to read. The bottom line is that even the people who are very interested in your topic are in a hurry and want to get the goods fast.

- *Be consistent with your layout:* If the first item on your list of bullet points starts with a verb, make sure the first word of every item starts the same way. For example, in this list of five points, each opening sentence—the one in italics—starts with the imperative form of a verb: *try, use, be.*

4.15.5 Written Exercise: It is time to write the body of your article. You need to elaborate on and fulfill the promise made in your introduction by backing up your statements with facts. Refer back to the points listed previously if you get stuck. And remember that you don't have to get all the words perfect in the first draft. Much of writing is about rewriting and editing. At this point, concentrate on the broad strokes and allow yourself to enjoy the process.

The conclusion: Have you said everything you wanted to say? Then it's time to wrap it all up. The conclusion is easy because it's simply a summing up of everything you just wrote. The point is to leave your readers with an easy-to-remember summary of your main theme so that it is reinforced in their minds.

If you were simply to finish your article on point nine of a list of tips, your readers would feel they were left hanging. It's human nature to crave a satisfying ending to a story. You can leave them on an even sweeter note if you share with them how they can best use the information to their advantage, and you can offer a few words of encouragement.

Write a conclusion using these guidelines:

- Restate your main points, wrapping them up in a neat summary.
- Encourage readers to try your advice.
- End on a positive note.

4.15.6 Written Exercise: End your article with a strong closing. Write a conclusion by summarizing your key points from the body of the article and tell the readers how they can best use the information you just gave them.

The author's resource box: This is where you get to take a bow, share something pertinent about yourself or your business, and invite your readers to take an action. It's also an important opportunity to offer your services.

At the end of every article is a separate paragraph of about five or six lines (this depends on the guidelines of each publication, so check with them before submitting). This resource box or author's bio can be used in several ways. Most authors put the following information in their resource boxes:

- A brief explanation of who they are and their expertise
- A line or two about their business or the special offer they want to promote
- A call to action that prompts readers to either phone, click a link, or make contact in some other way
- *Optional:* The offer of a gift or other incentive to motivate action

The key to writing your resource box: To make sure your resource box is effective, clearly invite action and explain why this action would benefit your readers. This applies to whether it's signing up for a free report, a newsletter subscription, or simply a visit to your website to learn more about your products, services, and programs or to read more of your scintillating articles!

4.15.7 Written Exercise: Create your author resource box. Remember to include your area of expertise, your business or offer, a specific call to action, and pertinent contact information and links.

Let it simmer and proofread: Now take that article you have so carefully and lovingly created—and ignore it. Set it aside for *at least* a day. Return to it later and take the time to read it out loud. This is when any dropped words or weird phrasing will become apparent. Check your grammar and spelling. Polish your work to perfection. Ten rereads are not excessive; each time you'll see something that could be said better, tighter, or more accurately. Always read your writing out loud. Many people—like me—will hear errors that their eyes don't see on the page.

A word about spelling checkers: your word processing program has a spelling and grammar checking function. Use it but don't depend on it. You could use a spelling checker and still make spelling errors. For example, you might have typed *here* when you meant to type *hear*. The English language is a mess, and, although they're getting better, most spell checking programs can't comprehend which word you meant to use or should have spelled differently based on how you used it. Also, share your articles with others and accept their help to spot any spelling or grammar problems that you may have overlooked.

4.15.8 Booked Solid Action Step: Compile all the accumulated elements of your research and writing to complete one article of 500 to 750 words on the topic of your choice, including the resource box. When it's polished to your satisfaction, share it with friends, colleagues, or a writing group to gain valuable insight on your writing progress.

Part 5: Getting Your Article Published

This is when the fruits of your writing labor pay off. After you have completed writing your article, you'll want to search for websites and the publications that will help share your writing with the world.

Getting published on the web: The internet offers a number of unique environments to display your written work, thereby generating traffic to your website, building your credibility, and increasing visibility for your products, programs, and services. Here are some examples:

- Niche websites and blogs
- Social media sites
- Numerous online magazines
- Email newsletters

Let's take a closer look:

- *Niche websites and blogs:* The owner of a niche website or blog requires quality content written on specific topics relevant to their audience. The web owners' agenda is to keep their website fresh with articles that cater to their targeted readers; they look to writers like you to supply them with this free content.

- *Social media platforms:* Many social media platforms provide you with the ability to publish your long-form content. It's never a bad idea to publish broadly, but don't get into the situation where you're only preaching to the choir, or writing articles for an audience that is already actively following you. We want to reach new prospects with our self-promotion strategies, not just engage with our existing prospects.
- *Numerous online magazines:* There are hundreds of online magazines that serve your target audience, and they're constantly trying to find content providers like you to fill their "pages."
- *Email newsletters:* Electronic newsletters come in all shapes and sizes on varied topics. You write the content, share it with these publishers, and immediately gain access to their readers who are also your target audience. The publisher gains credible content without needing to write the articles, and you reach a larger group of prospective customers.

Where should you start? Consider your target audience and where they're most likely to spend their time online. These are the hot spots you'll leverage to display your writing on a consistent basis. However, before you start the submission process, there are a few more details you need to consider:

- *Researching relevant environments:* Locate the specific environments that cater to your target audience, familiarizing yourself with the article submission guidelines.
- *Creating an article summary:* Write a short synopsis of your article.
- *Choosing keywords and keyword phrases:* Make a list of your keywords and keyword phrases. (These should be the same keywords and keyword phrases you used to prepare your title and article copy for the search engines.)
- *Listing the word count:* Some content sites will require a word count of your article. The total word count usually includes all words plus the title and resource box that make up your entire piece.
- *Checking your spelling and grammar:* Check your article before submission. I agree with Mark Twain, who said, "I don't give a damn for a man that can only spell a word one way." Unfortunately, not everyone agrees. One misspelled word can really turn people off.

- *Preparing an email:* Write a letter to the publishers detailing what your article is about and why it would benefit the content provider's readership. Insert a copy of your article into the body of the email correspondence.

4.15.9 Written Exercise: List five online magazines that serve your target market.

4.15.10 Booked Solid Action Step: Submit your article once you've followed the preceding Book Yourself Solid writing process.

4.15.11 Written Exercise: List five email newsletter publications that serve your target market.

4.15.12 Booked Solid Action Step: Submit your article once you've followed the preceding Book Yourself Solid writing process.

Consistency is the key to writing and publishing articles as a marketing tool. The idea is to saturate your target market so when a potential client is searching for valuable information, your name and articles come up again and again within the search engines' results.

Getting published in print: Once you're comfortable with sharing your written work online, you might consider branching out and offering articles to print publications. Writing for the print market can be a more competitive process, but it's also very rewarding.

Plan your print publishing strategy:

1. Think big but start small.
2. Request the writing guidelines.

3. Analyze the contents.
4. Write a query letter.
5. Send the letter.
6. Follow up with the editor.

Let's examine each step in more detail.

Think big but start small: Rather than going for the large mainstream magazines, shoot for the small, focused publications such as local newspapers and magazines, trade journals, or neighborhood community newsletters. These publications are more likely to accept your work and even help edit your articles for suitability.

Once you've been accepted to write in one of the smaller publications, you can build your portfolio of printed pieces and approach the larger markets. This is important because many large-publication editors won't consider your writing ability unless they can see you have been previously published. It's similar to when you're trying to break into the speaking circuit: you start at the local level, step up to the regional level, then to the national level, and finally to the international level. It's the same concept when you're trying to get your writing in print publications.

Request the writing guidelines: Never submit articles without understanding what the publication is looking for and accepts. You need to be aware of word count, spacing format, style, and the type of information each publication is looking to include. For more detailed information on writing guidelines for thousands of print publications, pick up a copy of *Writer's Market 100th Edition* (Robert Lee Brewer, Editor, Writer's Digest Books, 2021).

Analyze the contents: Your chances of getting an article accepted for print will greatly improve if you take the time to become familiar with the publication. Either purchase a subscription or several back issues; then analyze the contents by looking at items such as article length, the tone of the writing pieces, the topics covered, the balance of short articles versus long, and how many illustrations or photos were used.

Write a query letter: Now that you know which topics you want to write about and have identified the publications you want to write in, it's time to write a letter to send by email. A query letter is basically a proposal that pitches your article idea. You can send a query letter about an article that has already been written or an article that hasn't yet been created as a way to feel out the publication's enthusiasm for your idea.

Your query letter should follow the rules of a good business letter. It must immediately grab attention and convincingly sell your article idea. Use bullets to list key points for easier reading.

Send the letter and follow up with the editor: After sending your query letter by email and waiting the appropriate time for a response, follow up by telephone. Your objective is to inquire whether the editor is interested in your article and if they require additional information. If the editor's response is no, don't be pushy and try to change their mind. Instead, ask if there is a different slant to the article that might interest them or whether they know someone else who might be interested in your piece.

4.15.13 Written Exercise: List three print publications that serve your target market.

4.15.14 Booked Solid Action Step: Submit your query letter to the print publications you identified in Written Exercise 4.15.13.

Help Editors Help You

Every publication has an insatiable hunger for good content. They're looking for articles that will inform and entertain their readers—pieces that will help them improve their lives, whether it's how to save money, lose weight, build self-esteem, or build a shelving unit.

Most editors need good writers who also happen to be experts in their field—like you. They usually have to pay staff writers or freelancers. So if you can give them good articles at no charge, the publication saves time and money, and you get great exposure.

A solid relationship with an editor can help you gain insight to the following:

- What type of information is being considered for future publication
- What kind of story may be needed in the future
- How to strengthen your chances of being interviewed to write a particular story

Consideration goes a long way in the print publishing business. You'll discover that the most vital component for building relationships with editors is listening and providing the best information to meet their needs. If you stay in contact with them and consistently work to supply them with good stories, you'll successfully build relationships that will provide publicity for you and your business over time.

4.15.15 Written Exercise: Decide on an ongoing schedule for submitting your articles. This can be weekly, every other week, or monthly.

4.15.16 Booked Solid Action Step: Schedule the time you'll need to write and submit new articles and then do it.

It's important to learn the art of delayed gratification. Although it's natural to want instant results, this is a process, not a magic formula for overnight fame and fortune. One of the greatest mistakes I see service professionals make is giving up too quickly when their initial efforts don't produce immediate results. It's the cumulative effect that will pay off, so be consistent and be tenacious. Don't give up.

16

The Book Yourself Solid Web Strategy

When I took office, only high-energy physicists had ever heard of what is called the World Wide Web . . . Now even my cat has its own page.
—Bill Clinton

Most very successful coaches have a web presence. It's likely you need the same. Why? Well, you know this but I'll say it anyway: the web is a powerful tool for starting and continuing conversations with potential clients. So, yes, you need a brand-building website that starts conversations with potential clients to turn them into current clients. That said, using web marketing as a primary strategy for promoting your services is not essential, nor is it necessarily effective for marketing your services. The web can be *very* effective, but hardcore internet marketing is not for everyone and every business. If the highly specialized internet marketing gig is not right for you, then it won't be effective.

If you don't want to become an internet marketing maniac, don't. Mastering tactics like search engine optimization, pay-per-click advertising, and the many other tools are for those who want to spend their time online. If that's not where your passion lies, you'll quickly become overwhelmed, and the last thing you, or I, want is for you to feel overwhelmed.

If you are simply not driven to spend your energy learning a new technology, but you still want to leverage the power of the internet, hire or partner with others who have the skills, talents, and desires that you do not.

These days working solo does not mean working alone—far from it. At present, I have a 5,300-square-foot campus that is filled with talented, hard-working, dedicated, and caring people. But I started with one employee—me. But even in the beginning, I outsourced much of the work that I didn't like to do and wasn't very good at to assistants and technical experts. You can do much more with others than you can alone.

There is something for everyone in this chapter, novice and expert alike, so I've divided this chapter into three parts:

Part 1: Designing Your Website
Part 2: Getting Visitors to Your Website
Part 3: Building Your Social Media Platform

The web is an extraordinary vehicle for self-expression. It offers huge opportunities for sharing who you are and what you offer, as well as the privilege of connecting with others. There is a learning curve, but all great opportunities require that we learn something new. Two of the most important rules for doing big things in the world are learning in action and working with others.

Learn in real time and in action. Don't wait until everything is perfect to go out and do what you want to do. If you wait for perfection to go out in the world and do big things, it's unlikely you're going to get there, or get anything done, for that matter. Many people hold themselves back because they think they have to know everything about how to do something before they actually do it. This is not true. You can learn while doing.

You cannot learn how to run or become a better runner without actually running. You can certainly read an article about how moving your arms in a particular way can help your stride, but until you put the tip into action, you won't really know or experience its truth. The same is true for marketing or any other new skill you're interested in learning. As you embrace each of these self-promotion strategies by learning in action and working with others who have more experience than you, you will be pleasantly surprised at what you're able to accomplish in a very short time.

PART 1

DESIGNING YOUR WEBSITE

Design is not just what it looks like and feels like.
Design is how it works.
—Steve Jobs

In this first part, I walk you through the purpose and benefits of having a website, how to structure the content on your website, the most effective website formats for coaches, what to look for in a website designer, along with the biggest mistake most people make online. I'll try to make it as easy to understand as a day at the beach—or at least a day at the beach with your laptop.

Purpose and Benefits of Having a Website

There are numerous purposes and benefits to having a website and developing a strong web presence, many of which I'm sure you've considered. Your own website can help you do the following:

- *Positions you as an expert:* Having your own website increases your visibility, credibility, and trustworthiness.
- *Builds your brand identity:* Your website represents you and your business in the marketplace.
- *Reaches a global marketplace:* If you have a product available on your website, you'll expand your geographic marketplace from your local neighborhood to the entire world.

- *Creates a 24/7 passive-revenue profit machine:* The web never sleeps, which means that you can turn your computer and website into a cash register around the clock, and many, if not all, of the processes can be automated.
- *Builds your database:* A website can instantly increase the effectiveness of your sales cycle by building a targeted list of potential clients who have given you permission to follow up with them. A website with an opt-in feature enables you to provide value while building your database (by offering something of value in exchange for email addresses). Remember, your visitors must see your offers and your services as opportunities worthy of their investment, even if that investment is as small as an email address.
- *Allows for filtering out unsuitable clients:* All of your marketing materials can guide potential clients to your website, where you save precious time by allowing them to familiarize themselves with you, your services, your procedures, and maybe even your prices before they contact you for more information. They can then determine whether they feel they'd be well-suited to work with you.
- *Provides an opportunity for bold self-expression:* Your website is a fantastic vehicle through which to express yourself. It is an extension and a representation of you and what you offer.

The Biggest Mistake Most People Make Online

Before we get into the technical aspects of what makes a great website, consider the biggest mistake most people make online: they don't know what they want their visitors to do when viewing the site, and if they do know, they don't know how they're going to get the visitor to do it.

Most people consider a website to be one thing. It's not. On the contrary, a website is made up of a collection of pages that live on the same domain and may be related to one another. For each page on your site, you should be able to answer the following three questions with complete clarity:

- Who is coming to the page?
- What do you want them to do?
- How are you going to get them to do it?

Knowing the answer to these three questions will ensure that the content on each page of your site is perfectly designed for the type of person who visits the page. Why? Because you will consider what kind of true story you're going to tell, and how you're going to tell it, to get your visitor to reach the goal you've set for that page. Your website can be a remarkably effective tool for attracting and securing clients—if it's done right.

A pretty website does not necessarily a good website make. Sure, you may get a few calls because someone visited your site, or sell a few products, but the majority of the people who visit your site will not come back again just for its prettiness. Site visitors' behavior is not necessarily because they don't like what you have to offer, but because people are busy and most don't even remember how they found your site in the first place. Pretty is forgettable. Content that answers the needs of the visitor sticks in people's memories. Ease of use enables them to consume it.

As a successful online marketer, you will focus on attempting to convert the traffic that comes to your site into a potential client, someone who eagerly anticipates your marketing messages. These messages will come in the form of the next great service offering that will help someone advance an aspect of their life. You might do this by giving these clients something of value, like a special report or a free video series in exchange for permission to stay in touch with them. Remember how important building trust over time is. If your primary objective is to offer extraordinary value upfront in exchange for an email address and permission to follow up, then you can make relevant and proportionate monetized offerings later on, once you've built trust.

Content and Structure The content and structure of your website includes the information you wish to convey and how you organize and label it for easy navigation. Just as you can leverage the same content for an information product into several different formats, you can choose a variety of formats to lay out your website's content.

As you consider your content and structure, your focus should be on your target market. It is especially critical when you're working with a designer to think like your target audience. What do they want? Design to meet their needs.

Your content and structure are key elements in determining whether your website is effective. The content has to be relevant to your target market and the layout should make it obvious where the visitor needs to go and what the visitor needs to do.

Visitors to your site want information and resources that will assist them in their work and their lives. If they can't find what they need, they'll get frustrated with your site and with you. The result is a lost connection. Make your site easy to navigate and easy to use, and you'll establish an immediate rapport with your visitors because they will feel that you already know and understand them.

4.16.1 Written Exercise: Consider the home page of your website. Who is coming to this page (potential client, current client, past client, referral partner, or the press, for example)?

4.16.2 Written Exercise: Consider the home page of your website. What do you want the visitor to do (opt in to a newsletter so they can get access to a special report, sign up for the webinar that is your always-have-something-to-invite-people-to offer, and so forth)?

4.16.3 Written Exercise: Consider the home page of your website. Now that you know what you want the visitor to do, how are you going to get them to do it (with a compelling true story in your copywriting or in a video, or maybe a free report, and so on)?

4.16.4 Written Exercise: Now repeat the previous three steps for each page of your website (if you have one). If you are in the process of building your website, complete these exercises for each page of the site as you build it.

Website Basics   Your website can make you look like a superstar, offering valuable content, experiences, and opportunities for your target market. With a professional, up-to-date modern design, and loads of great content that serves your target market, you will position yourself as an expert and the go-to person in your field.

As challenging as the journey to website success may seem right now, you might be pleasantly surprised that the work you've already done in the book has set you up for success. Your website is your opportunity to decide and control how you're known. Your tagline boldly expresses why you do what you do. Your site should speak to the values of your ideal clients and demonstrate how dedicated you are to your target market, their needs and desires, the number one biggest result that you help them get, along with the financial, emotional, physical, and spiritual benefits they will receive from investing their time with you.

Your website also demonstrates your platform and helps you build trust and credibility. Also, each of the Six Core Self-Promotion Strategies can be integrated into the way you promote and use your site. Your website can help you start a conversation with a potential client by offering free information products or experiences for new potential clients, and it's an effective way to introduce them to your sales cycle so you can build trust over time. Your site is an avenue through which you can offer various pricing incentives for your products and services, leading to super simple sales conversations with ideal clients.

Here are some specific ideas of how you can integrate the Book Yourself Solid Six Core Self-Promotion Strategies right into your site:

- *Networking Strategy:* You can invite people to join you on various social network platforms where you're active. You can also use it to connect with new people every day through your subscriber list, blog posts, and "contact me" forms.
- *Direct Outreach Strategy:* You can use direct outreach to get to know others in your field by commenting on their posts and also asking them if you can reprint some of their blog posts. You can even offer to write posts for them to publish on their blogs. Not only is your website a great tool for starting conversations with potential clients but also it's a great way to start conversations with influencers in your

industry. It's often the first thing a potential business associate will review when they are evaluating you and your relevance to them.

- *Referral Strategy:* You can implement the referral strategy by writing blog posts or articles that refer to another colleague who can help your clients with a particular problem they may be having for which you are not the expert. Or you can create a resource page in which you profile various referral partners. Your newsletter is another opportunity to offer referrals.

- *Speaking Strategy:* You can advertise your webinars, classes, and events on your site. You can also feature your podcast through your website.

- *Writing Strategy:* A blog can be integrated into your site and you can have a page with articles that help position you as an expert in your field.

By integrating the Six Core Self-Promotion Strategies into your site, you will attract potential clients with whom you will build trust, and who will ultimately become ideal, life-fulfilling, and career-making clients.

The Seven Most Effective Website Home Page Formats for Coaches

The Brochure   A brochure website is usually about five pages and is the online equivalent of a written brochure. It's the most common format of website for the coach. Generally, a brochure website includes information about you, your services, and some resources, for starters.

The risk you take when using this format is that it can appear to be all about you rather than the people you serve, and if you aren't creative, your website may not look much different from every other coach's website.

The Email Converter   The email converter format—aka the squeeze page, or landing page, or lead magnet page—is the ultimate one-step website. There's only one thing to do on an email converter web page—give your email address in exchange for something of value, like a special report or white paper, a mini-course, or access to your always-have-something-to-invite-people-to offer. You must have a very compelling offer right out front that prompts visitors to engage because you've got only one shot at getting that all-important email address.

Just be careful with a site like this. You may capture email addresses that help you build a list of subscribers, but some people will be put off by this type of website. Essentially, you're asking for something before you give anything. By now, you probably get that the Book Yourself Solid way is to give first before you ask for something in return. Feel free to test it out and see how your target market and ideal clients respond. That's the true indicator of any marketing tactic—how the people you serve respond to it, what results does it produce, and how do those to whom you are marketing feel about the tactic?

You will need a tool that allows you to capture email addresses and automatically send customers a confirmation and follow-up with delivery of the value in exchange. There are many programs that will help you do this:

- Convertkit.com
- ActiveCampaign.com
- ConstantContact.com
- AWeber.com
- MailChimp.com
- Keap.com
- Hubspot.com

Some are full-service customer relationship management systems that integrate payments, marketing, website building, community and project management tools. Others just focus on email. If you're just starting out, you may do better with one of the simpler email-only solutions. They're simpler to operate and more affordable as well.

The One-Page Sales Letter   A one-page sales letter is designed specifically to encourage buying a product, program, or service. You may have come across one-page sales letters that you found hyped up, over-the-top, and all about the hard sell.

That's not who you are, so your one-page sales letter won't come off that way. Remember, all of your marketing must be designed to speak to your target market. If your target market responds to hyped-up, over-the-top, and hard-sell marketing messages, well then, that's what you'll use. I have a feeling, though, that that's not the case with you. The reason so many online marketers use the long form one-page sales letter is that when it's done well, it's a good tool for selling products. It is designed to elicit a direct response from the reader. Long-form one-page sales letters work well because they're not really meant to be read in their entirety. They're designed to be scanned. That's why they often boast big colorful headlines and bullets and bold text and highlighted text, for example. The important point here is this: know your market and how they'll respond to this type of sales page.

The Assessment   Offering an assessment that speaks directly to the urgent needs and compelling desires of your target market is a wonderful way to create an immediate connection and help your potential clients assess how much they actually need your services. Assessments can be created in the form of a quiz, survey, or personal profile. They're effective because they're interactive, they engage the client, and they invite a qualifying action. To receive answers to the assessment would require the assessment takers to enter an email address. The entire process can be automated, and you can create new assessments or quizzes to have on your website to draw repeat visitors back to your site.

The Blog   A blog originated simply as an online diary. It has become so much more than that. Most recent entries appear on the home page of the blog. Older entries, known as *archives*, are organized by date and often categorized by topic. Most blogs offer the reader the opportunity to post comments, share the post on other social media platforms, as well as rate the post. As opposed to static websites, blogs are appealing to readers (and search engines alike) because they are instantly updatable, offering fresh, timely, and relevant content. Of course, you can integrate a blog into any other of these other types of sites. The biggest drawback to a blog is that it works only if you post to it regularly.

The Social Network   Social networking is the grouping of individuals into specific groups, like a political or religious group or people who collect model trains. Certainly, social networking can be, and always has been, organized in person. Now we do it online more often. Hundreds of millions of people are online, and they are looking to meet others that share their interests and can offer advice, support, or connections about golf, basket weaving, entrepreneurship, swimming, parenting, addiction, and more. When you want to organize people online you can use a type of website typically referred to as a social network platform. It functions like a community center with places for discussions and posting of information, pictures, video, and more. When a new person is granted access to the community, they can usually set up a profile and immediately begin to socialize.

The social network website format is a generous and effective way to stand in the service of the community you wish to serve. It's free and enables the people you serve to connect and collaborate.

Basically, you can create your own community but specifically for your target audience. Your smaller, but not necessarily less powerful, site will serve the personal and professional needs of your clients and will be an effective tool for you to build relationships with potential clients as the leader of the community. Or, simply use the most established social media platforms to host your community. You don't own it but because your target audience is already there, they don't have to go far to find you. For example, I'm a boater and host a private Facebook group for other people who own the same brand of boat as I do. I don't do it for financial reasons, and it has nothing to do with my business, but it's a lovely way to meet other people with similar interests. And, we use Facebook groups for both the Book Yourself Solid and Heroic Public Speaking businesses as well. They are incredibly effective for creating a sense of community in the way we serve our clients.

The Personal Brand Identity Site   If you're promoting your personal brand rather than the brand of a company, you may want to consider this format. I created one for myself at MichaelPort.com. It's one page that demonstrates what I do, what I stand for, and whom I serve. It's really pretty simple. It displays the books I've written and the businesses I own. When a visitor is interested in one of the businesses they click on a button that opens a new browser window and sends them to that site.

4.16.5 Written Exercise: Go online and find three or four websites you like and three or four that you dislike. List the formats they use and the features you like and dislike, and why. These will be useful as examples of what you want—and don't want—to show to your designer. If possible, choose websites for this exercise that provide services to your target market and note what they're offering and how they present their offering. This will give you a sense of what's already out there and may spark new ideas.

What to Look for in a Web Designer

When I started my business, I spent over $6,000 on a website with lots of funky animation that I never used—or I should say, I used it for five months to no avail. The site may have looked cool, but it wasn't effective because it was all Flash-based and all about what I did rather than what I could do for my clients. I learned pretty quickly to look for a web designer who is proficient in all three of the critical skills of web design: design, marketing, and programming. I encourage you to do the same. Web design is becoming more democratic with many tools and hosts offering templates and drag-and-drop interfaces. But if you are not a designer, please enlist a professional to help you. You will thank me later.

Now you know how you want to *design* your website. Next up is how to get people to *land (and stay)* on your website. You're in the right place. Turn the page and you'll be on your way to traffic school—where you'll learn how to drive traffic, quickly (and safely), to your site.

PART 2

GETTING VISITORS TO YOUR WEBSITE

*I think the internet is uniquely suited to this free
market idea . . . we all need each other.*
—Pete Ashdown

Here is where we look at how to create a steady flow of traffic to your site and how to convert that traffic into business, a process that's called *generating traffic*. I'll cover the most important and easy-to-understand, tried-and-true techniques and strategies for generating more traffic to your site, along with the two essential principles of *visitor conversion*, so that when someone does visit your site, they give you permission to keep in touch (market to them).

Optimize Your Site

Search engine optimization (SEO) is all about how to get the search engines to notice your site and, ideally, to give you a good ranking. Then, when someone searches for what you're offering, your listing will be displayed in a high position in the search results. SEO is a big topic. Entire books are written about it so I'll touch on only the basics, and if you choose to make SEO a primary traffic generation strategy, I trust that you'll continue your learning elsewhere.

As the sheer amount of content on the internet expands by millions of bits and bytes every day, SEO is a game that is increasingly tough to "win";

however, a basic understanding of how the search engines index and read your site is excellent to have so that you're not losing out on potential traffic.

Make sure your site is optimized with the best keywords, that is, words or phrases that your target market types into the search engine to find what you provide, along with the proper metadata, including descriptive keyword–rich page names. Because every search engine has different criteria for ranking websites, and none of them actually want you to know what these criteria are, the most effective strategy for search engine optimization is to build content-rich pages that your visitors want to see, pages that are legitimately filled with the same keywords and phrases they use to search for what you are offering.

How do you determine what keywords and phrases will help you drive the most traffic? You focus on the urgent needs and compelling desires of your target market. What would a potential client type into a search engine to find what they're looking for? The best keywords and phrases are the emotional, benefit-filled terms that do the following:

- They have the most number of searches.
- They have the least amount of competition.
- They draw targeted traffic that is ready, willing, and able to invest in your services.

In fact, there are a number of tools that tell you exactly how many people are searching on your chosen keywords and phrases. Google offers a free keyword search tool. To find it, just search on Google for "Google Keyword Planner." When you find the right keywords and phrases for your site, optimize your site using these same words and phrases. Understanding your best keywords is essential for the success of all your online marketing.

4.16.6 Written Exercise: Identify the top five keywords and phrases for your site.

Leverage Your Email Signature   One of the most often overlooked methods of promoting your services is through your email signature. This is the information that you put at the close of your email. It's a simple and effective way to tell people about what you have to offer and to encourage them to sign up for your newsletter or any other no-barrier-to-entry offer that you make.

You could consider asking a question in your signature and include a link to your site where the answer to the question will be waiting.

4.16.7 Booked Solid Action Step: Create a compelling email signature and begin using it immediately.

Participate in Online Communities   There are hundreds of thousands, if not millions, of groups online discussing the issues of the day: discussion boards, forums, social networks, and others. Getting involved in the communities in which your target market hangs out offers you an opportunity to become a leader of the community by offering advice, support, and any other value. Many of these communities give you the opportunity to create a profile that displays your bio, email address, website address, and more. When you make a (good) name for yourself in a community made up of your target market, members of that community will be compelled to visit your website to learn more about you and how you are able to serve them. You find these groups by searching Google. Input the various keywords and key phrases that your target market would use to find communities built on their industry, situation, needs, and so on.

4.16.8 Booked Solid Action Step: Find the most active online communities that serve your target market and are focused on topics you know a lot about. As a member of the group, you can make intelligent, thoughtful posts that add value to the discussion topic. You might answer other members' questions or you might suggest helpful resources or simply provide your opinions on issues that relate to your industry. And you never know—you may learn a lot by reading what others have to say.

Cross-Promote Through Marketing Partners This is one of my favorite online marketing strategies because it enables me to partner with, and promote, other people I think are fabulous while they do the same for me. We've talked about how important it is to get other people to talk about you so you can quickly build trust with new potential clients. Well, cross-promoting through marketing partners is the best way to do so.

If my colleague sends out an email to their newsletter subscribers endorsing my services, products, or programs, those subscribers are more likely to trust me. When I promote my colleague, the same will be true. It makes it much easier to build relationships with potential clients that way. It's just like meeting a great friend of a great friend of yours. You love your friend, and if your friend loves that person, you assume that person is great. The same goes for cross-promoting online (and offline).

You can cross-promote like this on many levels: between you and another coach who happens to serve the same target market or with larger associations and organizations. If you're a business coach who serves small business owners, and you develop a relationship with the membership director for a small business association that has 75,000 members, and they promote your services to their membership, just think about all of the newsletter sign-ups you can get. And just think about all of these new potential clients who turn into actual clients. The possibilities are limitless.

Here are some other strategies to consider:

- Co-produce special promotions you could not afford on your own.
- Have a contest with the prizes contributed by your partners. For the next contest, roles change, and you contribute your product or service as a prize for a partner's contest.
- Give clients a free product or service from a participating partner when they buy something that month from all of the partners listed on a promotional piece.

Online cross-promotion has the potential for a big marketing payoff because partners can successfully expand through one another's client base. Both you and your marketing partners can gain an inexpensive and credible introduction to more potential clients more effectively than with the traditional lone-wolf methods of networking, advertising, or public relations.

4.16.9 Written Exercise: Come up with several of your own unique ideas for cross-promotions and identify who might be a good marketing partner.

4.16.10 Booked Solid Action Step: Reach out, connect with, and share your ideas with the people you identified in the preceding exercise.

Use Tell-a-Friend Forms A significant percentage of your clients will come from referrals. If your current raving fans are telling others about you offline, don't you think they would like to tell others about you online as well? Well, they can with a tell-a-friend form. Imagine that a visitor to your site likes what they see and believes they have a friend who could benefit from your services, too. People use social sharing buttons regularly—Facebook, LinkedIn, and so on, but with a click on your tell-a-friend link, they can refer your site directly to that friend. You can even customize it so that it automatically sends a personalized email promoting your site and its web address.

It's an amazingly simple and effective strategy. Again, you're getting others to talk about you and help build trust between you and a potential client.

4.16.11 Booked Solid Action Step: Create, or hire someone to create, a tell-a-friend form and begin using it.

Take Advantage of Online Press Releases The internet has unleashed so many new opportunities to connect with your target market and get free publicity online. Online press releases are one marketing tactic often underused, yet effective for increasing web traffic. Online publicity opportunities can improve your site's search engine ranking while, at the same time, enhance your credibility and increase exposure to media outlets.

Consider using online press releases to do the following:

- Increase traffic to your website quickly (usually within 24 to 48 hours).
- Boost your credibility—it increases the know, like, and trust factors.
- Make you stand out from the crowd because it's a marketing tactic that few coaches use.
- Deliver traffic for months and years to come because online press releases are permanently indexed by search engines.

So, what's the difference between an online press release and an offline press release? When a small business has news, online press releases are the fastest and easiest way for the media to find them. Sites like PRWeb.com and PRNewswire.com take your press release and place your news directly on leading sites like Yahoo! News, Google News, Ask.com, and other sites, which reach hundreds of thousands of news subscribers and media publications, including bloggers, journalists, and consumers. Online press releases can increase traffic to your website and increase your search engine rankings. For small business owners, PRWeb.com is by far the most feature-rich and affordable service. (Please note: I have no financial or personal connection to this service.)

Your press release must be well written and targeted. To optimize your press release for online distribution, use keywords for your business throughout the body of the press release so that when someone does a search on your business or topic, your press release shows up prominently in search engines. Keywords should be used in the headline, subtitle, and body of the release.

If you're not a writer, you can easily outsource press release writing to a freelance writer or PR agency. Many sites have press release distribution services (some may require a waiting time of 24 to 48 hours), most have a fee, but some offer various free options as well.

Another useful tool is an online press kit. You can add a page to your website titled "Press Kit" or "Media Resources." The page should include a personal bio, company bio, any press releases written, article placements, and a professional photo of key business personnel. In addition to adding a page to your website, you can also host your press kit with online press page services. Journalists and bloggers frequently visit these sites for story ideas and interviews.

> **4.16.12 Booked Solid Action Step:** Write a press release about the most impressive result one of your clients achieved and submit it to PRWeb.com. You can get tips at the site on how to craft a solid press release.

Profit from Pay-per-Click Advertising   Using pay-per-click ads on search engines can be an effective marketing tool. Pay-per-click means that you pay a fee for each person who clicks on the ad. You may be surprised to realize that this is the first time I've mentioned spending money on advertising. Until now our other online strategies haven't cost much besides time. You should not be spending much, if any, money online to generate traffic. But if you want to speed things up, or if you have more money than time, then this is a great way to get targeted exposure for a small investment with the potential for a big return.

Paid advertising is a complex beast, and unless you have the time and inclination to learn how to create and manage online advertising campaigns on your own (which can be a full time job), I'd encourage you to find an advertising agency that comes highly recommended by your peers, that specializes in coaching businesses of your level, and that suits your budget.

It's also important to note that advertising platforms, the features that they offer, and even the legislation that surrounds online advertising is in a state of permanent flux. What is true today may not even be possible tomorrow, which is even more reason to work with professionals if you want to put your money to play to generate visitors to your site.

The most common form of online advertising is called pay-per-click (PPC). Pay-per-click advertising means that you will make an offer (bid) on how much you are prepared to pay for somebody to visit your website. You can target visitors either according to what they are doing (often called *search intent*) or who they are and what they are interested in, for example, the city where they live, the groceries they buy, the car they drive, and where they spend their time online.

Google and Meta are the largest PPC advertising companies at the moment, but they are far from the only players. They will serve your ads to their visitors on the various platforms they own and on third-party websites, where your target market will be most likely to interact with your ads and click through to your website.

Then, when the visitor arrives on your website, and because you have very carefully worked out who they are, what you want them to do, and how you're going to get them to do it, a certain number of them will (hopefully) do exactly what you want them to do.

This is where measurement and math become critically important. Let's imagine that you are selling a $97 mini-course and you have a daily budget of $100 for advertising. Over the space of one day, your advertising attracts 20 visitors to your page, and 1 of those visitors buys your course. Congratulations! You've made a $3 profit.

But the next day, you get another 20 visitors for another $100, and nobody buys. So you're down $97 across two days.

Or another scenario: You run a campaign to get people to sign up for a valuable free information product. You spend $100 and of the 20 visitors to your page, 5 of them join your mailing list, and 1 of them buys your $297 online course a day later. You're temporarily in the money!

Of course, these are simplistic examples and don't take retargeting, custom audiences, pixels, testing, machine learning, and campaign tweaking into consideration, all of which will be carefully considered by a good agency.

But advertising can be volatile and requires very strict monitoring and measurement. If you can crack the code and turn $1 into $2 over a time frame that you're comfortable with, then that's a wonderful position to be in. But all advertisers will tell you: it works until it doesn't, and continuous vigilance is required.

So my advice is this: if you are in a position to do some marketing experiments with paid advertising without suffering financial hardship, then go for it, with the right support and guidance.

Spending money rather than time and energy on client attraction can be a very attractive and sensible option for the time-poor coach who's got a solid financial foundation. But you don't need to run advertising to get booked solid, that I can tell you for sure.

The Two Essential Principles of Visitor Conversion

You want to attract visitors to your website and turn them into friends, then potential clients, and finally, current clients. You can generate all the traffic you want, but if that traffic does not want to stay or come back and get more information, advice, or resources from you in the future, it's not doing much good.

There are two essential principles of visitor conversion: enticement and consumption. Understand them, implement them, and profit from them, but never abuse them.

Enticement   Your website is like your home. What's the first thing you do when someone comes to visit? You offer a drink and a bite to eat. You ask, "Are you hungry? Can I get you something to eat? How about a glass of water or some iced tea?" If you know your visitors well, you can offer them their *favorite* snack and beverage. In fact, when family or close friends come to visit, you make an extra trip to the supermarket to get all their favorites.

This is the principle of *enticement.* You offer something of value to your website visitors as soon as they land on your site in exchange for their email address and permission to follow up. They give it to you because they're interested in your enticement, and they believe you'll deliver more good stuff in the days and months to come.

Be careful not to hide your enticing offers in the crevices of your website. When you have a dinner party, do you hide the food around the house in strange places or set it just out of reach? Of course you don't. You put the hors d'oeuvres and munchies in the most obvious, accessible places possible. And sure enough, the places you put the hors d'oeuvres are exactly where everybody ends up hanging out! Have you ever been at a party where the host skimped on the hors d'oeuvres? Did you find that everybody started hanging around the kitchen as they got hungrier and hungrier? We're always searching for what we want and need, and your website needs to speak to your visitors' needs and desires. So please, put your opt-in form in the most obvious place possible. I suggest you place it above the fold (the part of your home page that is visible without having to scroll down).

4.16.13 Booked Solid Action Step: If you don't already have an e-course, special report, or other enticement to offer your visitors, create one using the easy steps I outlined in Chapter 8. Then ensure that you have an opt-in feature for your offer displayed prominently on your site.

Consumption   The principle of consumption follows the principle of enticement. When your visitors have been enticed and have given you their email address in exchange for a mini-course, white paper, special report, e-book, article, audio recording, or other free offer, you must follow up to help them consume the valuable information or experience they just received. Most people don't take advantage of all the opportunities available to them. It would probably be impossible to do so. An even smaller number of people follow up on all of the opportunities available to them through the internet and email, even the ones they've asked for. When someone does opt in to receive your free offer, they may not really consume it—use it, learn from it, and benefit from it. It's your responsibility to help them do so by following up with an email.

Does it sound like it would be a lot of work? Oh, no, my big-thinking friend, it's not. You can use an automatic email responder system to set up a series of email messages that are automatically sent to a new contact at any frequency you specify. You can send one a day, one a week, or one a month for a year—it's up to you. Your messages will check in with your new friend and begin to deliver the services you provide or other helpful resources.

The principle of consumption should follow the principle of enticement. It's just as you would ask your guest, the one you generously supplied with their favorite snack and beverage, "How is the tea? Is it cold enough? Would you like more ice? Is it helping quench your thirst?" Maybe you'd offer a suggestion, "You know . . . if you squeeze the lemon like so, it tastes even better." You'll ask your new friends how they're doing with the information you gave them, and you'll help them consume it. If you do this well, you'll increase your likeability, and you'll create a more meaningful and lasting connection with your new friends, turning them from new friends into potential clients or maybe even into current clients.

4.16.14 Booked Solid Action Step: If you don't already have an autoresponder system to help potential clients consume your offer, set one up right now.

Okay, take a break. Take a walk. Take it easy. Then, come on back as we move into part 3 of the Book Yourself Solid Web Strategy: building your social media platform.

PART 3

BUILDING YOUR SOCIAL MEDIA PLATFORM

The internet is becoming the town square for the global village of tomorrow.

—Bill Gates

Social media sites come and go. Two decades ago, when I wrote the first edition of *Book Yourself Solid*, Ryze was one of the most popular business networking sites on the internet. You've probably never even heard of Ryze. Why? Because it got wrecked, never to rise again. So, it's important to understand the principles that support successful social networking and personal platform building (how well you're known) before you focus on any particular platform.

There is so much conflicting noise about the necessity of social media, and there are so many shiny attractions promising overnight success if you just use this one new social media toy. More important, however, is to tie your web strategy back to Module Two—establishing oneself as a category authority, building trust and credibility, leading back into the sales cycle process and keep-in-touch strategy.

What most folks miss in the midst of all the noise is that social media (and the greater web) is just a tool. Many people obsess over getting lots of likes, followers, and views. They miss the critically important concept that your followers are not your email subscribers, and as a consequence, they fail to build a real community, a real tribe, and wonder why they aren't getting the traction they want and deserve.

255

In previous editions of *Book Yourself Solid,* I attempted to detail all the ins and outs of how to use Facebook, LinkedIn, and X. However, they just change too quickly to keep the information current. So, for this edition of the book, I'm going to focus on the big picture. If you understand what makes someone popular on any of these sites, you can transfer and apply that understanding to any other social media site so you can play to your heart's delight.

Like all relationship and platform development, when your focus comes to social media or online social networking, you must be willing to make a long-term commitment to the cause if you want to see long-term positive results. And, contrary to some expert advice, I don't believe in outsourcing your social media marketing to an assistant or outside firm—especially when you're just starting out. Sure, get help with the technical aspects of organizing a Facebook page or LinkedIn profile, if you need it, but if you really want to build your social network online, you've got to show up to do it. I mean *social* is the operative word here. And really . . . how hard can that be? You don't even have to leave your house. You just need to make the time for it. And, as you know, we need to make the time to do our marketing to earn clients. *Earn* is the operative word.

The Goal Is Marketing

When you do build a large platform of fans or followers on whatever social media platform is the site du jour while you're reading this, over time, you'll be able to turn your networking and publishing efforts into marketing initiatives that drive sales.

Social media platforms primarily allow for both publishing and networking. You can choose to publish and broadcast new content that you have created, you can choose to interact with other users, or you can choose to do both. There is a growing school of thought that argues that all coaches (and other small business owners) should also be publishing new multimedia content to position themselves as thought leaders on a regular basis.

This is not true. Many very successful coaches don't use social media for anything other than keeping tabs on their grandchildren or finding new dinner recipes. They network and practice direct outreach online and offline, and that is more than enough to fill their client roster. However, if you like the idea of being a regular publisher on social media, and you find it joyful and rewarding, then please be my guest. You will certainly attract new leads and visitors to your website if you are consistent.

Your return on investment on social media is both quantitative and qualitative. You are likely to see more leads for new clients and increased profit and, at the same time, enhance your brand identity through positive, professional, and valuable interaction with and service to your community, industry, or field.

Historically, traditional media was controlled by professional news organizations and their advertisers. As you know, online media, along with social media, is more democratized. Issues, ideas, and discussions are driven by public discourse more than they have been in the past. There are both positive and negative consequences associated with this change.

For this section of the chapter, I assume two things: First, that you have already done the work on building your Book Yourself Solid foundation. Second, I assume that you have a basic knowledge of social media. You're probably active on one or all of the most popular social media platforms. Social media enables a coach to make a large presence within a very short time. Social media makes it possible for you to reach out to the most prominent figures in your field. It can accelerate the process of gaining credibility and trust—all for little or no cost.

Most of these platforms smoothly interface with your website, blog, and even other social media platforms. Your blog posts can be instantly pushed onto your social media pages, and your social media posts on platform A can be automatically distributed to your followers on platform B.

All of this is great but . . . yes, there's a but . . . you may actually be spending too much time on social media platforms for very little return on your time investment. Generally, I don't need to encourage people to use social media more. On the contrary in fact, I very often encourage folks to pull back. Spending a little time on each of the different platforms takes up a lot of time in total but often disperses your efforts and waters down any chance of building a real presence. However, focusing your efforts on one platform—one that you enjoy and is filled with your target audience—is often a better and faster way to build an audience when you're starting out.

Instead of allocating 10 minutes a day to five different sites, use the same time building up a community and a following on one site where you focus your efforts.

How you choose where to focus is entirely personal. When I was more active on social media I preferred Facebook, because that's where my target market would hang out and I enjoyed our interactions. I had close to 25,000 followers on X at one point, even though I didn't spend any time there. I found it completely unsatisfying for a host of reasons.

Whichever platform you find most rewarding is the platform where you should spend most of your time growing your footprint. Just don't waste your time watching cat videos and call it marketing.

As a teacher, I attempt to help my students understand how to behave in a given situation, culture, or environment and how things fit together (context). Identifying (and then learning to master) the important details is pretty easy once you know what you're looking for. How to do something becomes pretty easy once you know the rules, how it works, and how the pieces fit together. You can see the pieces more easily if you know what you're looking for.

I encourage you to focus on the big picture of social media and how you're going to use it before getting worried about all the clever little marketing hacks you think you're supposed to be doing on these platforms.

Don't Mix the Personal with the Professional

It's lovely that you can make personal connections with potential clients, current clients, and colleagues on social media. However, get clear on what you feel is appropriate to share. Yes, share your interests and some of your family life. People like to know who you are and what you value. However, in my humble opinion—and this is my opinion only—others will take a different approach—keep your political and personal issues off the social media channels that you use for business purposes.

If your brand is based on taking provocative positions—religious, political, or otherwise—then fine, fire away with fierce posts. But, sometimes, it's hard to strike the right balance, to mix the right amount of personal and business sharing. It's a good idea to keep a separate, completely private profile exclusively for friends and family so that you can post anything you please. Then, have a separate page or profile where you are your professional self. Be personal in the way that you interact with people, share your knowledge, network, and compassion, but be above the fray of unnecessary conflict-oriented subjects.

Plus, if you have any desire to build a coaching business that is sellable to someone else in your field or transferable to your children someday, then keeping your personal and business profiles separate on all the platforms might be a good idea.

How to Use the Book Yourself Solid System on Social Media

Almost every aspect of the Book Yourself Solid system can be used on social media once you have done the work on your foundation:

1. *Who knows what you know and do they like you?* One of the most powerful uses of social media is to showcase your expertise in your field. You are able to list your qualifications in your profiles. By making frequent valuable posts to the sites, people get to know what you know. All the social media platforms have the ability to accelerate the process of gaining credibility.

2. *Book Yourself Solid Sales Cycle process:* By being actively engaged with prospective and active clients on social media, they know that they can find you there and what you can do for them. Since you know who is online among your friends or followers, you can connect through a real-time conversation. By having information that is salient to your target market, you can make your profiles "sticky" through content-rich, informative, interesting posts that invite interaction. Social media can also provide the platform for sales conversations (when the time is right) for those who are following you. You can also announce your always-have-something-to-invite-people-to event on your platform of choice. The key is to motivate people to go to your website and subscribe to your mailing list. If you can do that, you can market to them appropriately, moving them through your sales cycle process.

3. *The power of information products:* It is very easy to promote your information products on social media. Again, you can direct people to your website for your free information product in exchange for their email address or other contact information.

4. *Super simple selling:* Facebook enables you to have many interactions with people and gives them easy access to you when they want to reach you. Because you can connect, you are able to have real-time sales conversations right when it counts.

5. *Networking strategy:* All of the platforms make it easy to share your network, knowledge, and compassion with others.

6. *Direct outreach:* Because social media enables so many connections, it can be easier through social media to meet people you wish to get to know. However, it is very important to note that when you do reach out, do it with a message that introduces yourself and recognizes the person for their accomplishments. Never send a message to someone you do not know asking them to do something for you. I know I've said this before.

7. *Referral strategy:* Social media makes it easy to not only give referrals to others, but to promote others' efforts. One of the best ways to get others to help you promote your business is for you to promote their business.

8. *Keep in touch:* All social platforms make it easy to stay in touch. You can easily send messages or engage in a chat.

9. *Speaking and demonstrating:* You can hold streaming events and you can promote your webinars or live events. Your podcast or YouTube channel can make your name as a speaker and thought leader.

10. *Writing:* Some platforms are designed to give you a phenomenal platform for writing. Not only can you write short posts that inform your audience of what you do, but you can also write long-form articles, provide information of value, and write posts that encourage interaction. Writing on these sites will enhance your credibility and help position you as an expert in your field.

11. *Web strategy:* All the social platforms easily interface with your website for generating and converting traffic.

Social Media: Pulling It All Together

If you are serious about adding social media to your self-promotion strategy, consider starting with a plan and schedule time in your day to devote to your chosen platforms. Effective use of social media requires consistency and commitment. Results are not always apparent right away. Give your social media plan three to six months to start working.

Social media expert Nancy Marmelejo suggests that the return on investment for social media is threefold:

- Return on interaction
- Return on involvement
- Return on investment

Return on interaction and involvement speak directly to the time you put into finding ideally matched followers and turning them into raving fans. These fans are the ones who gladly and voluntarily do your marketing for you. Return on investment starts coming in when your loyal legion of followers also become email subscribers and start responding to your offers at different stages of your sales cycle. Your interactions and involvement transform followers into folks who are ready to buy.

Start using social media by developing your own routine.

Daily
- Post your updates a minimum of once a day.
- Schedule 15 to 20 minutes of time in your calendar each day to post and monitor your social networks.
- Get involved in relevant discussions, conversations, and respond to direct messages and invitations.

Twice a Week
- If you are using social platforms for publishing, consider posting new content, whether in video, audio, or text format, once or twice a week.
- Your content can be repurposed for different platforms. For example, you can take an edited transcript from your podcast and reproduce it in your newsletter.

Posting, publishing, networking, commenting, broadcasting—sometimes it can all sound so exhausting. "Do I have to?" a little voice in your head continues to protest. No, you don't, as I said at the outset of this chapter. Perhaps you have the kind of business that can flourish without social media. Great. But, for many of us, an online strategy is important and effective, and using a social media platform to its fullest helps us reach our goals more quickly, plus, maybe it's not nearly as daunting as it might seem at first. Why? Because being social about what you love to do (that is, your business) is not that hard. In fact, it can be downright inspiring to connect with others and share what you know. After all, if you love to serve your target audience, what could be better than serving them better, faster, and more easily. The internet is your friend. Use it to make more friends. And more money.

Final Thoughts

This is not the end. It is not even the beginning of the end.
It is, perhaps, the end of the beginning.
—Sir Winston Churchill

Wow. You just read over 91,000 words. I imagine it took considerable time and effort. That demonstrates commitment and the pursuit of mastery. The Book Yourself Solid system is provoking, challenging, sometimes scary, often exciting, and always powerful. The rewards you reap as a result of all your hard work will be well worth the time and effort you've devoted to this process. I hope you'll take the time now to acknowledge all that you've done because it's no small task. In fact, it's really big. We've covered a lot of ground, and you stuck with me, step-by-step, from beginning to end. Not everyone can say that.

You now know who your ideal clients are and how to ensure that you're working only with those who most inspire and energize you. You've identified the target market you feel passionate about serving, as well as what their most urgent needs and compelling desires are, and what investable opportunities to offer to them. You've developed a personal brand that is memorable, has meaning for you, and is uniquely yours, and you know how to articulate whom you serve and how you serve them in a way that is intriguing rather than boring and bland.

You've begun thinking of yourself as the expert you are. You're continuing to enhance your knowledge to better serve your market, and you understand the importance of your likeability factor. You know how to develop a complete sales cycle that will enable you to build trust with those you want to serve. You've learned how to begin developing the brand-building products and programs that are a key part of that sales cycle, how to price your products and services, and how to have sincere and successful sales conversations with your potential clients.

You are networking with others in a way that is genuine and comfortable, and you've learned how to build a website that will get results, how to reach out to others in a personal and effective way, how to generate a wealth of referrals, how to use speaking and writing to reach more of your potential clients, and then how to keep in touch with the multitude of potential clients you'll connect with when implementing all of the Book Yourself Solid Core Self-Promotion Strategies.

Everything you've learned is important, but even more important is to remember the philosophy that underlies the entire Book Yourself Solid system: there are people you are *meant* to serve, and they are out there waiting for you. When you find them, remember to give so much value that you think you've given too much, and then be sure to give them more.

I mentioned at the beginning of our journey that the people who don't book themselves solid either don't know what to do or do know what to do but aren't doing it. You now know exactly what to do. There are no more excuses, no more reasons to procrastinate or drag your feet, or hide in your office.

The question now is what are you going to do with what you've learned? Throughout the course of this book I've given you written exercises and Booked Solid Action Steps that can earn you more clients than you can handle. Have you been doing them throughout the book? If you have, fantastic, keep going. If you haven't, are you going to start doing them right now? Your success hinges on your continued action.

To that end, at www.BookYourselfSolid.com, you can continue to get support and advice about all of the concepts I've laid out in this book. This may be the end of this book, but that doesn't have to mean the end of our work together. Your business is a generative and iterative process. You will be changing and evolving as you adapt to the ebb and flow of your growing booked-solid business, and I look forward to continuing to serve you in the best and most effective ways I can. You might want to read one of my other books like *Steal the Show* if you're interested in improving your public speaking.

I sincerely thank you for spending this time with me by learning the Book Yourself Solid system. It means so much to me that you've taken the time out of your busy schedule to read this book. It's not really mine anymore. It's yours now. I am simply honored to serve you. I hope these principles, strategies, techniques, and tips make a true difference in your life and in the lives of those you serve.

I hope the Book Yourself Solid path helps you to look in the mirror every morning and have a mad, passionate love affair with yourself, do the work that you love to do, and book yourself solid while standing in the service of others and making a difference in their lives.

I love you very much (and not in a weird way).

Think Big,

Michael Port
MichaelPort.com
questions@michaelport.com
P.S. I don't charge for typos; they're my gift to you.

References

Baer, Jay. 2016. *Hug Your Haters*. New York: Portfolio.

Bayan, Richard. 1984. *Words That Sell*. Chicago: McGraw-Hill Contemporary Books.

Brewer, Robert Lee. 2021. *Writer's Market 100th Edition*. Cincinnati: Writer's Digest Books.

Collins, Jim. 2001. *Good to Great: Why Some Companies Make the Leap and Others Don't*. New York: HarperCollins.

Covey, Dr. Stephen. 1989. *The 7 Habits of Highly Successful People*. New York: Simon & Schuster.

Crum, Thomas F. 1987. *The Magic of Conflict: Turning Your Life of Work into a Work of Art*. New York: Touchstone.

Curtis, Glade B., and Judith Schuler. 2004. *Your Pregnancy Week by Week*. Cambridge, MA: Da Capo Press.

Godin, Seth. 1999. *Permission Marketing*. New York: Simon & Schuster.

_____. 2004. *Free Prize Inside! The Next Big Marketing Idea*. New York: Penguin Group.

Goleman, Daniel. 2017. *Social Intelligence: The New Science of Human Relationships*. New York: Bantam.

Hogshead, Sally. 2016. *Fascinate*. New York: Harper Business.

Jantsch, John. 2010. *Duct Tape Marketing*. Nashville: Thomas Nelson.

Levinson, Jay Conrad, and David Perry. 2005. *Guerrilla Marketing for Job Hunters*. Hoboken, NJ: John Wiley & Sons.

Meyerson, Mitch. 2005. *Success Secrets of the Online Marketing Superstars*. Chicago: Dearborn Trade Publishing.

Michalowicz, Mike. 2017. *Profit First*. New York: Portfolio.

Mitchell, H. 2017. *Wimbledon Wisdom: Every Good Deal Has to Have Something in It for Everybody*. Australia: The Sydney Morning Herald.

Peters, Tom. 2006. *In Search of Excellence*. New York: Harper Business.

Sandberg, Sheryl. 2013. *Lean In*. New York: Knopf.

Sanders, Tim. 2002. *Love Is the Killer App: How to Win Business and Influence Friends*. New York: Crown.

_____. 2005. *The Likeability Factor: How to Boost Your L-Factor and Achieve Your Life's Dreams*. New York: Crown.

Slim, Pam. 2013. *Your Body of Work*. New York: Portfolio.

Stratten, Scott. 2016. *UnMarketing*. Hoboken, NJ: John Wiley & Sons.

Vascellaro, Jessica E. 2009. "Why E-Mail No Longer Rules." *Wall Street Journal* (October).

Voss, Chris 2016. *Never Split the Difference*. New York: Harper Business.

How to Reach the Authors

Michael Port

Skip on over to www.HeroicPublicSpeaking.com and you'll discover insights, inspiration, and information you can't find anywhere else in the world. You'll read articles that challenge your current ideas and infuse you with new ones. You'll get moments of inspiration that stir you to make changes and try new things.

Fulfill your destiny.

Thousands of others have turned their passion for what they do into an abundant career that profoundly affects others. You can too.

Matthew Kimberley

Head over to www.DelightfulBusiness.com and check out the guides, resources, and email support that Matthew has cooked up for coaches like you.

Plus, you can always contact him by email at contact@matthew kimberley.com. He reads every email and replies to most of them.

About the Authors

Michael Port is an American entrepreneur, author, and angel investor. A *New York Times* and *Wall Street Journal* best-selling author, Michael's nine books have been translated into 29 languages. After spending a decade delivering thousands of paid speeches on the world's biggest stages, Michael sold his first company, Book Yourself Solid Worldwide, and founded Heroic Public Speaking with his wife, Amy Port, where they develop and nurture the next generation of thought leaders, as well as CEOs and founders, best-selling authors, business owners, and movement leaders. For more, visit www.HeroicPublicSpeaking.com.

Matthew Kimberley is a British entrepreneur, author and cowriter of this book. He is the host of the Marketing for Coaches podcast, creator of the School for Selling, the Principles of Professional Persuasion, Delightful Emails, and more. His first book, *How to Get a Grip* sold extensively in the UK, Germany, and Czechia, and was re-released as *Get A F*cking Grip* more than a decade after its first edition. Long-time CEO of Book Yourself Solid Worldwide, Matthew now runs Delightful Business, which helps coaches and consultants enjoy more fun, freedom, and (cash) flow. Find out more at www.MatthewKimberley.com.

Index

271